E UNIV
NCHESTER

D1757706

WITHDRAWN FROM
THE LIBRARY

UNIVERSITY OF
WINCHESTER

KA 0328606 1

Studies in the History of Medieval Religion
VOLUME VIII

A

BROTHERHOOD OF CANONS
SERVING GOD

English Secular Cathedrals in
the Later Middle Ages

This study focuses on the canons of the nine secular cathedrals in England in the later middle ages, men who were amongst the most able and successful clerics of their age. After considering the functions of the cathedrals which provided them with a comfortable income and considerable status, Dr Lepine turns to the canons themselves, tracing their geographical, social and educational origins and analysing their careers in the service of Church and state: this was the surest route to a canonry, an honour for which clerics were prepared to go to considerable lengths. Of central importance to this survey is an examination of canons' residence at their cathedrals, establishing how many were resident in the close and how much time they spent there.

The residentiary canons are the main subject of the second part of the book. The author explores their grand and liberal lifestyle, modelled on that of the nobility, and uses archaeological evidence to reconstruct the houses from which they dispensed hospitality; their religious, intellectual and artistic interests and activities are also described. The study concludes by presenting two case studies to show the vigour and diversity of capitular life in the later middle ages: Salisbury between 1398 and 1458 (its so-called golden age) and Lichfield from 1490 to 1540, on the eve of the Reformation.

Dr DAVID LEPINE teaches history at Dartford Grammar School.

Studies in the History of Medieval Religion

ISSN 0955-2480

General Editor
Christopher Harper-Bill

A
BROTHERHOOD OF CANONS
SERVING GOD

English Secular Cathedrals in
the Later Middle Ages

DAVID LEPINE

THE BOYDELL PRESS

© David Lepine 1995

All Rights Reserved. Except as permitted under current legislation
no part of this work may be photocopied, stored in a retrieval system,
published, performed in public, adapted, broadcast,
transmitted, recorded or reproduced in any form or by any means,
without the prior permission of the copyright owner

First published 1995
The Boydell Press, Woodbridge

ISBN 0 85115 620 7

The Boydell Press is an imprint of Boydell & Brewer Ltd
PO Box 9, Woodbridge, Suffolk IP12 3DF, UK
and of Boydell & Brewer Inc.
PO Box 41026, Rochester, NY 14604–4126, USA

British Library Cataloguing-in-Publication Data
Lepine, David
　　Brotherhood of Canons Serving God: English
　　Secular Cathedrals in the Later Middle Ages. –
　　(Studies in the History of Medieval Religion,
　　ISSN 0955–2480; Vol.8)
　　I. Title II. Series
　　274.2050922
　　ISBN 0–85115–620–7

Library of Congress Cataloging-in-Publication Data
Lepine, David, 1955–
　　A brotherhood of canons serving God : English secular cathedrals
　　in the later Middle Ages / David Lepine.
　　　　p.　　　cm. – (Studies in the history of medieval religion,
　　ISSN　0955–2480 ; v. 8)
　　Includes bibliographical references and index.
　　ISBN 0–85115–620–7 (Hardback : alk. paper)
　　1. Canons, Cathedral, collegiate, etc. – England – History.
　　2. England – Church history – 1066–1485. I. Title. II. Series.
　　BR750.L46　　1995
　　271'.08042–dc20　　　　　　　　　　　　　　　　　　95–18236

The paper used in this publication meets the minimum requirements
of American National Standard for Information Sciences –
Permanence of Paper for Printed Library Materials, ANSI Z39.48–1984

Printed in Great Britain by
St Edmundsbury Press Ltd, Bury St Edmunds, Suffolk

Contents

Illustrations

To my mother and
the memory of my father

Acknowledgements

My greatest debt is to Professor Nicholas Orme who supervised my thesis on the Exeter canons and has been a source of encouragement and advice in writing this book. He has read much of it and improved it considerably. Professor Barrie Dobson has also given encouragement and advice about cathedral canons for which I am grateful. The archivists at Exeter, Hereford, Lichfield, Lincoln, Salisbury and York have provided courteous and efficient service, particularly Mrs A. Erskine at Exeter and Miss S. Eward at Salisbury. The British Academy made a generous grant enabling me to research in the archives at Hereford, Salisbury and Lincoln. Two colleagues at Dartford have given their expertise and skill freely. Mr T. P. Smith drew the maps and appendix 2 and Mr S. Geeves introduced me to the mysteries of the word processor.

Abbreviations

AASRP	*Associated Architectural and Archaeological Reports and Papers*
Bod. Lib.	Bodleian Library
BRUC	*Biographical Register of the University of Cambridge*
BRUO	*Biographical Register of the University of Oxford*
BRUO 1500–1540	*Biographical Register of the University of Oxford 1500–1540*
BL	British Library
Cal. Misc. Inq.	*Calendar of Miscellaneous Inquisitions*
CCR	*Calendar of Close Rolls*
CFR	*Calendar of Fine Rolls*
CPL	*Calendar of Papal Letters*
CPP	*Calendar of Papal Petitions*
CPR	*Calendar of Patent Rolls*
CYS	Canterbury and York Society
D&C	Dean and Chapter
DCRS	Devon and Cornwall Record Society
DNB	*Dictionary of National Biography*
DRO	Devon Record Office
ECA	Exeter City Archives
EETS	Early English Text Society
EHR	*English Historical Review*
GL	Guildhall Library
HCA	Hereford Cathedral Archives
HMC	Historical Manuscripts Commission
Inq. Post Mortem	*Inquisitions Post Mortem*
JEH	*Journal of Ecclesiatical History*
LAO	Lincolnshire Archives Office
LJRO	Lichfield Joint Record Office
LPFD	*Letters and Papers Foreign and Domestic, Henry VIII*
LRS	Lincoln Record Society
MCR	Mayors Court Roll
PRO	Public Record Office
RCHM	Royal Commision on Historical Monuments
Reg.	Register
s. a.	sub anno
SAC	*Sussex Archaeological Collections*

SRS	Somerset Record Society
SS	Surtees Society
Staffs. Rec. Soc.	Staffordshire Record Society
Taxatio	*Taxatio of 1291*
TDA	*Reports and Transactions of the Devonshire Association*
Test. Ebor.	*Testamenta Eboracensia*
VCH	*Victoria County History*
WRS	Wiltshire Record Society
YAJ	*Yorkshire Archaeological Journal*
YAS	Yorkshire Archaeological Society
YML	York Minster Library

1

The Secular Cathedrals
of Later Medieval England

Among the churches of the whole world the church of Salisbury shines
like the sun in full orb . . . shedding her beams on every side
Salisbury Cathedral Statute of 1256[1]

the fame of [York Minster] stands out among the celebrated churches of
the world . . . with its excellence and dignity.
Papal Letter to the Dean and Chapter of York in 1407[2]

This study concerns the canons and in particular the residentiary canons of the
nine secular cathedrals of medieval England. But before examining them in detail
it is necessary to consider the cathedrals in whose shadow much of their lives
were passed and where the bones of so many still lie. The descriptions of Salisbury
and York quoted above reflect the important and influential position cathedrals
occupied in the medieval Church. By the late middle ages they had developed
into complex, wealthy and largely independent corporations with a multiplicity
of functions. Their constitutional and administrative history has been set out
with admirable lucidity and clarity by the pioneer in this field, Kathleen Edwards,
to whom all subsequent scholars are greatly indebted.[3] This evolution will only
be briefly sketched here together with some discussion of the few developments
that took place in the century and a half up to 1541. Cathedrals were first
introduced into England by St Augustine at Canterbury in the seventh century.
After 1133 and for the rest of the medieval period there were a total of nineteen
of which ten were monastic and served by monks, except Carlisle served by
regular canons, and nine were secular, served by secular canons. The distinction
between the two emerged gradually in the eleventh and early twelfth centuries.
During the Anglo-Saxon period there was a trend to a communal life at
cathedrals and in the tenth century Benedictine monks were introduced in four
of them. This was followed in the mid eleventh century by the introduction of

---

[1] D. Greenway, *Fasti Ecclesiae Anglicanae 1066–1300, iv Salisbury Diocese*, 1991, 90.
[2] *CPL vi*, 137–8.
[3] The rest of this paragraph and the next two are based on Edwards, *Secular Cathedrals*,
  1–22, 33–41, 135–55, 159–66, 176–222.

a quasi-monastic life based on the Rule of St Chrodegang, or a version of it, with a common refectory and dormitory, at five others. After the Norman Conquest, under Archbishop Lanfranc the trend towards monastic cathedrals was strength-ened and their number increased to nine. Yet elsewhere, by the end of the eleventh century the move to a quasi-monastic life was reversed. Instead of the communal ownership of property that was the basis of a monastic life, separate incomes were created, usually from estates or churches, known as prebends and named after the place they drew their income from, which were allocated to individual canons who could now live in their own houses. This happened gradually at St Paul's but was the result of major reforms by Norman bishops at Lincoln, Salisbury and York in the years 1089–91. Salisbury was the model for the reorganisation of Chichester, Lichfield and Wells as secular cathedrals. The emergence of Exeter and Hereford as secular cathedrals at about the same time was more gradual.

Between the twelfth and fifteenth centuries these nine secular cathedrals developed into large corporations numbering between fifty and over a hundred clerics with a complex organisational structure of dignitaries, canons and minor clergy. The dignitaries were the chief officers who together administered the cathedral. By the early thirteenth century all nine had adopted a 'four square' constitution with four principal dignitaries, dean, precentor, chancellor and treasurer, in that order of precedence, each with their own separate responsibili-ties. They were usually, but not always canons, some having prebends attached to them, and with the exception of the dean who was elected by the canons, appointed by the bishop. The dean was the head of the chapter, though his authority varied from cathedral to cathedral according to the powers of bishops and chapters. If a canon, he presided over meetings of the chapter and his agreement was required for its decisions. He also had pastoral and disciplinary responsibility for the cathedral clergy. The precentor's duties concerned the cathedral's music: overseeing the choir, leading the singing and sometimes providing service books. The chancellor's primary responsibilities were for sec-retarial and educational activity in the cathedral. His duties were mainly to supervise the grammar school and theology school, as the actual teaching was often done by others, though in most chapters he was required to lecture or preach. He was also nominally responsible for the secretarial work of the chapter and preserving its archives, both of which were carried out by other junior officials. In some cathedrals care of the library was one of the chancellor's functions. It was the treasurer's duty to look after the cathedral's valuables, the plate, ornaments, vestments and relics. He also had to supply the materials needed for services, candles, incense, bread and wine. The dignitaries, who were often absentees, were assisted by deputies, normally members of the minor clergy, who carried out most of the day to day administration. Alongside the four principal dignitaries the subdean and archdeacons were sometimes considered dignitaries or to have a similar status, the practice varying from cathedral to cathedral. When they were canons, which was not always the case, they were usually given precedence over ordinary canons. In cathedrals where the subdean was a dignitary he acted for the dean in his absence, though rarely exercising his disciplinary powers. It was more common for his duties to be more circumscribed. At three cathedrals he was also the penitentiary of the diocese. Archdeacons' duties lay almost entirely outside the cathedral in which they played only a small part unless they were canons. Dignities were generally more valuable than canonries. The *Valor Ecclesiasticus* of 1535 shows just how wealthy many cathedral dignitaries were. The deans of York and Lincoln enjoyed an income of over £300 each. At the much poorer cathedral of Hereford it was £38 6s 1d. The majority of dignitaries could expect an income of at least the Hereford level and over half of them were valued at more than £50. Only at Hereford were there dignities worth less than £20 a year; the chancellorship worth £14 4s 4d and the treasurership £15 8s.[4]

Canons were the next most important of the cathedral clergy. Their numbers varied from chapter to chapter and had been fixed by the end of the thirteenth century. The largest – Lincoln, Salisbury and Wells had over fifty – with fifty-eight, fifty-two and fifty-five canons respectively. The four medium sized had around thirty; Chichester and St Paul's both thirty, Lichfield, thirty-two and York thirty-six. The two smallest were Hereford with twenty-eight and Exeter with only twenty-four.[5] The value of their prebends varied as widely, both from cathedral to cathedral and within chapters; the poorest worth £4 or £5 annually and the richest over £60. In the valuation of benefices undertaken in 1291 to calculate papal taxes the average value of Lincoln prebends was £40 whereas those of St Paul's were worth between £3 and £7. York had the most valuable prebends and the greatest number of them, with an average value of £48 in the 1291 assessment, about £8 more than the average at Lincoln, also one of the wealthy cathedrals. In the 1535 valuation at a typical middle-sized cathedral, Lichfield, three prebends were worth more than £40, five were worth between £20 and £40, eight between £10 and £20, and the remaining sixteen less than £10.[6] At the extremes were the prebend of Pratum Minus at Hereford, worth only a truss of hay in 1291 and 4s 4½d in 1532, and the aptly named 'golden' prebend of Masham at York worth £120. Exeter was unique in having prebends of equal value, worth only £4 each. One of the earliest and most serious problems chapters faced was canons' residence, which will be dealt with fully in chapter five. Many were absent, engaged in diocesan administration or in the service of kings and popes who used canonries as rewards for their officials. As a result a substantial proportion of the cathedral's wealth was lost. The solution to this problem was to distinguish between residents and non-residents and reward them accordingly. The common fund, a reserve of the chapter's property kept after the creation of individual prebends, was used to make daily payments to resident canons and thereby encourage residence by making it financially attractive. Even so at most cathedrals residentiary canons were a minority, between a third and

---

4 Lehmberg, *Reformation of Cathedrals*, 27.
5 Edwards, *Secular Cathedrals*, 33–4.
6 Kettle and Johnson, 'Lichfield Cathedral', 144.

a quarter of the chapter at their height, but often as few as five or six by the late fifteenth century.[7]

The minor clergy formed a third group of clergy serving secular cathedrals; it was also the largest.[8] Even in the smaller cathedrals they numbered over fifty, far outnumbering the residentiaries who often found them unruly and difficult to manage. They were divided into four groups: vicars choral, chantry priests, altarists or secondaries and choristers. The vicars choral were the canons' deputies whose principal function was to perform the daily services, the *Opus Dei*. The chantry priests, as their name suggests, were employed to say mass at the increasing number of chantries founded in cathedrals. 'Clerks of the second form', or secondaries as they were often called, made up an intermediate rank between the choristers and the vicars. They were adolescents, too old to be choristers but too young to be ordained priest and become vicars, whose duties were to assist the other clergy in the cathedral's worship. The choristers' function, then as now, was to share in the singing of the liturgy. In the absence of the majority of canons the minor clergy played an essential part in the cathedral liturgy and without them the performance of the *Opus Dei*, the eight daily offices, would have broken down. In addition the vicars and chantry priests had an important and equally vital role in the administration of cathedrals, occupying the minor offices, as deputies of the dignitaries and officials of the chapter. This growing importance was reflected in the increasing independence they gained during the later middle ages. A fourth and final category – the servants, both clerical and lay – as large and sometimes larger in number than the minor clergy, completed the cathedral community. This comprised two groups: those in the service of the cathedral itself, the lay gentry employed as stewards, the washer-women, grave diggers and other humble servants, and a much larger number living within the close and associated with it. Members of canons' households, diocesan administrators and a host of unbeneficed clergy, all of whom owed their presence in the close to the cathedral, made up this second group. Together the two groups of servants might equal the number of cathedral clergy.

By 1300 the constitutional and administrative form of the nine medieval secular cathedrals was virtually complete. Over the next two and a half centuries there were few formal developments until the Henrician Reformation. The main institutional changes affected the minor clergy whose status gradually increased. All four ranks were clearly established by 1300 and at some cathedrals the vicars and choristers had acquired their own income and property and lived a commu-nal life. The vicars choral achieved most and by 1500 all but those of Lichfield had gained corporate status in their own right. Choristers, because of their youth, were provided with a separate house in most cathedrals by the mid fourteenth century. Only at Hereford, where there were only five choristers, did this not happen by the Reformation, though it had only recently been achieved at

---

[7] For a full discussion of this see chapter 5.
[8] Edwards, *Secular Cathedrals*, 251–317; Lehmberg, *Reformation of Cathedrals*, 12–25.

Lichfield where a hall was built as late as 1531. Chantry priests began living a communal life at St Paul's and Wells in the 1390s and at Lichfield they had their own hall soon after 1414. The most important and prestigious chantry foundation was St William's College at York, established in 1461. Exeter was the last cathedral to provide a communal life for its chantry priests, in 1527, but at the remaining four cathedrals this was never achieved. The secondaries did not gain the corporate status of the rest of the minor clergy, except at Lincoln where from the late thirteenth century they had their own accommodation.

At Chichester, Lincoln and York there were minor alterations to a handful of prebends. In 1413 the prebend of Wilmington in Chichester cathedral, which had been held by an alien religious house, was suppressed and converted into a chantry foundation.[9] The precentorship and chancellorship at Lincoln had their revenues augmented in 1379 effectively creating two new prebends but without increasing the size of the chapter as they were held simultaneously with the dignities.[10] The same two dignities at York each a had prebend attached to them by Archbishop Rotherham in 1484.[11] There were innovative changes at Chichester just before the Reformation. The first, in 1498, was the refounding of the prebend of Highleigh by Bishop Story to create a unique teaching prebend. The mastership of the grammar sc hool was combined with the prebend whose future occupants had an explicit duty to teach.[12] Twenty years later in 1520 and 1523 Bishop Sherborne founded four 'Wiccamical' prebends. Intended as a means of promoting learning in the Church and the cathedral in particular, they were reserved for alumni of either Winchester College or New College Oxford, both of which Sherborne had attended. Their status in the cathedral was somewhat anomalous, somewhere between the canons and vicars choral. They were not members of the chapter though they had separate stalls in the choir and their incomes were greater than most other canons, but like the minor clergy they had a duty of residence. This had been part of Sherborne's intention when creating them and they were given their own separate accommodation in the Close.[13] An educational motive also lay behind the impropriation of the York prebend of Wetwang to the deanery of Henry VIII's new college at Oxford in 1533. This proved to be a temporary loss and was recovered in 1557.[14] The Henrician Reformation, while it plundered the wealth of the secular cathedrals, especially their shrines and some of their endowments, made few other changes to them. A number of prebends and dignities were lost, beginning with the confiscation by the crown of the treasurership at Lincoln in 1538 after the execution of Henry Litherland for treason.[15] On the dissolution of the larger monasteries the few

---

9 *Chichester Fasti*, 49; CPR 1413–16, 76–7; CCR 1413–19, 89–91.

10 *Lincoln Fasti*, 23, 109–9, 114–15, 20, 71–2.

11 J. M. Horn and D. Smith, *Fasti Ecclesiae Anglicanae, 1541–1857, iv York Diocese*, 1975, 33, 47.

12 *VCH Sussex*, ii, 48, 402–3.

13 *Chichester Fasti*, 52–4; Kitch, 'Chichester Cathedral', 277, 279.

14 *York Fasti 1541–1857*, 65.

15 *Lincoln Fasti*, 23.

prebends of those whose heads were members of cathedral chapters were also confiscated; three were lost at Salisbury, five at Wells and two at York.[16] This had little impact as these monastic canons did not play an active part in the life of the cathedral. The creation of new dioceses and cathedrals in 1541 was partly at the expense of the existing ones. Three archdeaconries and the prebends attached to them were transferred to new cathedrals, Northampton to Peterborough, and Dorset to Bristol, while Chester was detached from Lichfield to the new see there.[17] During the 1540s both Salisbury and York lost three further prebends each, and the latter, like Lincoln, lost its treasurership.[18] Much more radical change was brought by the Edwardian Reformation, particularly the dissolution of the chantries in 1548, which transformed cathedrals' functions and appearance and reduced the number of clergy.

The Functions of Secular Cathedrals

The importance of the nine secular cathedrals in medieval society is revealed in the variety of their functions. Physically they dominated their cities and their spires and towers were landmarks visible for miles around. Lincoln Minster still towers above the city at the top of Steep Hill and familiarity does not diminish the impact of Salisbury's spire. These and some of the larger monastic churches were the largest buildings most medieval people encountered in their lives. Their grandeur was enhanced by an imposing West Front which in medieval times would have been brightly painted. As institutions they were among the largest religious houses in the kingdom, significantly larger than most monasteries. The clerical poll tax returns of the late fourteenth century enable us to begin to estimate the numbers of clergy at several cathedrals. Even at the smallest, Hereford, in 1383–84 there were forty-six. Salisbury (in 1380–81) and Wells (in 1377) had double the number, 106 and ninety-five respectively.[19] A smaller residentiary body probably accounts for the lower total of seventy-five at York in 1379–80, though outside the close the city was teeming with clergy; 143 are listed only twenty-one of whom were beneficed.[20] The largest community was at Lincoln where there were 137.[21] To these totals, which include all the clerics living in the close, should be added the many lay servants of the cathedral, its minor clergy and canons' households, who together certainly numbered a hundred and probably considerably more depending on the size of the residentiary

---

16 *Salisbury Fasti*, 64, 76, 84; *Wells Fasti*, 21–2, 54, 58, 60; *York Fasti*, 39, 78.
17 *Lincoln Fasti*, 12; *Salisbury Fasti*, 9; Kettle and Johnson, 'Lichfield Cathedral', 166.
18 Edwards, 'Salisbury Cathedral', 185; Cross, 'Reformation to Restoration', 196–7.
19 PRO E179/30/12; *Clerical Poll Taxes in the Diocese of Salisbury, 1377–81*, ed. J. L. Kirby, in Collecteana, WRS, xii, 1956, 163–4; PRO E179/4/1.
20 PRO E179/63/12.
21 A. K. McHardy, *Clerical Poll Taxes in the Diocese of Lincoln, 1377–81*, LRS, lxxxi, 1992, 1–2.

body.[22] By comparison Durham Priory, an important and prestigious monastic house, had sixty-nine monks in 1406 and at least as many servants.[23] The numbers in cathedrals tended to decline in the fifteenth and early sixteenth centuries as financial hardship reduced the numbers of some of the minor clergy and fewer canons kept residence. Despite this there was still a large community at Lincoln in 1501 when 102 were cited to appear at Bishop Smith's visitation, and even at the smaller cathedral of Exeter there were fifty-eight in 1492.[24]

Cathedrals were dedicated to the perpetual worship of God. Their principal function was the performance of the liturgy, the daily offices and above all the mass. The mass was at the centre of medieval religious life and thought. Its continual offering was a re-enactment of Christ's Passion, a means of intercession for the living and the dead, and the pre-eminent source of spiritual benefits. More and more masses were said and cathedrals were redesigned and rebuilt to enable the increasingly elaborate liturgy to be performed.[25] New lady chapels were constructed at the east end in response to the growth of the cult of the Virgin during the thirteenth and early fourteenth centuries. Simultaneously space was created for shrines for the veneration of local saints, usually behind the high altar. Room was also needed for processions and new altars as the number of masses multiplied. The remodelling of the east end at Wells in the early fourteenth century followed the adoption of the more complex Sarum liturgy soon after 1298.[26] Altars proliferated, in side chapels, transepts and the nave, some the result of new chantry foundations. Twenty-three medieval altars have been identified at Exeter and twenty-seven at Lincoln and Salisbury, though these totals were not reached until the eve of the Reformation.[27] A list of altars in York Minster made in 1344 contains twenty-eight.[28] Quite how many masses were said at them is difficult to quantify but it was considerable. In 1531 the dean and chapter of Lincoln decreed that thirty masses should be said in succession between 5 a.m. and 11 a.m. so that there would always be a mass in progress for visiting laity to attend.[29] This was a reorganisation of the daily masses that chantry priests were required to say as part of their duties and they were said at sixteen of the cathedral's altars. At least three other daily celebrations took place,

22 For a discussion of canons' households and their size see chapter 6.
23 Dobson, 'Cathedral Cities', 23–4.
24 LAO Reg. XXIV (Reg. Smith Lincoln) fos 237r–v, this figure includes a handful of laymen; Reg Morton Canterbury, ii, 74–5, to which have been added fourteen choristers and the nine resident canons.
25 For a broader discussion of this see P. Draper, 'Architecture and Liturgy', in Age of Chivalry, Art in Plantagenet England, 1200–1400, ed. J. Alexander and P. Binski, 1987, 83–91.
26 A. Klukas, 'The Liber Ruber and the rebuilding of the East End of Wells', in BAA, Medieval Art and Architecture at Wells and Glastonbury, 1981, 30–5.
27 Orme, Exeter Cathedral, 22–3; P. B. G. Binnall, 'Notes on the Medieval Altars and chapels in Lincoln Cathedral', Antiquaries Journal, xlii, 1962, 68–80; Wordsworth, Salisbury Ceremonies and Processions, 277–306.
28 YML M2/4g fos 36r–43v.
29 Cole, Lincoln Act Book, 1520–36, 142–4.

low mass or chapter mass, high mass, at which the resident canons would be present, and the mass said in honour of the Virgin in the Lady Chapel.[30] In addition a variety of special masses were said for important visitors, or occasions such as an episcopal enthronement, and – most frequently – for funerals. The most regular of these were the annual obit masses celebrated for the soul of the founder. These tended to increase steadily through the fifteenth century; at Wells there were twenty-eight in 1372–73, thirty-two in 1480–81 and forty-three in 1524–25.[31] Practically incalculable are the multiple masses requested shortly after death by so many, clergy and laity alike, some of which would have been said in the cathedral by its ministers. The masses celebrated by chaplains for an individual's soul for a few years, temporary chantries, fall into the same category. On a typical day there may have been as many as forty masses a day in a cathedral.

As we have seen this multiplication was largely a consequence of the increasing numbers of chantries and obits being founded, which itself was a reflection of the doctrine of purgatory and a desire for intercessory prayers. At their dissolution in 1548 there were between fourteen and twenty in the smaller cathedrals, Chichester, Exeter and Hereford and over thirty at Lincoln and York.[32] Eighteen were functioning at Wells in 1487–88.[33] In the course of the later middle ages considerably more had been established but as their endowments dwindled and priests could not be found to serve them some were amalgamated or dissolved. Only fifteen of the twenty-five set up in Exeter survived in their original form to be suppressed in 1548.[34] York, Lincoln and St Paul's were exceptional in the numbers of chantries they attracted. There were more than sixty at York, twenty-nine of them listed in 1344, and seventy at St Paul's at the beginning of the fifteenth century.[35] While most were founded by bishops and wealthy canons a number were established by the nobility, the Courtenays' at Exeter, the Hungerfords' at Salisbury and the Scropes' at York. A handful of leading citizens also did; William Swayne, a merchant and mayor of Salisbury, founded a chantry in the cathedral in 1470.[36] Obits were even more numerous if more shortlived than chantries and the work of a broader cross section of society. Alongside the seventy chantries at St Paul's at the beginning of the fifteenth century were 110 obits.[37] As the Wells figures show the rate of foundation was usually higher than the rate of decay leading to an overall rise in

---

[30] For a general discussion of cathedral liturgy see Orme, *Exeter Cathedral*, chapters 6–8 and Bowers, 'Music and Worship to 1640'.

[31] Colchester, *Wells Escheators Accounts*, i, 14–16, ii, 204–6, 293–5.

[32] There were twenty-one at Hereford and fourteen at Chichester; Lehmberg, *Reformation of Cathedrals*, 23.

[33] *Wells* HMC ii, 107.

[34] Orme, *Minor Clergy of Exeter Cathedral*, 133–7; L. S. Snell, *The Chantry Certificates for Devon and the City of Exeter*, Exeter, 1960, 2–10.

[35] Dobson, 'Later Middle Ages', 95; YML M2/4g fos 36r–43v; G. H. Cook, *Medieval Chantries and Chantry Chapels*, 1968, 145.

[36] Salisbury D&C Reg. Machon fo. 19r.

[37] Cook, *Chantries and Chantry Chapels*, 145.

their numbers. It was customary for canons and dignitaries to found obits in their cathedrals and they were joined by the nobility and citizens in considerable numbers. In the early sixteenth century several mayors of Exeter were commemorated by obits in the cathedral.[38] Deans and chapters encouraged the foundation of chantries and obits because, by adding to the number of masses, they increased the 'divine service', honouring and glorifying God. They were an important way in which the wider community participated in the spiritual benefits provided by the cathedral.

Repetition of the mass, though the most important, was not the only form of worship and source of spiritual benefit in the cathedral. The liturgical day was built round the eight daily offices beginning with matins and lauds at around midnight or dawn according to local custom.[39] Prime was followed by low mass and then terce, high mass, sext and nones which would be complete by 11 a.m. Vespers and compline were sung in the afternoon. The lady chapel had its own liturgy in honour of the Virgin Mary. On feast days and in the lady chapel more generally the liturgy was longer and more elaborate as processions and polyphonic music developed. Worship was dignified and made more splendid by processions which marked the greater feasts. The most important were concentrated in the spring and early summer between Palm Sunday and Corpus Christi and involved the whole community. Like masses, processions were a means of securing benefits for souls and additional ones were specially founded by individuals. At Wells in 1480–81 six such processions were observed. All took place on the eve of a favoured feast day, five of them connected to Our Lady. Indeed such was the devotion to the feast of the Assumption that there was a procession at both first and second vespers.[40] Prayers for the dead, the placebo and dirigie, were said in as much and sometimes greater profusion than masses. Cathedrals had a wider intercessory role offering up prayers regularly for all Christians in general, both living and dead, and to their benefactors in particular. In the fifteenth century a bidding prayer was read in English to the laity before high mass. The one used at Salisbury began with prayers for the Holy Church, the cathedral and all other churches, the pope, archbishops and bishops and the bishop of Salisbury. It went on to list the cathedral clergy by rank and then prayed for the recovery of the Holy Land. Next in priority was the king and royal family and the nobility all carefully distinguished by rank from dukes to barons, followed by peace between England and France and uniquely a named individual and benefactor the earl of Shrewsbury. Prayers were then asked for members of the cathedral fraternity and all the cathedral's parishioners (perhaps worshippers) and friends and 'all true Christian people'. After further prayers a list of the names of the cathedral's benefactors was recited.[41] The value of cathedrals' intercession lead to special requests for prayers by the king for victory in battle or in

[38] DRO Exeter D&C 3675 fos 35v, 62v, 71v–72r.
[39] See note 30.
[40] Colchester, *Wells Escheators Accounts*, ii, 206.
[41] Wordsworth, *Salisbury Ceremonies and Processions*, 22–32.

thanksgiving. The Chichester chapter made particularly lengthy prayers for the good estate of Henry VII and the scattering of his enemies.[42]

To some the cathedral and its cemetery offered a Christian burial. In Exeter, Hereford and Lichfield the cathedral had sole burial rights in the surrounding city and the majority of citizens were buried in its cemetery or acknowledged its rights by paying mortuary dues.[43] Those of sufficient wealth and status could ask to be buried in the cathedral or its cloisters alongside the clergy. Relatively few chose to, preferring instead to gain permission for burial in their parish churches or a religious house. When members of the nobility were buried in cathedrals this was a personal choice of the individual rather than the continuation of a family tradition. The second earl of Devon's interment in Exeter cathedral in 1377 was a temporary break with the family tradition of burial in one of the religious houses where they were patrons or a parish church they were connected with.[44] This seems to have been the pattern elsewhere with the exception of Salisbury where in the fifteenth century the Hungerfords established a tradition of burial as well as a series of chantries.[45] The building of a tomb housed in a chantry was an opportunity for heraldic display and family pride which was also visible elsewhere in the cathedral, in stained glass windows, on roof bosses and embroidered on vestments. The Courtenay burials at Exeter were accompanied by their patronage of a major reglazing scheme that gave prominence to their arms and family lineage.[46] Increasingly in the fifteenth century leading citizens wished to be buried in their local cathedral, probably as a mark of status. A Lincoln chapter act book for the years 1451 to 1465 records twelve lay burials in the cathedral, most of them citizens or their wives. The standard fee was 20s, a sum that would have been beyond the reach of most.[47]

The nine secular cathedrals were important centres of pilgrimage if not quite of the front rank like Canterbury and Walsingham. The majority were the burial place of their own saint around which diocesan and regional cults developed. All were bishops of the cathedrals where they were later venerated: Chad at Lichfield, Erkenwald at St Paul's, Hugh at Lincoln, Osmund at Salisbury, Richard at Chichester, Thomas Cantilupe at Hereford and William at York. Wells and Exeter were alone in not having their own canonised saints. However, they shared with the other seven in having unofficial cults also based on bishops. Three bishops of Wells had a reputation for saintliness, which led to cults: William Bitton II, William de Marchia and Ralph Shrewsbury. There was an unsuccessful attempt to canonise Bishop Marchia in 1324.[48] For at least thirty years after his death Bishop Shrewsbury (d.1363) was attracting offerings from

42 Peckham, *Chichester White Act Book*, 9–11.
43 Orme, *Exeter Cathedral*, 1–2; Bannister, *Hereford Cathedral*, 76–7; Kettle, 'Cathedral and Close', 160–1.
44 Lepine, 'Courtenays and Exeter Cathedral', 52–3.
45 Edwards, 'Salisbury Cathedral', 181–2.
46 See note 44.
47 LAO D&C A/2/35 fos 9r passim.
48 Gransden, 'Wells Cathedral', 36–7.

the pilgrims visiting his tomb.[49] A similar cult of about the same duration grew up around Bishop Berkeley (d.1327) at Exeter and a subsequent holy bishop, Edmund Lacy (d.1455), was also the focus of veneration.[50] Indeed, Osmund's status at Salisbury was unofficial until his relatively late canonisation in 1457. The early fourteenth century saw the peak of these unofficial cults with one around Bishop Dalderby of Lincoln (d.1320) contemporary with those of Marchia and Berkeley.[51] The most persistent unofficial cult was that of Archbishop Scrope of York, who was executed in 1405, which survived government disapproval and was still active up to the Reformation.[52] All these saints were honoured with shrines, sometimes richly decorated, partly paid for by the offerings of pilgrims, an indication of their popularity. The best descriptions of them are often those of their despoilers in the 1530s who recorded the splendour with which they had been adorned. St William's shrine at York, which has been reconstructed from its archaeological remains, consisted of a silver coffin raised on a marble pedestal and was adorned with gold, silver and jewelled offerings from the faithful.[53] As well as their own saints cathedrals had significant collections of the relics of other saints that drew pilgrims to them. St Paul's possessed a miraculous rood, the Crux Borealis, which was kept in the north transept and said to have been carved by Joseph of Arimathea.[54] Once a year there was a special festival to venerate a cathedral's relics which were also displayed on special occasions such as a royal visit. In the fourteenth century the bones of St Chad were taken round the diocese to raise money for the fabric and his head was displayed in the cathedral on Sundays and double feasts.[55] In addition a cathedral's other patron saints drew pilgrims. Salisbury had a vigorous cult of Our Lady, its patron alongside St Osmund. Several pilgrim badges of this cult have been found and show that it was more than a local one within the diocese, since examples are known as far away as Brabant.[56]

Cathedrals set the liturgical standards for the parishes of medieval England. Their influence was transmitted by their 'uses', the service books that set out how they performed the liturgy. The most famous of these was the Sarum use, which after 1543 was the only one permitted, but all the others except Wells had their own.[57] Even before 1543 the Sarum use was predominant in the province of Canterbury and taken up in parts of the province of York particularly the

[49] Colchester, Wells Fabric Accounts, 67.
[50] Bishops Berkeley and Lacy, see Orme, 'Two Saint-Bishops'.
[51] Owen, 'Historical Survey 1091–1450', 135–6.
[52] Swanson, Catholic England, 179–81; for a fuller discussion see J. W. McKenna, 'Popular Canonisation as Political Propaganda: the Case of Richard Scrope', Speculum, xlv, 1970, 608–23.
[53] C. Wilson, The Shrines of St William of York, York, 1977, 18–20.
[54] Brooke, 'St Paul's Cathedral', 77.
[55] Jenkins, Lichfield Cathedral, 22.
[56] B. Spencer, Salisbury and South Wiltshire Museum: Medieval Catalogue, Part 2 Pilgrim Souvenirs and Secular Badges, Salisbury, 1990, 33–5.
[57] This paragraph is largely based on R. Pfaff, New Liturgical Feasts, Oxford, 1970, 6–8.

diocese of Durham. The Salisbury chapter consciously promoted their use, the most important part of which, the ordinal, had been compiled the precentor Thomas Welewick in 1341–43.[58] Richard Ullerston, a leading residentiary in the early fifteenth century called it 'incomparable in the world' and with pardonable exaggeration 'the chief among other uses in the whole world'.[59] The diocese followed the practice established in the cathedral. When the chapter elevated the status of the feast of the Translation of St Nicholas in 1447 it was ordained that the rest of the diocese would also.[60] The advent of printing secured the pre-eminence of the Salisbury use. Most of the other uses were confined to their cathedrals or dioceses. Of them the York use was the most widespread, across much of northern England. The Hereford and Lichfield uses gained some acceptance in their dioceses, particularly the former, partly because of its remoteness and insularity. During the later middle ages the Lincoln use was only followed in the cathedral, its city and the surrounding area; the diocese was too large for its wider adoption. This pattern was repeated in the diocese of London where the St Paul's use was not widely taken up outside the cathedral. In all cathedrals the Sarum use was acknowledged as a model and parts of it were gradually introduced. Wells was the first to do this at the beginning of the fourteenth century when the complete use was adopted and St Paul's followed in 1414.[61] The same fate befell the Chichester use which had been introduced across the diocese by St Richard in 1250.[62] When improving the liturgy at Lichfield in 1523 the chapter looked to the Sarum use for guidance.[63] However, local uses were not given up lightly. In 1391 the Exeter chapter reacted warily on being presented with an ordinal of the Sarum use. They agreed to use it except when it differed from the Exeter Ordinale that had been drawn up by Bishop Grandisson in 1337 and like the Hereford use was widespread in the diocese.[64] Liturgical standards were transmitted by the ministry of the minor clergy who after being trained in the cathedral brought its practices to the parishes many of them went on to serve. In an eminently practical way the canons of Hereford were in the habit of lending copes and 'jewels', probably ornaments, to the parish churches of the diocese for special services. The chapter banned this in 1519 unless the canons wore them themselves, in what seems like an attempt to prevent them going missing.[65]

The cathedral's authority and influence partly derived from its status as the mother church of the diocese, a claim that seems to date back to Norman times

---

[58] Edwards, 'Salisbury Cathedral', 173.
[59] Jacob, 'English Conciliar Activity 1395–1418', in E. F. Jacob, *Essays in the Conciliar Epoch*, 3rd edn, Manchester, 1967, 80–1.
[60] Salisbury D&C Reg. Hutchins, fo. 54r.
[61] Brooke, 'St Paul's Cathedral', 77; for Wells see note 26.
[62] Swainson, *Chichester Statutes*, 85.
[63] LJRO D&C D30/2/1/3 fo. 139r.
[64] DRO D&C 3550 fo. 75r.
[65] HCA Baylis, i, fo. 19v.

and probably to St Augustine.[66] As the Lincoln chapter put it in 1321 'Our cathedral church of Lincoln which is the mother and mistress of all other churches in the diocese of Lincoln'.[67] This was an attempt to forge a link with all the people of the diocese, to many of whom the cathedral was a remote institution, and not just with each parish. The principal expression of it was a demand for a small annual offering of perhaps a farthing from every household, which came to be known as pentecostals because of the time of year that it was made. Once a year the people would be reminded of the cathedral and involved in its affairs. Originally the offerings were brought to the cathedral in processions by representatives of each parish. In a large diocese like Lincoln they were usually collected in each archdeaconry; thus pentecostals from the archdeaconry of Leicester were collected in Leicester. By the later middle ages in some dioceses they were simply paid to archdeacons' officials but parishes close to the cathedral still made annual processions which were often boisterous occasions. Local parishes still brought their pentecostals to Lichfield in procession as late as 1532 and 1534 when there were arguments between parishes over which was to have precedence.[68] It is impossible to know how close to the mother church of the diocese medieval parishioners felt, but their wills make it clear that there was a convention to make small bequests to the cathedral and the standard phrase used in them was the 'mother church'. Even in the archdeaconry of Buckingham, one of the remoter parts of the large diocese of Lincoln with a tradition of Lollardy, this convention remained strong in the early sixteenth century.[69]

Cathedrals had a surprisingly wide range of what would now be regarded as secular functions. In 1385 Bishop Braybrooke of London made a thunderous denunciation of what he regarded as the desecration of St Paul's by the commerce and sport taking place in the nave. As well as ball games breaking windows, for which choristers at all cathedrals were frequently admonished, there was shooting at the birds nesting in the walls.[70] St Paul's was unique in the amount of secular activity within it because of its position in the capital; even its close had shops.[71] Elsewhere there was much less disruption but it should not be imagined that cathedrals in medieval times were oases of spiritual tranquility. Much of the time they were noisy and busy, not only with pilgrims and worshipers, but those who came to do business. Some of them brought their dogs; the vicars' dogs at Salisbury followed their masters in and barked during services.[72] The minster at York was the setting for councils and meetings, especially in times of war with the Scots. It was there that Archbishop Greenfield held a council of magnates

---

66 For a general discussion of this see Orme, *Exeter Cathedral*, 54 and Owen, 'Historical Survey 1091–1450', 131–2.

67 Owen, 'Historical Survey 1091–1450', 131–2.

68 Cox, *Lichfield Muniments*, 93.

69 E. M. Elvey, *The Courts of the Archdeaconry of Buckinghamshire, 1483–1523*, Buckingham Record Society, xix, 1975, passim.

70 Brooke, 'St Paul's Cathedral', 89.

71 Macleod, 'Topography of St Paul's', 1–14.

72 Salisbury D&C Reg. Burgh fo. 49v.

in January 1315 and in the chapter house that news was announced in the presence of the leading citizens; after news of the king's victory over Lambert Simnel in 1487 a Te Deum was sung.[73] When Parliaments met at Lincoln in 1315, 1316 and 1327 members used the deanery and chapter house for some of their meetings.[74] When news of the absolution of the murderers of Archbishop Scrope arrived in Lincoln in 1408 it was posted on the cathedral door.[75] Cathedrals were a fittingly public place for the excommunication of criminals and the performance of penance, especially by heretics. Public penance usually consisted of ritual humiliation with the penitent required to join the Sunday procession barefoot and bareheaded.[76] To those in danger cathedrals, like all other churches, were places of sanctuary. As late as 1521 a condemned man fled into Chichester cathedral after surviving a botched hanging.[77] It was no doubt this sense of security that led many magnates to store their cash, jewels and plate in cathedrals whose treasuries, like those of monasteries, acted as bank vaults. In 1326 the earl of Arundel had £524 of cash and jewels worth £52 stored in Chichester cathedral, which he used as a subsidiary depository for his considerable wealth.[78] Yet, though normally secure, cathedral treasuries were not always inviolate. Following the brutal murder of Nicholas Radford in 1455, the perpetrators, henchmen of the earl of Devon, extorted £600 of his goods from the dean and treasurer of Exeter cathedral.[79] Crime and violence took place from time to time, mainly cases of theft and brawling, but bloodshed in the cathedral was rare, though it was more common in the close. In one case a conspiracy was hatched in the cloisters at Exeter to overthrow Henry VII and replace him with the Yorkist earl of Warwick.[80] In a more prosaic way cathedrals regulated the daily lives of citizens; its bells and the opening and closing of the gates of the close marked the passing of the hours. Cathedrals were one of the few places in cities to have public clocks in medieval times. Furthermore, for kings and bishops cathedral chapters were a vital source of patronage and rewards for the clerks in their service and canons households an important route of advancement into it, as we shall see in later chapters.[81] To the inhabitants of their cities the cathedral offered a market for their goods, the chance of employment, facilities for education and, in times of hardship, charity.[82]

As this examination has shown, many of the functions of secular cathedrals

---

[73] *Historical Papers and Letters from Northern Registers*, ed. J. Raine, Rolls Series, lxi, 1873, 243; *York Civic Records*, ii, ed. A. Raine, YAS, vol. cvi, 1942, 24.

[74] Owen, 'Historical Survey 1091–1450', 157.

[75] *Reg. Repingdon Lincoln*, i, 135–40.

[76] For examples of this see Orme, *Exeter Cathedral*, 61–2 and Owen, 'Historical Survey 1091–1450', 133.

[77] R. F. Hunnisett, 'The last Sussex Abjurations', SAC, vol. cii, 1964, 39–40.

[78] C. Given-Wilson, 'Wealth and Credit, Public and Private: The Earls of Arundel 1306–1397', EHR, cvi, 1991, 1–26.

[79] R. L. Storey, *The End of the House of Lancaster*, new edition, Gloucester, 1986, 170.

[80] Orme, *Exeter Cathedral*, 60–1.

[81] This is discussed more fully in chapters 2 and 4.

[82] Space precludes fuller consideration of this subject here but for an analysis of the

reflected a significant lay presence. Although cathedrals were primarily the private churches of their clergy whose liturgy required no congregation, the laity were encouraged to attend from an early date.[83] The laity's first loyalty remained to their parish churches but they became an integral part of cathedral life. They visited in large numbers as pilgrims to their shrines, encouraged by the spiritual benefits of the many indulgences granted by successive bishops and popes. They were regularly present at services, not only masses but some of the daily offices. The Salisbury chapter successfully petitioned the pope in 1479 to say matins at dawn instead of midnight to encourage the laity to attend by removing the dangers of going to the cathedral in the dark.[84] At Lincoln in the fifteenth century the cathedral was still full of people and pilgrims when vespers was being said.[85] The courses of sermons preached in the vernacular on Sundays and other festivals were intended for the lay congregation.[86] There would be larger numbers at funerals and on special occasions such as the enthronement of a new bishop or the election of a new dean. The processions and plays that formed part of the liturgy drew crowds. On St Anne's day 1483 at Lincoln a play depicting the Assumption of the Virgin was performed in the nave during the citizens' procession in the nave.[87] Lay attendance in the cathedral was encouraged by chapters. Salisbury was not alone in scheduling its services for the convenience of worshipers. At Exeter from the late fourteenth century and Lincoln from 1531 the chantry masses were said continuously and in succession from early in the morning so that there would always be one for visiting laymen to attend.[88] The Lincoln chapter was particularly worried that if there were none in progress the congregation would go elsewhere to 'inferior churches'. Indulgences were another means of attracting visitors. In 1290–91 the cathedrals of Hereford, St Paul's, Salisbury, Lincoln and York acquired papal indulgences granting a relaxation of a year and forty days penance to all those visiting them on certain feast days.[89] We can never know how many came as visitors' books were not kept, but some impression is given by the offerings made at shrines and the many collecting boxes in cathedrals, though this is difficult to interpret. Anecdotal evidence, for all its shortcomings, suggests they were well attended. The pressure of pilgrims to the shrine of St Richard at Chichester led Bishop Storey to impose some discipline in 1479 by allocating parties from each archdeaconry of the diocese a specific time for their devotions and requiring them to form orderly processions with their crosses and banners instead of chattering. Two years later after a

relationship between cathedrals and their cities see Dobson, 'Cathedral Cities', and Kettle, 'City and Close'.
[83] Cathedrals did not serve as parish churches, Lehmberg, *Reformation of the Cathedrals*, 271.
[84] *CPL xiii*, part 2, 662–3.
[85] Hamilton Thompson, *English Clergy*, 90.
[86] For a fuller consideration of this subject see chapter 7.
[87] LAO D&C A/3/1 fo. 22r.
[88] Orme, *Exeter Cathedral*, 56; note 29 above; Cox, *Lichfield Muniments*, 88.
[89] *CPL i*, 521, 526, 537–8, 540.

visitation he ordered the doors of the choir to be shut on major feasts to keep out the laity who were disrupting the offices.[90]

The laity were involved on a more formal basis. The mayor and aldermen of most cathedral cities attended services on the major feast days and were received with due solemnity, though sometimes the processions were marred by arguments over precedence.[91] At York, Lichfield and St Paul's city guilds operated from within the cathedral. The guild of St Christopher and St George at York used the altar of St Christopher in the Minster where it collected the offerings and contributed to the liturgy by presenting a chaplain.[92] The guild of the Name of Jesus at St Paul's and the fraternity of Jesus and St Anne at Lichfield were well supported fifteenth-century foundations.[93] All nine cathedrals had fraternities or guilds providing spiritual benefits for their members which were open to the laity. Their roots lay in the twelfth century when they were used to raise funds for the great building projects. Some, notably Lichfield and Wells retained this function up to the Reformation.[94] Several underwent a revival in the fifteenth century; there were flourishing fraternities at Lincoln and Salisbury both of which had a distinguished membership from among the nobility, gentry and city oligarchy.[95] There is some evidence to indicate that the Lichfield fraternity was particularly large and included many of the ordinary people. A list compiled in 1532 containing over 50,000 names from the archdeaconry of Stafford was probably a register of its members, both living and dead.[96] Such a figure seems very large but may not be unreasonable. In one year alone, 1488–89, there were nearly 300 bequests to the Lincoln fabric fund, a total of £29 18s 7d.[97] Bequests were another formal expression of lay involvement in their cathedrals. The Lincoln fabric accounts show a healthy income from bequests in the late fifteenth and early sixteenth centuries, ranging from a low point of £21 17s 4d in 1491–92 to a peak of £70 19s 10½d in 1500–01 and rarely falling below £25.[98] Some of the laity chose to live in the close. Lincoln attracted the most distinguished occupants, among them John of Gaunt's wife Katherine Swynford who spent two periods in the close, the first c. 1386/7 to 1392/3 and the second after her husband's death in 1399 until her own in 1403.[99] She is buried in the cathedral in a magnificent chantry tomb. Her daughter, the countess of Westmoreland (d.

90 Swainson, *Chichester Statutes*, 100, 102.
91 *HMC Fourteenth Report*, part 8, 25; for a Hereford example see HCA 2957, 2958.
92 E. White, *The St Christopher and St George Guild of York*, Borthwick Paper no. 72, York, 1987, 7–8; for a Lincoln example see Owen, 'Historical Survey 1091–1450', 156.
93 Brooke, 'St Paul's Cathedral', 98; Kettle, 'City and Close', 163.
94 Jenkins, *Lichfield Cathedral*, 18. A fraternity operated at Wells throughout the later middle ages, see *Wells* HMC ii, 923 under Brotherhood of St Andrew.
95 LAO D&C A/2/35 passim and A/2/36 passim; Edwards, 'Salisbury Cathedral', 177.
96 A. J. Kettle, *A list of the families in the archdeaconry of Stafford, 1532–3*, Staffs. Rec. Soc., Fourth Series viii, 1976, vii–xi.
97 LAO D&C Bj/1/4 fos 50v–63v.
98 The figures are taken from LAO D&C Bj/1/4.
99 Jones, *Lincoln Houses*, i, 52–3.

1440), also spent some of her declining years in the close and lies in the cathedral.[100] Indeed, noble dowagers seem to have found cathedral closes an attractive place to live; four others are known at Lincoln and one at Lichfield.[101] Several fifteenth-century Lincoln townsmen also lived in the close.[102]

The responsiveness of cathedrals to the needs of society accounts for the relatively small amount of contemporary criticism specifically directed at them, unlike the vast amount aimed at wealthy pluralists, corrupt monks, the episcopate and the papacy. Nevertheless, a strand of criticism and satire can be found running through poems and sermons from the fourteenth to the sixteenth centuries. In one fourteenth-century polemical sermon cathedrals were denounced as full of 'flesh and blood, the nephews and grandnephews of bishops'.[103] The author of *Mum and the Sothsegger*, a fourteenth-century poem, described canons as gluttons who in spite of their wealth gave nothing to the poor.[104] In the *Dance of Death*, a French poem translated into English in the mid fifteenth century 'Sir dean or chanon' was reminded that he would not escape death despite his 'distribucions in gret array, your tresour to dispende with all your richnesse and your possessiouns'.[105] The Lollards were no friends of cathedrals. A Lollard sermon on the ministers of the church taught that the elaborate ritual of cathedral liturgy was irrelevant to salvation, 'For Salusbury us, ne York us, be not nedfulle to come to heuene. But as yche cathedral chyrche hath an us bysyde the pope, so Crist wolde teche eche cristene mon how he schulde prey and serue hym.'[106] An abortive Lollard rising in May 1431 planned to attack and destroy Salisbury cathedral, plundering its ornaments and relics.[107] Archbishop Cranmer was scathing; in a letter to Thomas Cromwell in 1539 he complained that 'the sect of prebendaries have . . . spent their time in much idleness and their substance in superfluous belly cheer . . . commonly a prebendary is neither a learner, nor teacher, but a good viander'.[108] As we shall see, though there was some truth in these criticism, Cranmer was unduly harsh in his generalisation. Cathedrals performed functions that medieval society valued and retained the support of the community which helped them survive the upheaval of the Reformation. In the end, despite being able to contemplate living without monasteries, friaries and chantries, the leaders of Tudor England could not imagine a Church without cathedrals: indeed, they even enlarged the number.

---

[100] Ibid., 78.
[101] Jones, *Lincoln Houses*, i, 78–9, iii, 38, 70; Lady Matilda de Pipe was living in the close at Lichfield in 1379–80, see Boyd, *Poll Tax for Offlow and Cutlestone*, 168.
[102] Jones, *Lincoln Houses*, iii, 92–3.
[103] Owst, *Literature and the Pulpit in Medieval England*, 2nd edn, Oxford, 1961, 245.
[104] *Mum and the Sothsegger*, ed. M. Day and R. Steele, EETS, Old Series, cic, 43–4.
[105] *Dance of Death*, ed. F. Warren, EETS, Old Series, clxxxi, 41.
[106] *English Wycliffite Sermons*, ii, ed. P. Gradon, Oxford, 1988, 362–3.
[107] Ball, 'Thomas Cyrcetur', 235.
[108] *Miscellaneous Writings and Letters of Thomas Cranmer*, ed. J. E. Cox, Parker Society, Cambridge, 1846, 396–7.

2

The Scramble for Preferment:
Acquiring a Canonry

On All Saints Day 1338 William Gulden burst into Exeter cathedral with a gang of armed men. He marched them into the choir where some canons and the minor clergy were singing the office. Interrupting the service, he demanded to be admitted to the stall of Reginald Chambernoun, who had died in 1333. The disturbance continued through high mass as he pressed each canon in turn, but without success. On hearing of this, the indignant Bishop Grandisson excommunicated him. The affray was the culmination of a five year campaign to effect a papal provision. Gulden had already received one sentence of excommunication in 1333 for obstructing the bishop's nephew over a prebend. Despite two excommunications, being accused of adultery, and suspected of heresy, he did briefly become a canon in 1339, presumably on the strength of his provision. The chapter then began a lawsuit against him but he persisted in his claim, even against a powerful royal nominee, John of St Pol, the keeper of the great seal, backed by a royal prohibition in 1343. In the end St Pol bought him off with an exchange of benefices in 1344.[1]

Few were as reckless as Gulden in their pursuit of a prebend but many were as determined. Such was the desirability of canonries that by his death in 1351 Robert Kildesby had faced three challenges over eleven years for his prebend at Lichfield despite the intervention of the king on his behalf.[2] Canonries were highly sought after not only for their wealth and status but because they were deemed to be without cure of souls (except deaneries and archdeaconries) and could be held in plurality. This made them attractive to patrons as well as ambitious clerics; popes, cardinals, bishops, kings and lay aristocrats used them as rewards. The high demand for prebends intensified competition for them in which some like Gulden were unsuccessful or like Kildesby challenged and others ejected after temporary possession. Though originally all canons and dignitaries, except deans, were appointed by the bishop there were, in practice, four principal means of acquiring a canonry: collation by the bishop, royal grant, provision by

---

[1] Reg. Grandisson Exeter ii, 893–4; Exeter Fasti, 30; Lepine, Canons of Exeter Cathedral, 36–7.
[2] Lichfield Fasti, 67.

the pope, and exchange. Access to all four means lay through a network of patronage and kinship much of which is now hidden. Of these four episcopal collation was the commonest, royal grants were generally limited to short periods during episcopal vacancies, papal provisions, though a serious threat in the fourteenth century, died out in the fifteenth; and exchanges were relatively infrequent. Apart from exchanges all methods of appointment were ultimately dependent on the number of vacancies. This was determined by the size of the chapter and the longevity of canons the majority of whom tended to retain their prebends until they died. Thomas Austell at Wells and Richard Wynwyk at York both held their prebends for over fifty years.[3] In a small chapter such as Exeter or Lichfield, with twenty-four and twenty-five prebends respectively, there were limited opportunities for making appointments. This led Bishop Grandisson in 1331 to complain of the 'very small number of canons' at Exeter.[4] On average there and probably at other small chapters the bishop could expect one or two vacancies a year, rising to four or six in an exceptional year and falling to none in others; between 1300 and 1455 there were thirty-nine years with none.[5] In the much larger chapter of Wells, with fifty-five prebends, vacancies were comparatively plentiful. There was rarely a year without one, just twelve years in the fifteenth century, and often between two and five rising to ten or more in exceptional years.[6]

Episcopal Appointments

In theory, if frequently not in practice, the right to appoint canons and dignitaries, with the exception of the dean who was elected by the chapter, lay with the bishop. His right arose in the eleventh century when cathedrals were served by clerks from his household. Though chapters developed considerable autonomy during the twelfth and thirteenth centuries they never managed to dispute episcopal patronage of their dignities and canonries. However, such was the desirability of prebends that from at least the second half of the thirteenth century up to the Reformation and beyond bishops came under considerable pressure when making appointments from popes, kings and lay magnates as well as ambitious clerics. At its greatest this pressure resulted in the loss of a considerable amount of their power to make appointments; for much of the fourteenth century papal provisions were used to fill canonries and in the 1530s the king and lay aristocracy acquired the right to present to a number of prebends in many cathedrals. Between these two periods, during the fifteenth and early sixteenth centuries, the pressure is largely hidden but undoubtedly remained. Bishops certainly felt increasing pressure. As early as 1287 Bishop Swinfield of

3 *Wells Fasti*, 79; *York Fasti*, 90.
4 *Reg. Grandisson Exeter* i, 106.
5 These figures are based on *Exeter Fasti*.
6 These figures are taken from *Wells Fasti*.

Hereford wrote to a royal clerk explaining that he was unable to collate him to a prebend because he already faced other royal and papal requests.[7] By the early fourteenth century episcopal concerns had become complaints, particularly about papal provisions. Bishop Grandisson of Exeter protested vigorously and frequently in 1328, 1331, 1342 and 1349 using characteristically forthright language denouncing 'self-seekers' and the 'burdensome multitude of provisions'.[8] He was not alone. Bishop Martival of Salisbury, where there were double the number of prebends found at Exeter, made a more temperate complaint to the pope in 1327 and as late as 1389 Bishop Scrope of Lichfield chided his chapter about their readiness to accept provisions.[9] The same year Bishop Trefnant of Hereford asked the pope to provide well educated and suitable pastors to prebends rather than the ambitious clerics who sought them.[10] As provisions died out so did episcopal complaints.

Such complaints had some justification and were not simply excuses. During the fourteenth century bishops found their right to collate to prebends and dignities considerably restricted, principally by the pope but also by the king and private exchanges. At York during Archbishop Greenfield's episcopate (1306–1315) only a third, ten, of the thirty-four new canons were appointed by the bishop, and twelve each by the king and the pope.[11] Table 1 shows the position at Exeter from 1307 to 1541.[12] Bishop Stapeldon (1307–26) appointed to ten out of twenty-six vacancies, and Bishop Grandisson to only twenty-one of the seventy-six new canons in his forty-two year episcopate. Brantingham's experience is more difficult to quantify because the method of appointment of a quarter of the new canons of his reign is unknown. Even so of the fifty-five new canons thirty-one, nearly two-thirds, were not appointed by the bishop. The decline of papal provisions and exchanges enabled future bishops to collate the overwhelming majority of canons from the fifteenth century up to the Reformation. Exeter's experience in the fourteenth century was repeated at Lichfield and is set out in Table 2.[13] Bishop Grandisson's experience was not unique. His contemporary Bishop Northburgh fared worse, appointing only twenty-two of the ninety-eight new canons during his slightly shorter episcopate of thirty-six years. In the second half of the century Bishop Stretton at Lichfield found to an

---

7   *Reg. Swinfield Hereford* 150–3.
8   *Reg. Grandisson Exeter* i, 163, 106, 111, 175–6.
9   *Reg. Martival Salisbury* ii, 549–52; LJRO D30/2/1/1 fo. 20r.
10 *Reg. Trefnant Hereford* 11–12.
11 *Reg. Greenfield York* i, xiv–xv.
12 This table is based on *Exeter Fasti* with additions from the editions of the papal registers published in Rome and Paris and Lunt and Graves, *Papal Accounts*. Exchanges of prebends within the cathedral have been excluded as have appointments to dignities. Canons who resigned and were later reappointed or who were removed by a rival but subsequently gained another prebend have been counted for each appointment. Episcopal vacancies have been taken to last until the new bishop was granted the temporalities of the see.
13 This table is based on the figures in Jenkins, *Lichfield Cathedral*, 172, 176, 185–6.

TABLE 1 METHODS OF APPOINTMENT OF EXETER CANONS, 1308–1541

Episcopate	Bishop	King	Pope	Exchange	Unknown	Total
Stapeldon 1308–26	10	0	6	5	5	26
Vacancy 1326–27	0	1	0	0	0	1
Berkeley 1327	0	0	0	0	0	0
Vacancy 1327–28	0	1	0	0	0	1
Grandisson 1328–69	21	5	38	5	7	76
Vacancy 1369–70	0	6	0	0	0	6
Brantingham 1370–94	8	2	15	14	16	55
Vacancy 1394–95	0	1	0	1	0	2
Stafford 1395–1419	38	0	7	3	2	50
Vacancy 1419	0	0	0	0	0	0
Catterick 1419	0	0	0	0	0	0
Vacancy 1419–20	0	2	0	0	0	2
Lacy 1420–55	42	0	0	5	6	53
Vacancy 1455–56	0	1	0	0	0	1
Neville 1456–65	2	0	0	0	11	13
Vacancy 1465	0	0	0	0	0	0
Booth 1465–78	8	0	0	1	17	26
Vacancy 1478	0	0	0	0	0	0
Courtenay 1478–87	7	0	0	0	7	14
Vacancy 1487	0	0	0	0	2	2
Fox 1487–92	5	0	0	2	4	11
Vacancy 1492	0	0	0	0	0	0
King 1492–95	4	0	0	0	7	11
Vacancy 1495–96	0	0	0	0	0	0
Redmayn 1496–1501	3	0	0	0	3	6
Vacancy 1501–02	0	0	0	0	0	0
Arundel 1502–04	3	0	0	0	2	5
Vacancy 1504–05	0	0	0	0	0	0
Oldham 1505–19	20	1	0	0	9	30
Vacancy 1519	0	0	0	0	0	0
Veysey 1519–41	25	1	0	1	6	33
TOTAL	196	21	66	37	104	424

TABLE 2. METHODS OF APPOINTMENT OF LICHFIELD CANONS, 1296–1400

Episcopate	Bishop	King	Pope	Exchange	Unknown	Total
Langton 1296–1321	28	1	13	7	7	56
Northburgh 1322–58	22	10	47	16	3	98
Stretton 1360–85	12	6	28	24	5	75
1386–1400	17	13	6	11	0	47
TOTAL	79	30	94	58	15	276

even greater extent than Bishop Brantingham that the decline in provisions was offset by an increase in exchanges and that together they greatly reduced his ability to appoint canons. Bishops often found greatest difficulty collating to dignities and the richest prebends in their cathedrals because they attracted most attention from the pope and king. During the fourteenth century the archbishop of York and bishop of Lincoln each made only three collations to the three richest prebends, worth over £100 each, in their respective cathedrals.[14] Even the much poorer archdeaconry of Cornwall, valued at £50 in 1535, was outside episcopal appointment from 1308 to 1397; it was, however, unusual for a bishop to be excluded for nearly a hundred years.[15] More typical is the subdeanery at Exeter where a royal grant and exchanges kept the bishop out from 1369 to 1399.[16]

From the fifteenth century, with the ending of papal provisions, episcopal collation was the normal route to a canonry. The episcopal registers suggest that up to the Reformation bishops controlled most appointments to prebends and dignities in their cathedrals. However, the registers are largely silent on the demands of patrons and clerics which remained despite the removal of provisions. The absence of collections of episcopal letters from the fifteenth century makes it difficult to observe and measure this pressure closely but there is enough other evidence to show that it could be considerable and there were real constraints on a bishop's freedom to appoint to his chapter. Much routine correspondence from clerics seeking preferment and patrons requesting rewards for their protégés has been lost. An echo of it can be heard in the formularies of letters drawn up at Oxford University which contain many requests to bishops for benefices, though none survives asking for a canonry. Sixteenth-century letter collections enable us to see the workings of patronage more clearly. One of the most illuminating is a letter written by Bishop King of Wells in June 1502 to Sir Reginald Bray which shows the pressures bishops could face, in this case from

---

[14] The York prebends of South Cave, Masham and Wetwang (*York Fasti*, 41–2, 66–7, 90) and the Lincoln prebends of Corringham, Sutton and Thame (*Lincoln Fasti*, 54–5, 113–14, 115–16).

[15] *Exeter Fasti*, 15–16.

[16] Ibid. 6.

the crown.[17] In his letter the bishop reveals that on his consecration, in 1495, he had promised to accept royal nominations to the chapter and had kept it in appointments to the archdeaconries of Wells and Taunton and the prebend of Yatton between 1496 and 1500. The method of appointment in two of these cases is not recorded but that of Robert Sherborne, a prominent royal clerk and secretary to Henry VII, to the archdeaconry of Taunton was by episcopal collation.[18] This suggests that other royal clerks who were collated by the bishop were, in practice, appointed directly at the king's request. In Bishop King's case it was relatively easy for him to meet Henry VII's demands as there were thirty-seven vacancies in the years 1496 to 1500.[19] His letter sought Sir Reginald's intercession with the king to recover some of his patronage to appoint a resident precentor rather than have an absent royal nominee.

Lay magnates made requests alongside the king. In 1536 Bishop Longland of Lincoln was asked for a prebend for Richard Scrivener by Lord Lisle and had already promised to promote one of his chaplains.[20] Scrivener received his prebend later that year, perhaps partly because he was also one of Longland's chaplains. Just how central and extensive patronage was is well illustrated in one of Thomas Cromwell's letters. In 1538 he wrote to Roland Lee, a former protégé and tutor to his son, now bishop of Lichfield asking for a prebend for a 'nere frende' of his nephew Richard Cromwell.[21] Though such requests may have been difficult to refuse and limited bishops' control of their chapters it would be wrong to assume that they were reluctantly granted. Most bishops owed their advancement to precisely this sort of patronage which could bring many advantages, not least the goodwill of the king and great magnates. As Thomas Cromwell wrote in his letter to Bishop Lee 'Wherein your so doyng [granting the prebend] ye shall administer unto me suche thankfull pleasour as I shall not faile to have the same in remembrance when occasion shall occurr.'

Episcopal attitudes to the large scale alienation of the right to present to canonries and dignities over a short period in the later 1530s and 1540s are harder to gauge. At most of the nine secular cathedrals from 1531, bishops granted to others the right to present to the next vacancy in a named prebend or dignity. Only York and perhaps Hereford seem to have escaped this process. These alienations were most numerous at Chichester, where thirty-six were made between 1535 and 1543, and Lincoln where thirty-two were made by Bishop Longland from 1531 to 1547. At Lichfield twenty-three are known between 1536 and 1554 but fewer than ten are recorded at Wells, St Paul's and Exeter.[22] Richard Sampson, a prominent servant of Henry VIII, upholder of the royal supremacy and successively bishop of Chichester in 1536–43 and Lichfield in 1543–54, was responsible for no less than forty-seven grants of presentations, twenty-eight at

[17] Robinson, 'The Correspondance of Bishop Oliver King', 1–10.
[18] Wells Fasti, 17.
[19] These figures are taken from Wells Fasti.
[20] M. St C. Byrne, The Lisle Letters, 6 vols, 1981, iii, 275.
[21] R. B. Merriman, The Letters of Thomas Cromwell, 2 vols, Oxford, 1968, ii, 137.

Chichester and nineteen at Lichfield. The recipients of grants ranged from the king, his ministers and courtiers to local gentry in the diocese and other canons. At Wells the king was granted an archdeaconry, six other alienations went to royal ministers or courtiers and one was made to the bishop's brother whereas at Chichester local gentry were more prominent.[23] In contrast Bishop Veysey's grants at Exeter were more often to trusted resident canons.[24] The motives for these alienations apparently varied. At Lichfield two seem to have been straight-forward financial transactions and others related to finding places for dispossessed monks for whom lay purchasers of monastic estates were responsible.[25] The grants also reflect anxiety at the religious turbulence of the 1530s in particular the visitation and subsequent dissolution of the monasteries and the known hostility towards cathedrals in some quarters at court. Some were intended as placatory grants to the king and prominent noble courtiers; at Lincoln Bishop Longland attempted to gain the support of the Boleyn faction at court by granting the advowson of the prebend of Aylesbury to Thomas Boleyn in 1534.[26] Others made by the same bishop were intended to protect the conservative religious sympathies of the chapter by granting patronage to reliable clerics, such as Bishop Gardiner, and local gentry. In the same decade Longland sought to protect the chapter's prebendal lands from permanent loss by making long leases to trustworthy individuals. At Wells Bishop Clerk's grants were a response to political uncertainty. In 1537 he asked Thomas Cromwell for his help to improve his standing with the king and subsequently granted patronage to Cromwell and his associates. Like Longland, Bishop Clerk was a religious conservative and felt vulnerable to and out of sympathy with reform. His fears of change seemed justified in January 1539 when commissioners arrived to investigate the wealth of the cathedral.[27] An assessment of how much these alienations affected the character of cathedrals awaits detailed research but it is clear that the new patrons were affecting the composition of chapters until the 1550s and 1560s.

Royal Grants

Appointments by the king were based on his 'regalian right' by which he took over the bishop's temporalities during a vacancy which included his rights of patronage as well as his lands and income.[28] A vacancy was therefore a valuable

---

22 *Chichester White Act Book*, 174 et seq.; Bowker, *Henrician Reformation*, 100–1; Kettle and Johnson, 'Lichfield Cathedral', 166; P. M. Hembury, *The Bishops of Bath and Wells 1540–1640*, 1967, 62–6, 74–5; DRO D&C 3551 fos 126, 128v, 129, 130v, 136v; J. M. Horn, *Fasti Ecclesiae Anglicanae 1541–1857*, i, St Paul's, 1969, 17, 35.
23 *Chichester White Act Book*, 174 et seq.; Hembury, *Bishops of Bath and Wells*, 62–6, 74–5.
24 DRO D&C 3551 fos 126, 128v, 129, 130v, 136v.
25 Kettle and Johnson, 'Lichfield Cathedral', 166.
26 Bowker, *Henrician Reformation*, 96–100.
27 Hembury, *Bishops of Bath and Wells*, 62–6, 74–5.
28 For a general discussion of this topic see M. E. Howell, *Regalian Right in Medieval*

source of profit to the king and fully exploited by him. Royal interventions were usually confined to short periods until a new bishop was appointed, though attempts were made to stretch them out further. The king's regalian rights date from the Norman Conquest and were developed and extended in the thirteenth and fourteenth centuries. Edward I extended them further by claiming them retrospectively. He sought to appoint the successors of those he granted prebends to during a vacancy. Edward II pursued them more vigorously still trying to extend regalian right to include vacancies in his father's reign as well as his own. The process of extension reached its apogee under Edward III who in the 1340s attempted to make regalian rights permanent. Cathedral prebends became the main focus of this because, lacking cure of souls they could be held in plurality which made them attractive rewards for royal servants. However, the growth of royal activity provoked disputes and litigation. During the 1340s the number of appeals to the Curia increased as clerics sought to fend off rivals. The king used his courts to back up his claims. From the time of the Constitutions of Clarendon of 1163 the king had claimed that his courts rather than Rome were the final court of appeal in cases of ecclesiastical patronage. Writs of *venire facias* and *quare impedit* were used to force bishops to block opponents to royal nominees and prevent them from appealing to Rome, and to force the bishop himself to appoint the royal candidate. In defence of his claims Edward III could draw on the Commons' petitions against papal provisions. The issue came to a head in 1351–52 after a particularly fierce dispute between Bishop Grandisson of Exeter and the king. In 1349 the defiant bishop had his temporalities confiscated for repeatedly refusing to appoint a royal nominee to a canonry. It was the third attempt by the king to extend regalian right retrospectively to appoint a successor to a canonry granted by his father during a vacancy in 1326. Grandisson's loss of his temporalities, which lasted two years, provoked the clergy to include attempts to make regalian right permanent among the grievances they presented to the king.[29] The statute *Pro Clero* of 1352 acknowledged this complaint and in it Edward III agreed not to extend regalian rights beyond his accession The compromise struck in 1352 lasted for the rest of the century. Retrospective claims to appoint to canonries were briefly revived under Henry IV, most notably in 1411 when a Lichfield prebend was granted on the basis of a vacancy in Edward III's reign.[30] This and a handful of other cases seem to have been instigated by royal clerks rather than the king himself. They did not lead to a permanent revival of retrospective appointments. Thereafter regalian right was confined to episcopal vacancies up to the Reformation, a reflection of the declining demand for prebends caused by the growing laicisation of the royal bureaucracy.

The application of regalian right in cathedral chapters provided the crown

England, 1962; Heath, *Church and Realm*, 32–3, 100, 124–5, 214–15, 250–1, and W. M. Ormerod, *The Reign of Edward III*, 1990, 124–7.

[29] Lepine, *Canons of Exeter Cathedral*, 18–19.

[30] Heath, *Church and Realm*, 250.

with a steady but relatively limited flow of patronage despite the attempts to extend it. In the two and a half centuries 1300 to 1541, mainly during vacancies, the king made ninety-two direct appointments to canonries and dignities in St Paul's, all but eighteen of them successful, and thirty-nine at Exeter.[31] Over the shorter period 1296 to 1400 he made thirty successful appointments to prebends at Lichfield.[32] Though there were few years without one at one of the nine secular cathedrals it was unusual for episcopal vacancies to last more than a few months and rare for them to extend over a whole year. At Exeter the average was between six and nine months. Like other patrons the king was dependent on the number of prebends falling vacant during these periods which could be quite small depending on the size of the chapter and other chance factors. At St Paul's there were twenty-six episcopal vacancies between 1303 and 1539 during which sixty-four royal grants were made, typically between one and three each time.[33] Yet in seven of these periods the king made no grants at all. Despite an unusually long eighteen month vacancy in 1448–50 there were only two royal appointments. However, there were eighteen in the nine month vacancy of 1361–62 caused by the return of the plague which carried off the bishop as well as many of his chapter. Though episcopal vacancies were generally relatively short there were a few lengthy ones, at Chichester and York, which gave the king more scope for intervention. The premature death of the new bishop extended a vacancy at Chichester to three years between 1415 and 1418 when five crown appointments were made and there was a two year vacancy in 1506–08 resulting in four grants.[34] During the early fourteenth century there were two year vacancies at York in 1315–17 and 1340–42 which were fully exploited by the king who made thirteen grants during the former and nine in the latter.[35] The delays in finding a successor to Archbishop Scrope caused another extended vacancy in 1405–07, when nine grants were made. Royal grants outside an episcopal vacancy, often made at the request of ambitious clerics and based on retrospective regalian right, were less likely to be effective; at St Paul's 40 per cent made outside a vacancy failed whereas only 10 per cent made during one were ineffective. The normal flow of patronage following the death or translation of a bishop was occasionally supplemented by exceptional confiscations of episcopal temporalities by the king. Most of these took place in the first half of the fourteenth century and were precipitated by the turbulent politics of Edward II's reign, though Bishop Grandisson's punishment was by Edward III. Bishop Langton of Lichfield's loss of his temporalities during his trial in 1307–08 did not result in any royal appointments.[36] Bishop Burghersh of Lincoln in 1321–24 and Bishop Orleton of Hereford in 1324–25 were not so lucky and found vacancies had been filled

---

[31] The figures are calculated from *St Paul's Fasti* and *Exeter Fasti*.
[32] See Table 2.
[33] The figures are taken from *St Paul's Fasti*.
[34] *Chichester Fasti*, 24, 29, 30, 38, 40, 45, 47, 49.
[35] *York Fasti*, 10, 13, 19, 25, 29, 33, 35, 39, 42, 44, 48, 58, 59, 62, 64, 66, 75, 78, 84.
[36] *Lichfield Fasti*.

by the king.[37] After 1400 the seizure of temporalities was extremely rare though the threat of this was still felt in Henry IV's reign. The Lincoln chapter, in 1405, thought it prudent to prefer the royal nominee to the prebend of Empingham to his rival, a papal provisor, for fear of confiscation of the temporalities.[38] As in the 1320s it was political crisis that led to the confiscation of temporalities in the fifteenth century. Following Bishop Courtenay's involvement in Buckingham's rebellion in 1483 and subsequent flight, the temporalities of Exeter remained in Richard III's hands until Bosworth Field. Only a lack of vacancies prevented the king's nominees gaining a prebend.[39] At the Reformation there were occasional windfalls to the crown when canons opposed religious change, as in 1536 when Henry VIII presented Edward Whalley's successor to a Lincoln canonry after his attainder.[40]

The king's influence in appointments was not confined to his own presentations. Papal provisions were often granted at royal request. Petitions to the pope for benefices would regularly include canonries and dignities for royal chaplains and civil servants up to the 1360s. In 1378 pope Urban VI granted Richard II a faculty to appoint to the next two vacancies in all the cathedral and collegiate churches in the country.[41] As well as the king other members of the royal family made petitions. Queen Isabella, Queen Philippa, Edmund of Woodstock, earl of Kent, the Black Prince, and Henry, duke of Lancaster all made requests for their clerks. The Black Prince and Queen Philippa were particularly active in the 1340s and 1350s. Royal nominees to provisions tended to have a better chance of success than the average provisor. The king was also able to control unwelcome provisions in the second half of the fourteenth century by using the praemunire legislation, which had been passed to block provisions and prevent appeals to Rome. By the fifteenth century the very few provisions were subject to royal licences allowing them to be carried out, making them in effect a kind of royal nomination. The crown's indirect means of appointing canons extended beyond provisions. Many clerics known to have been in royal service were collated to canonries by bishops. The precise influence of their royal status in obtaining their canonries is difficult to gauge, but it must have contributed. Civil servant bishops, of whom there were many, would have found it hard to resist pressure from the king to appoint his clerks to their chapters. Direct evidence of this sort of pressure is rare, though many letters to bishops and chapters were undoubtedly sent as Bishop King's correspondence indicates.[42] The best documented cases

---

37 *Lincoln Fasti*, 6, 34–5, 48, 103; *Hereford Fasti*, 23, 34.
38 H. P. King, 'A Dispute between Henry IV and the Chapter of Lincoln', *Archives*, iv, 1959–60, 81–3.
39 The lack of vacancies did not prevent Richard III from pressing his claims. See R. Horrox and P. W. Hammond, *British Museum Harleian Manuscript 433*, 4 vols, 1979–83, i, 61–2.
40 *Lincoln Fasti*, 75.
41 Pantin, *English Church*, 51.
42 Robinson, 'Correspondance of Bishop King'. In 1391x95 Richard II wrote to Bishop

concern deaneries, the most important and valuable office in a chapter, where direct royal pressure was routinely applied. At Exeter in the late autumn of 1457 the queen, Margaret of Anjou, wrote to the chapter asking them to elect her chancellor, John Halse, as dean when the next vacancy occurred.[43] The incumbent, John Cobethorn, was about sixty years old and had been in office for nearly forty years. A vacancy was clearly expected, perhaps that winter. In the event Dean Cobethorn died in the summer of 1458 and Hals was duly elected his successor. The queen's letter contains interesting details of the lengths she went to. Some canons were not being co-operative. She had already written 'several' letters, and gave notice that a messenger with instructions was being sent. Royal correspondence about decanal elections survives at Wells in 1498, Exeter in 1509 and Hereford in 1529.[44]

Papal Provisions

The pope's intervention in the appointment of canons took the form of papal provisions and expectations: a provision being to a benefice already vacant and an expectation to a future vacancy.[45] The papacy justified its intervention by asserting that it was part of its *plenitudo potestatis*, a claim to sovereignty over the clergy and church property that included the right to appoint to all benefices. This was most clearly expressed by Pope Clement IV in 1265 and developed by his successors, most notably John XXII (1316–24), over the next half century. Provisions reached their peak in the mid fourteenth century during the pontificate of Clement VI (1342–52). The growth of provisions provoked complaints which increased in hostility as the numbers rose, culminating in protests in convocation in 1342 and in parliament the following year. The focus of these complaints was a belief that provisions were being used to swamp the English church with foreigners, particularly Frenchmen, at a time when war with France threatened. Edward III did not fully share these anti-papal attitudes but was prepared to use them to his diplomatic advantage. Though a royal ordinance against provisions was made in 1344 no statute followed until 1351, when the Statute of Provisors excluded papal provisions from the kingdom without the king's permission. It was followed in 1353 by the Statute of Praemunire which prevented appeals to Rome, though in practice the crown had exercised such power since the Conquest. Both statutes were intended as a warning to the

Waltham of Salisbury requesting him not to collate to the next vacant prebend without consulting him (M. D. Legge, *Anglo-Norman Letters and Petitions*, Anglo-Norman Text Society, iii, 1941, 462–3).

43 DRO D&C 3498/22–3.

44 HMC *Wells* ii, 151–2; J. A. F. Thomson, 'Two Exeter Decanal Elections, 1509', *Southern History*, vi, 1986, 36–45; HCA Baylis, i, fo. 47r.

45 For a general discussion of provisions see Pantin, *English Church*, chapter 4, Wright, *Church and Crown*, and Heath, *Church and Realm*, 125–7, 129–38, 213–18.

papacy rather than a ban on its activities. The flow of provisions continued in the 1350s and 1360s. Deteriorating relations with the papacy partly caused by Urban V's attempt to curb pluralism, which would deprive king's clerks of most of their benefices and wealth, led to the re-enactment of both statutes in 1365. Despite this and increasing anti-papalism in the 1370s provisions continued to be made by Gregory XI (1370–78) on a relatively large scale. The Great Schism and Richard II's increasing difficulties with his opponents, who objected to foreign provisors, brought a marked reduction. A revised and more severe Statute of Provisors was introduced in 1390 to be followed by a new Statute of Praemunire in 1393, though the latter was not enforced until the 1430s. Provisions continued at a low level through the reign of Henry IV controlled by the king using the anti-papal legislation. For the rest of the fifteenth century up to the Reformation they were virtually unknown. Isolated grants were made in the 1420s and 1430s but rarely implemented by bishops who feared royal displeasure; instead they preferred to collate papal candidates such as tax collectors.[46] As a papal collector Piero da Monte noted in 1438, England was a hopeless place for benefices.[47] After 1450 they were unknown. From the perspective of the whole medieval period papal provisions were a temporary phenomenon, but in the fourteenth century they loomed very large.

Fourteenth-century popes granted hundreds, perhaps thousands, of provisions and expectations to English cathedrals, but exactly how many is difficult to calculate; not even the papal scribes recorded all the grants made. Historians have three principal sources to work on, the nineteenth-century calendars of English material from the papal archives, the printed editions of the registers of the Avignon popes, and the accounts of the papal tax collectors, which are the only record of some grants. The picture is complicated by the different types of grants made and variations in the wording of the formula used in the grant. Furthermore full surveys of all nine secular cathedrals have yet to be undertaken. Despite these difficulties a clear view of the scale and pattern of provisions emerges. Though in many ways untypical of the other secular cathedrals, the pattern of provisions at Exeter does closely reflect and illustrate the national experience of them. Table 3 shows an analysis of papal provisions there.[48] After a modest start in the first three decades of the fourteenth century, when up to seven grants each decade were made, there was a substantial increase through the middle of the century. From the 1330s to the 1370s 112 provisions were made, three-quarters of the total. The Black Death brought a sharp increase. There were sixteen provisions in 1349 alone. From 1380 to 1400 there was a dramatic decline to the pre-1330 levels of up to half a dozen each decade. This was followed by an increase in the first decade of the fifteenth century to nine provisions. The

---

[46] M. Harvey, *England, Rome and the Papacy 1417–64*, Manchester, 1993, 94–8, 159, 166.

[47] Ibid., 166.

[48] For the basis of this table see note 12 above. The date of issue of provisions and expectations has been used.

TABLE 3. PAPAL PROVISIONS AND EXPECTATIONS TO CANONRIES AND DIGNITIES IN EXETER CATHEDRAL, 1300–1419

	CANONRIES			DIGNITARIES			TOTAL		
	Effective	Ineffective	Total	Effective	Ineffective	Total	Effective	Ineffective	Total
DECADE									
1300–09	2	0	2	0	0	0	2	0	2
1310–19	3	1	4	0	0	0	3	1	4
1320–29	4	3	7	0	0	0	4	3	7
1330–39	9	7	16	0	2	2	9	9	18
1340–49	14	12	26	3	2	5	17	14	31
1350–59	7	7	14	2	3	5	9	10	19
1360–69	12	4	16	2	2	4	14	6	20
1370–79	8	6	14	2	8	10	10	14	24
1380–89	2	1	3	2	0	2	4	1	5
1390–99	2	4	6	0	0	0	2	4	6
1400–09	3	3	6	1	2	3	4	5	9
1410–19	2	0	2	0	0	0	2	0	2
EPISCOPATE									
1300–7	1	0	1	0	0	0	1	0	1
Vacancy, 1307–08	0	0	0	0	0	0	0	0	0
Stapeldon, 1308–26	6	1	7	0	0	0	6	1	7
Vacancy, 1326–27	0	0	0	0	0	0	0	0	0
Berkeley, 1327	0	1	1	0	0	0	0	1	1

Vacancy, 1327–28	0	1	1	0	0	0	0	1	1
Grandisson, 1328–69	44	31	75	7	9	16	51	40	91
Vacancy, 1369–70	0	0	0	0	0	0	0	0	0
Brantingham, 1370–94	10	9	19	4	8	12	14	17	31
Vacancy, 1394–95	0	0	0	0	0	0	0	0	0
Stafford, 1395–1419	7	5	12	1	2	3	8	7	15
PONTIFICATE									
Clement V, 1305–14	3	0	3	0	0	0	3	0	3
John XXII, 1316–34	13	11	24	0	2	2	13	13	26
Benedict XII, 1334–42	2	0	2	0	0	0	2	0	2
Clement VI, 1342–52	15	16	31	2	3	5	17	19	36
Innocent VI, 1352–62	9	5	14	2	4	6	11	9	20
Urban V, 1362–70	9	2	11	2	1	3	11	3	14
Gregory XI, 1370–08	8	6	14	2	8	10	10	14	24
Urban VI, 1378–89	2	0	2	2	0	2	4	0	4
Boniface IX, 1389–1404	2	5	7	1	0	1	3	5	8
Innocent VII, 1404–06	3	3	6	0	1	1	3	4	7
Gregory XII, 1406–09	0	0	0	0	1	1	0	1	1
Alexander V, 1409–10	0	0	0	0	0	0	0	0	0
John XXIII, 1410–15	2	0	2	0	0	0	2	0	2

last was made in 1415, by which time they were rare. The first pope to make provisions to Exeter prebends on a large scale was John XXII (1316–34), who made twenty-six. Both his predecessor, Clement V (1305–14), and his successor Benedict XII (1334–42), were very modest, making two and three grants respectively. Clement VI (1342–52), well known for his generosity, was even more lavish than John XXII, granting thirty-six provisions, the most that any pope made. Under Innocent VI (1352–62) this momentum slackened somewhat. He made twenty provisions and under his successor, Urban V (1362–70), the number fell to fourteen. The last large-scale distribution of provisions was made by Gregory XI (1370–78), who made twenty-four, nineteen of them in the first two years of his pontificate. The Great Schism brought a substantial drop in provisions after 1378. Urban VI (1378–89) made only four, though this is probably an underrepresentation as little of his register survives, and his successors, Boniface IX (1389–1404) and Innocent VII (1404–06), eight and seven respectively. Innocent VII's grants, however, were made in a short two-year pontificate. In a longer reign Gregory XII (1406–09) made just one provision. The last two provisions were made by John XXIII (1410–15).

This pattern is confirmed by other studies. J. R. Highfield's broader survey of provisions to all benefices, not just cathedrals, by the Avignon popes from 1305 to 1378 shows that Exeter shared the overall trend in England.[49] In J. R. Wright's more detailed examination of provisions to cathedrals in the period 1305–34, set out in Table 4, a similar picture emerges showing John XXII as a prolific grantor of provisions in contrast to his predecessor Clement V. This study also enables us to compare the number of provisions at the nine secular cathedrals.[50] The wealth and to a lesser extent the size of the chapter determined the number of provisions made. The three richest, Lincoln, Salisbury and York, received most, often twice as many as the poorer Exeter, Hereford and Lichfield. With the partial exception of York, the three richest were also the largest chapters; their wealth and size made them of particular interest to provisors. The remaining three chapters, St Paul's, Wells and Chichester are all to some extent exceptions to this pattern, though all attracted noticeably less interest than the richest three. Though a medium sized chapter, St Paul's received a considerable number of provisions largely because of its prestige and convenient location in the capital for the many royal clerks who sought them. Despite being one of the largest chapters Wells did not receive as many provisions as the others of comparable size. This is probably a reflection of the relative poverty of many of its prebends. It is not clear why Chichester, a small and relatively poor chapter, received more provisions than comparable cathedrals such as Hereford and Exeter. T. N. Cooper's work on the diocese of Lichfield in the later fourteenth century enables a detailed comparison of provisions at Exeter and Lichfield in this period to be

49 Wright, *Church and Crown*, Appendix 1.
50 Ibid., Appendix 1, Table G.

TABLE 4. PAPAL PROVISIONS TO ENGLISH SECULAR CATHEDRALS, 1305–34

Cathedral	Number of Prebends	Clement V 1305–14	John XXII 1316–34
Chichester	29	0	46
Exeter	24	1	20
Hereford	28	2	25
Lichfield	32	5	37
Lincoln	55	6	73
St Paul's	30	3	52
Salisbury	52	4	77
Wells	55	0	49
York	36	5	65

TABLE 5. PAPAL PROVISIONS TO CANONRIES AND DIGNITIES
AT EXETER AND LICHFIELD CATHEDRALS, 1362–89

Pontificate	Lichfield	Exeter
Urban V 1362–70	26	14
Gregory XI 1370–78	33	24
1378–89	2	4

made.[51] This is set out in Table 5. At both Urban V (1362–70) was less prolific than the two outstanding grantors of provisions, John XXII and Clement V, but his successor Gregory XI (1370–78) nearly matched their high levels. In contrast provisions fell to a trickle in the pontificate of Urban VI (1378–89). The proportion of provisions made in 1362–89 to each chapter, with Lichfield receiving more than Exeter, broadly matches that found in the early fourteenth century. Detailed studies of other chapters would doubtless confirm this overall pattern.

Judging by contemporary complaints papal provisions had a widespread and damaging effect on the English Church. However, any assessment of their impact on cathedral chapters needs to bear in mind three factors. Firstly, that most clerics would have accepted the papal authority on which provisions were based and concentrated their objections on the way the system worked rather than rejecting it in principle. Secondly, the scale of provisions reflects the high demand for

[51] T. N. Cooper, 'The Papacy and the Diocese of Lichfield 1360–85', *Archivum Historicae Pontificae*, xxv, 1987, 73–103.

them by patrons and clerics alike, and finally many were never effected. One of the most articulate complainants was the chronicler Adam Murimuth. A suc-cessful canon lawyer, he acquired prebends in four cathedrals and the precentor-ship of Exeter. His campaign against papal provisions, especially to foreigners, forms a major theme in his chronicle, probably written in the 1340s at the time when the Commons was becoming increasingly anti-papal.[52] Murimuth was mainly concerned about the activities of foreign cardinals and provisions to bishoprics, but he also blamed bishops for not standing up to the pope, precisely because they had been provided to their sees. Despite his criticism of the system, he was prepared to use it to his advantage. In 1316 he received a provision to a canonry at Hereford and frequently acted as a papal 'mandator' or agent to carry them out including one for his kinsman Adam Murimuth junior.[53] In many respects his ambivalent attitude, with its emphasis on abuses in the way the system operated rather than fundamental objections to it, is typical of clerical views of the mid-fourteenth century. One of his most widely echoed criticisms was the way provisions enabled the English Church to be plundered by foreigners who occupied the richest benefices and diverted their incomes abroad. While there is some justification for such complaints they tended to be exaggerated. In the first half of the fourteenth century there was a significant presence of foreign provisors holding the richer prebends and dignities in the wealthier cathedrals. At Salisbury twelve foreigners were provided between 1329 and 1349, four of them to dignities.[54] Two dignities there were extensively occupied by foreign provisors, the deanery between 1308 and 1379 and the treasurership in 1317–40 and 1357–80. The proportion of foreign canons at York between 1296 and 1336 varied between a half and a third of the chapter.[55] However, their presence needs to be put in context. Native provisors were always much more numerous than those from overseas. Foreigners were a much smaller group at the poorer cathe-drals of Exeter, Hereford and Chichester. Even at Salisbury, where they were more numerous, many were Gascons and therefore subjects of the English crown, in whose employment many were engaged.[56] The resentment foreign provisors caused was much greater than their impact on the cathedrals where they were beneficed. The king's attitude to provisions has already been referred to. Like other patrons he found them a useful and cheap way of rewarding servants, some of them Gascons or papal officials. But his approach was determined by wider diplomatic issues in the course of Anglo-Papal relations. To this end he was prepared to use anti-papal sentiment and the legislation of 1351 and 1353 but at the same time continued seeking and using provisions up to the Schism.

---

[52] Gransden, Historical Writing, 63–7.
[53] CPL ii, 123; Jean XXII: Lettres Communes Analysee d'Apres les Registres Dits d'Avignon et du Vatican, ed., G. Mollat, Biblioteque des Ecoles Francaises d'Athenes et de Rome, Ser. 3, 16 vols, Paris, 1904–47, i no. 1920, ii no. 9350.
[54] Chew, Hemingby's Register, 11–13.
[55] Dobson, 'Later Middle Ages', 79.
[56] Chew, Hemingby's Register, 11.

Bishops had most to lose from papal intervention in appointments and as has been shown complained vigorously on occasion. A re-examination of Tables 1 and 2 reveals how much patronage some bishops lost to the pope. At Exeter provisions account for half the appointments during Bishop Grandisson's epis-copate from 1328 to 1369 and for almost as many (48%) at Lichfield during Bishop Northburgh's from 1322 to 1358. Yet, as we shall see, even bishops found provisions had their advantages.

When making provisions, popes were often responding to requests for them. Indeed, this was a major impetus behind their development. As Bishop Trefnant noted, much of the demand came from ambitious clerics. Robert Wodehouse, a leading royal clerk, pressed Edward II to write to the pope and two cardinals on his behalf to secure a provision.[57] The notification and recording of provisions by such men fills many of the surviving act books of cathedral chapters; one at Lincoln contains two lists dating from 1309 and 1330 with a total of thirty grants.[58] Registering a claim with the chapter was an important first stage in effecting them. Well placed royal and papal clerics acquired a series of provisions to desirable prebends. Andrew Offord, a leading royal envoy, was granted three in a single year 1343 and a further two in 1349.[59] Chapters themselves do not seem to have been hostile to the system which is not surprising given that many of their members had used it successfully. There are cases of chapters requesting provisions. In 1327 the Wells chapter sought one to a canonry in their own cathedral for Alan Conesburgh an ecclesiastical lawyer who had served them well.[60] They had even taken the precaution of ensuring the bishop's support and wrote to Conesburgh that they were confident that he would receive a prebend when there was a vacancy. Unfortunately their confidence was misplaced and he had to make do with a disputed claim to the provostship without a canonry. The majority of clerics had little chance of receiving a provision without an influential patron as few were important enough to make a petition in their own right. Patrons were as vigorous as clerics in pursuit of provisions. Chief among them was the king and other members of the royal family who secured the largest number of provisions. The lay nobility were as zealous, though on a smaller scale. Bishops, abbots and cardinals joined them in making requests for their clerks and relatives. The granting of provisions to bishops was one way of responding to their complaints about them. Bishop Grandisson's outspoken criticisms resulted in concessions in 1331 and 1344 which allowed him to nominate provisions to nine prebends and a dignity.[61] Like his fellow bishops Grandisson used provisions to reward his diocesan officials with canonries. This together with the undoubted learning and suitability of some provisors tempered his criticism of the system. Some enlisted the support of two or three patrons when requesting a provision.

[57] Ibid., 14–15.
[58] LAO D&C A2/21 33–4, 35–6.
[59] BRUO ii, 1390–1.
[60] HMC Wells i, 207, 250.
[61] Jean XXII: Lettres Commune, ii, nos 55156, 55961–2; Reg. Grandisson Exeter iii, 1360.

For those without access to individual patronage university petitions from Oxford and Cambridge for benefices for their alumni offered an alternative route.

A combination of high demand, prolific grants and the fixed number of cathedral prebends and dignities caused a relatively high failure rate of provisions. Such was the pressure on the papacy that multiple grants to the same prebend were made and provisions issued where there was no vacancy. Expectations to future vacancies in unspecified prebends were freely granted and not always recorded which only fueled disputes and litigation. In 1377 the papal collector stated that 288 provisions and 723 expectations to all types of benefice in England had yet to be effected.[62] Failure rates for provisions and expectations to cathedral prebends and dignities seem to have ranged from 40–60 per cent. In the pontificate of John XXII (1316–34) it was 40 per cent at Lincoln, 57 per cent at Salisbury and 50 per cent at Exeter.[63] The overall figure at Exeter for the period 1305–1415 is comparable at 46 per cent.[64] However, the failure rate at Lichfield between 1362 and 1389 was as high as 72 per cent, but over the same period at Exeter only 40 per cent.[65] Lichfield may have been exceptional but the figure may also reflect more accurate knowledge of the number of provisions made. Just why individuals failed to effect their provisions is less easy to explain. Being in the wrong place at the wrong time is probably the best explanation for some. There is little to separate the successful from the unsuccessful, either in terms of ability and office or powerful patronage. Distinguished and well-connected clerics like the theologian Walter Burley and the future archbishop of York Alexander Neville were unable to effect provisions to Exeter.[66] Delays (it could take several years to carry out a provision) and the prospect of litigation deterred some. Others fell foul of the anti-provisors legislation. At Exeter canons were twice imprisoned, in 1371 and 1381, for contravening it.[67] As a consequence the chapter was more circumspect in its acceptance of provisions. When John Abraham petitioned them for a prebend in 1390 they said they would do what they could bearing in mind the recently passed statute.[68]

Exchanges

It was, indeed, almost impossible for a cleric to obtain a canonry or dignity without the support of the bishop, king, pope, or another patron. There was, however, one other route open to him: to exchange his benefice for a canonry.[69]

[62] Chew, Hemingby's Register, 16.
[63] Wright, Church and Crown, Appendix 1, Table F; Table 3 above.
[64] See Table 3 above.
[65] See note 50.
[66] Exeter Fasti, 27, 15.
[67] PRO C47/52/3/124; CPR 1377–81, 521.
[68] DRO D&C 3550 fo. 63r.
[69] For a general discussion of this topic, on which few detailed studies have been made, see Thompson, English Clergy, 107–9; Chew, Hemingby's Register, 37–41.

In theory exchanges were under the bishop's control, required his approval and could therefore be prevented by him. In practice such permission seems to have been a formality and exchanges appear to have operated largely outside his control. The lack of obstruction and complaints about them suggests that bishops did not find them objectionable. For most of the later middle ages they had little cause to. There was a steady trickle of exchanges, on average five or fewer each decade, through this period. But in the later fourteenth century exchanges increased to the point where they were considered an abuse, and in 1392 Archbishop Courtenay issued a strong condemnation of the practice. At Exeter their increase happened suddenly in the 1370s, when there were fourteen, out of a total of fifty-seven in the period 1300 to 1541.[70] In one year alone, 1371, there were five: more in one year than in any other decade except the 1370s. On this scale exchanges reduced the bishop's ability to appoint canons considerably. It was mainly Bishop Brantingham who suffered from this; a quarter of the appointments to canonries in his episcopate were made in this way. Even so he was better off than Bishop Stretton at Lichfield (1360–85) where the proportion reached a third.[71] At St Paul's the pattern matches Exeter's closely, though because it was a larger and more prestigious chapter the total is higher, eighty-five exchanges occurred over the same period 1300–1541.[72] The peak was reached slightly earlier in the 1360s when eighteen were made. There was a second surge in the 1390s, a total of ten at the time when Archbishop Courtenay expressed his concern about the 'chopchurch' brokers who seem to have arranged many of them. Exchanges do not seem to have had much harmful effect on chapters. At Exeter most of those gaining a canonry in this way became resident and played an active part in the life of the cathedral. Generally the motives behind exchanges are not explicit and have to be inferred. In some cases there was a financial advantage, in others it marked a new stage in a career. Thomas Chandler intended to exchange his rectory of Milbrook near Southampton for a Wells prebend to be near his patron Thomas Bekington who was bishop there.[73] Disputed possession and legal challenges sometimes prompted clerics to cut their losses and exchange their prebend with a rival for another benefice. In the late fourteenth century series of the rapid exchanges, probably motivated by ambition and career advancement can be observed. At Exeter there was an outbreak in 1377 among a close knit group of royal clerks based at Westminster.[74] On 8 May Robert Crull, a chamberlain of the exchequer, exchanged his Exeter canonry with William Borstall, keeper of the rolls. Within a few weeks, by the end of June, he had exchanged his canonry with his kinsman Robert Braybroke, the

---

70 The figures are taken from *Exeter Fasti*.
71 See Table 2 above.
72 The figures are taken from *St Paul's Fasti*.
73 *Letters of Thomas Bekington* i, 265.
74 *Exeter Fasti*, 38, 40.

king's secretary, who held it for only a year before exchanging it. Exchanges of prebends within the same cathedral were on a much smaller scale and were undertaken for a similar range of reasons.

Disputes

In the seven weeks between 7 February and 23 March 1425 three different clerics were successively installed as archdeacon of Colchester in St Paul's cathedral.[75] While this was exceptional, the rivalry and determination to secure the office is typical of the intense competition for prebends and dignities among clerics. The combination of rivalry and determination led to disputed claims, some of which resulted in long and complex lawsuits. The most ambitious and ruthless clerics were prepared to go to considerable lengths in pursuit of a canonry. Disputes were almost entirely confined to the fourteenth and early fifteenth centuries. They were made possible by encroachments from the crown and papacy on bishops' rights of collation to prebends and dignities in their cathedrals, virtually disappearing as regalian right was more strictly confined to episcopal vacancies and provisions died out. With three alternative routes to a canonry, the scope for competition was much greater and more likely to result in disputes. There were far more provisions and royal grants than vacant canonries. Yet rivalry and competition did not always provoke disputes. Many royal grants and provisions remained ineffective because they do not seem to have been vigorously pursued, at least as far as the sources indicate. The usual procedure was first to register the claim with the chapter. Much then depended on whether there was a vacancy and any rival claimants. If there was no immediate vacancy vigilance was necessary to ensure the claim was pressed when one occurred especially if there were rivals. It could take several years to effect a provision. Duplicate grants by the pope and king, which added to the number of claimants, and papal expectations to unnamed prebends, which increased the uncertainty, together made it harder to obtain a canonry. When faced with a determined rival many were deterred by the expense and trouble of litigation and allowed their claim to lapse. Rivalry for a canonry escalated into a dispute when a claimant took steps to press his claim against another. At its simplest this might be a restatement of the claim at a chapter meeting, confirmation by the king of a royal grant or the bishop of his collation set out in the relevant documents. If a rival was not deterred by this the next stage was litigation in the course of which force and intimidation might be resorted to.

Most effort and rivalry was concentrated on the more valuable prebends and dignities which were more likely to be disputed. At the wealthy and large cathedral of Lincoln there were a considerable number, forty-eight can be identified; five of the eight archdeaconries and nearly half of the fifty-eight

---

[75] *St Paul's Fasti*, 13.

THE SCRAMBLE FOR PREFERMENT 39

prebends were disputed.[76] Of the twenty-six disputed prebends only three were worth less than £20, out of a total of fifteen below that value in the cathedral. Royal grants were overwhelmingly successful in contested claims at Lincoln and elsewhere against both papal provisors and those collated by the bishop. On the rare occasions when provisors overcame royal grants it was often with the king's support in the form of a confirmation of a provision or licence to accept one. Claimants were cautious in embarking on litigation; just under half the disputes at Lincoln were taken to court. The majority were settled in the royal courts, though up to 1351 and less frequently up to 1390 the papal courts were used. Thereafter anti-papal legislation proved an effective deterrent. A small number of cases were taken to the court of Canterbury, the final ecclesiastical court of appeal in England. The caution in bringing disputes to court was well founded as litigation could be complex and protracted. At Exeter Robert Broke's attempt to effect the provision he was granted in 1372 involved three appeals to Rome by various interested parties.[77] His first attempt to effect his provision was thwarted by a rival: Thomas Walkington. Undeterred Broke pressed his claim against another provisor, Ralph Tregrisiou, and appealed to Rome. Both Tregrisiou and the cathedral chapter made counter-appeals but Broke's persistence paid off and he became a canon in 1376. Some disputes became extremely tangled and it is hard to know who gained possession. The archdeaconry of Cornwall was in dispute from 1349 to 1371.[78] During this time there was effectively no archdeacon, though from time to time a candidate was instituted. Claims and counter-claims were passed down successive generations. The dispute was over whether the pope or king should appoint. Three provisors succeeded each other in 1350, 1355, and 1361. The two royal candidates succeeded each other by exchange in 1357. An appeal to the pope brought the intervention of the archbishop of York, who was appointed to decide the case in 1365. By this time the dean and chapter had become involved. They appealed to parliament against royal interference, but had no success.[79] Nor did another candidate, William Pyl, who found himself in the Marshalsea prison in 1371 as a result of his efforts to obtain the archdeaconry.[80] The king brought the matter to a conclusion that year by setting aside the rival candidates and making his own appointment.

The most ruthless were prepared to go to considerable lengths to overcome their rivals. Few were as brazen as William Gulden in bringing armed men into a cathedral but he was not alone in using force and intimidation. There were three cases of violence being used at Salisbury in the 1330s and 1340s.[81] Two of

---

[76] The figures are taken from *Lincoln Fasti*.
[77] *Exeter Fasti*, 39; *John Lydford's Book*, ed., D. M. Owen, DCRS, New Series, xx, 1974, nos 125–8, 148–9.
[78] *Exeter Fasti*, 15–16.
[79] CCR 1364–8, 126.
[80] PRO C47/52/3/124.
[81] Chew, *Hemingby's Register*, 35.

them involved attacks on prebendal estates at Bedminster and Grantham. In the third John Bredon in the course of trying to effect a provision to the treasurership was responsible for an assault on a rival provisor's proctor. Despite repeated excommunications in 1346 and 1348 and orders for the sequestration of his goods Bredon remained unrepentant and beyond the reach papal jurisdiction. David Calveley's defiance was more spectacular as he unsuccessfully sought to effect a papal provision to the Salisbury prebend of Blewbury from 1376 to 1381.[82] His rival William Salisbury had gained possession and must have felt secure as he had been presented by the king. This did not stop Calveley who began litigation contrary to the praemunire legislation and was consigned to the Marshalsea prison. While on bail he was alleged to have kidnapped Salisbury in an attempt to force him to give up his claim which resulted in his return to the Marshalsea in 1381. Events moved rapidly that year. In the course of the Peasants' Revolt he was released by the rebels and taken to Blewbury where he was put in possession of the prebendal manor. Calveley did not remain there long and was rearrested and imprisoned after the revolt collapsed. Subsequently he was released and in 1384 pardoned probably at the behest of his uncle Sir Hugh Calveley. Salisbury was luckier than some in suffering only a temporary loss of his prebend. Others were permanently ejected by their rivals. Men as unscrupulous as William Gulden and David Calveley were untypical, but most higher clergy appear in a rather unattractive light in the scramble for cathedral preferments. After all, they lived in a relatively lawless society, where violence was widely used and tolerated as a means of gaining one's end.

[82] Ibid., 241.

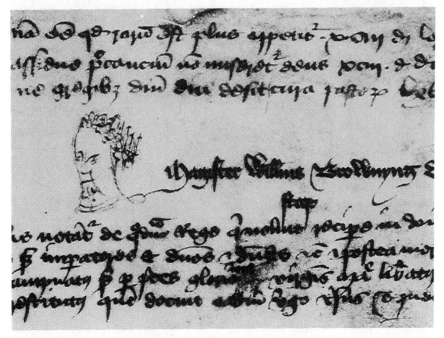

Plate 1. A rare thumbnail sketch of a canon, William Browning of Exeter (d.1454)

Plate 2. The chronicler Adam Murimuth (d.1347) from a donor panel in the east window of Eaton Bishop parish church, Herefordshire. In the course of a highly successful career he was briefly a canon of Hereford and in the service of Bishop Orleton.

3

Canons' Origins:
Geographical, Social and Educational

Cathedral canons and dignitaries were among the most privileged, wealthy and successful secular clergy of the later middle ages, ranking just below the episcopate. With just seventeen sees in England only a small elite could rise to be bishops, whereas a far larger group could aspire to be canons and dignitaries. At their peak just before the Reformation there were thirty-seven archdeaconries, forty-two dignities, and 350 canonries in the nine secular chapters, though some of the latter were attached to dignities or religious houses and not available as independent posts. Birth, education and service to either Church or crown were the surest route to one of these, as this chapter will show. Patronage or nepotism, and frequently both, eased the path and were usually found in successful careers. By the fifteenth century a university education and service were the most effective way to a prebend. In general the higher levels of the Church were relatively open to talent, and occupied by university educated administrators in Church and state from a wide range of largely landholding social backgrounds. In the course of these successful careers there was often a considerable degree of geographical mobility.

Geographical Origins

Canons were amongst the most highly mobile of the secular clergy. By the time they acquired their canonries, usually as mature and successful clerics, many had already travelled widely, first to university and then in the service of the king or a bishop. The secular clergy as a whole did not travel as far, at least in the early stages of their careers; their ordination records show them staying in their native dioceses or moving to contiguous ones. A study of the geographical origins of canons, for which a considerable amount of evidence exists, shows just how far they ventured, as an analysis of the holders of just one canonry demonstrates.[1] The prebend of Easton in Gordano in Wells Cathedral was held from 1300 to

---

[1] The problems encountered in determining canons' geograpical origins are discussed in Lepine, 'Origins and Careers', 88–92. The attributions used here are based on a wide range of printed and manuscript sources including the printed calendars of patent and close rolls, the printed papal registers and episcopal registers and a wide range of records printed by local record societies.

1541 by canons from as far away as Canterbury, Northampton, and Barrow in Furness, as well as from Somerset.[2] A broader survey of one cathedral over a short period reveals a similar diversity. At Salisbury in the twenty years from 1329 to 1349 there were canons from Swynnerton in Staffordshire and Cotterstock in Northamptonshire alongside those from the dioceses of Carlisle, Hereford and Norwich. Salisbury's wealth and prestige attracted many foreigners at this time with canons from the dioceses of Cahors, Limoges and Turin among several others.[3] From a systematic survey of two contrasting chapters, Exeter and Lincoln, over the two and a half centuries after 1300, clear patterns emerge.[4] Exeter is typical of the smaller, poorer and more remote chapters such as Hereford and perhaps to a lesser extent Chichester and Lincoln of the larger and wealthier including Salisbury and York. A good deal of information survives; at Exeter something is known of as many as 79 per cent of the chapter and at Lincoln for 66 per cent in the period 1300 to 1541. Two patterns emerge, combining a wide diversity of origins, with an important local element from the mother diocese. All chapters contained canons from across the country and in the fourteenth century, as a consequence of papal provisions, from abroad. Table 6 and Maps 1 and 2 give a breakdown of the geographical origins of the two chapters' canons and dignitaries by diocese. Despite their differences there are some striking similarities alongside the important differences between them. Both had some canons from every diocese, even the most distant Carlisle and Canterbury and abroad. However, the largest number came from the mother diocese. The second highest totals, though far smaller than the mother diocese, come, as might be expected, from the bigger dioceses elsewhere in England; at Exeter almost 10 per cent came from Lichfield and at Lincoln 14 per cent from York. The other dioceses of origin with larger totals also tend to be the larger ones; at Exeter they were, Lincoln and York with 6.9 per cent and 6.4 per cent respectively and at Lincoln, Lichfield with 9 per cent. The large diocese of Lichfield produced virtually the same proportion of canons at each chapter, 9.6 per cent at Exeter and 9 per cent at Lincoln. Canons from the rest of England and Wales originated from other dioceses in a remarkably even way; even medium sized dioceses like Norwich and Salisbury produced less than 5 per cent of the total of both chapters. At Exeter there was no marked predominance of canons from the neighbouring West-Country dioceses of Wells and Salisbury. Neither Exeter nor Lincoln attracted many canons from the south-east in spite of their large population. The five dioceses of Winchester, Chichester, Canterbury, Rochester and London, account for only 5 per cent of the Exeter chapter and 10 per cent at Lincoln. This broadly reflects the recruitment pattern of Oxford University where most

---

[2] *Wells Fasti* 46–7; Thomas Linacre from Canterbury (BRUO ii, 1147–49), John Seymour from Northampton (PRO PROB 11/13 fo. 170), Christopher Urswick from Barrow-in-Furness (BRUO iii, 1935–37) and from Somerset James and Peter Berkeley (BRUO i, 174–5).

[3] These attributions are taken from Chew, *Hemingby's Register*, 171–260.

[4] The method used is that outlined in note 1.

TABLE 6. THE GEOGRAPHICAL ORIGINS OF THE CANONS AND DIGNITARIES
OF EXETER AND LINCOLN CATHEDRALS, 1300-1541

Diocese of origin	Total EXETER	Percentage of total with known origins	Total LINCOLN	Percentage of total with known origins
Canterbury	6	1.6	13	1.7
Carlisle	4	1	11	1.4
Chichester	1	0.2	9	1.2
Durham	4	1	15	2
Ely	2	0.5	12	1.6
Exeter	176	46.9	18	2.4
Hereford	5	1.3	10	1.3
Lichfield	36	9.6	67	9
Lincoln	26	6.9	223	30
London	7	1.8	29	3.9
Norwich	10	2.6	23	4.3
Rochester	1	0.2	4	0.5
Salisbury	13	3.4	32	4.3
Wells	18	4.8	20	2.6
Winchester	9	2.4	21	2.8
Worcester	15	0.4	25	3.3
York	24	6.4	104	14
Welsh Dioceses	6	1.6	11	1.4
Foreign Dioceses	12	3.2	95	12.8
Total Known Origins	375	79	742	65.8
Total Unknown Origins	99		385	
Overall Total	474		1127	

canons, particularly at Exeter, were educated. No doubt these dioceses, close to the centres of royal and ecclesiastical administration, offered plenty of scope for ambitious clerics.

Lincoln canons were more cosmopolitan than their Exeter counterparts as Table 6 confirms. This is the main difference in their origins and is clearest in the number of foreign canons in each chapter. At Lincoln they form the third largest group, nearly 13 per cent of the total, whereas at Exeter they make up only 3.2 per cent. The valuable prebends at Lincoln attracted French and Italian clerics with papal connections. These foreign canons were most numerous in the fourteenth century in the period when papal provisions were at their height. The relatively poor Exeter prebends did not attract foreigners in such numbers. Salisbury and York, both wealthy chapters like Lincoln, also had relatively large

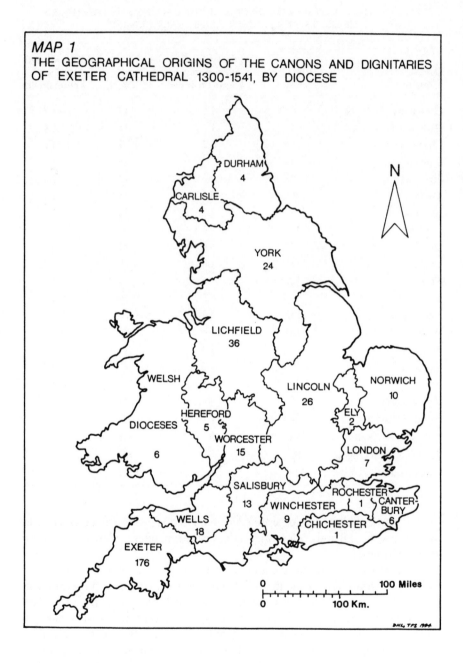

MAP 1
THE GEOGRAPHICAL ORIGINS OF THE CANONS AND DIGNITARIES
OF EXETER CATHEDRAL 1300-1541, BY DIOCESE

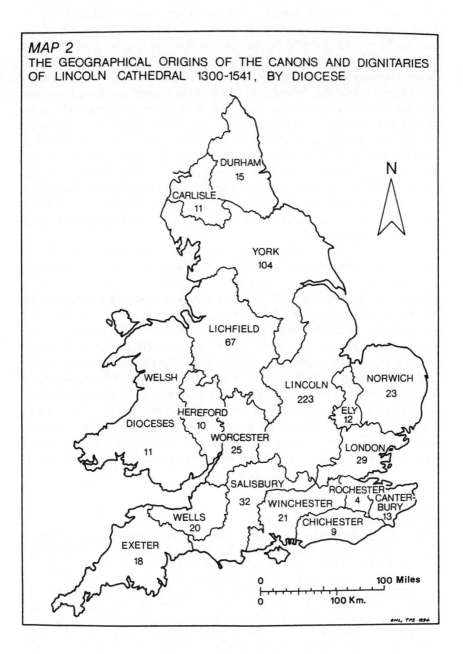

MAP 2
THE GEOGRAPHICAL ORIGINS OF THE CANONS AND DIGNITARIES
OF LINCOLN CATHEDRAL 1300-1541, BY DIOCESE

numbers of foreign canons at that time. At Salisbury they make up 18 per cent of the chapter in 1329–49.[5] Lincoln differs from Exeter in having a larger number of Northerners, where canons from the province of York form 16 per cent of the total, double the percentage at Exeter. The diversity of geographical origins found at Exeter and Lincoln is also found among the residentiary canons of York in the fifteenth century where two-thirds came from outside Yorkshire.[6] In all cathedrals a major reason for the influx of canons from outside the diocese was the appointment of bishops from elsewhere. They tended to bring in groups of canons from their previous centres of activity: men who were often related to them by family or service. During his episcopate from 1282 to 1317 Bishop Swinfield of Hereford, who was born in Kent, introduced a group of fourteen south-eastern canons into the chapter.[7] At Exeter a succession of northern bishops, George Neville and John Booth, began to introduce clerics from the north during their episcopates from 1456 to 1478. A further influx of Northerners arrived there during the episcopate of Hugh Oldham 1504–19, a native of Manchester, diluting the strong local presence.[8]

As mother churches cathedrals had an important place in their dioceses. Their standing and influence is reflected in the high proportion of canons from within the diocese. It seems that many a rising or successful cleric aspired to a prebend in his mother church, which was also the biggest source of such benefices in his locality. Even the cosmopolitan chapter of Lincoln contained nearly a third (30 per cent) who came from within the diocese. At Exeter the proportion was considerably higher reaching nearly half (47 per cent). The predominantly local character of Exeter's chapter was reinforced by the physical presence of the South-Western canons at their cathedral with three-quarters of those originating in the diocese becoming residentiaries, many in the course of local careers within the diocese of Exeter, apart from a period of study at university.[9] Patterns of recruitment within a diocese are largely dependent on the rather arbitrary survival of family property deeds. So far only the Exeter chapter has been studied at this level. For nearly half of those with geographical origins in the diocese it

5   See note 3.
6   Dobson, 'Residentiary Canons', 154–5.
7   Most of these attributions are based on their surnames being placenames which in individual cases is an unreliable method but with such a large group as this suggests a clear pattern in Swinfield's recruitment of canons. The five exceptions whose origins are known are three members of his family, his nephew John Swinfield and Richard and Stephen Swinfield, Thomas Cobham from Kent (BRUO i, 450–1) and William Sarden from Kent (Lincoln Fasti 1066–1300, 39). Those with toponymics are Roger Canterbury, Simon Faversham, Robert Icklesham, Richard Nonnington, Nicholas Reigate, Hamo Sandwich, Henry Shorne, Stephen Thaneto, and John Winchelsea.
8   Among the northerners introduced by bishops Neville and Booth were Robert and William Aiscough from the diocese of York and Thomas Rotherham from Rotherham (BRUC 27–8; BRUO iii, 1593–6). Bishop Oldham's 'Manchester mafia' is analysed in Thomson, Early Tudor Church, 69–70.
9   Lepine, Canons of Exeter Cathedral, Chapter 4.

is possible to provide a precise location based on attributions, family landholdings and ordination titles. The most convenient subdivision of the diocese is into its four archdeaconries. The archdeaconry of Exeter provided most canons: a total of thirty-three. This is not surprising as it included the city of Exeter, which was both the diocesan and regional capital – the largest town in the South-West apart from Bristol and Salisbury – and the well populated area of mid and east Devon. Twelve canons came from the city of Exeter, particularly during two periods: four in the first two decades of the fourteenth century, and two in the mid 1450s. A further six came from nearby villages. Almost as many came from the archdeaconry of Cornwall: a total of twenty-five canons. This territory, more or less identical with the county of Cornwall, was the remotest part of the diocese, separated by distance and slow roads, and distinguished west of Bodmin by language. Nevertheless, there was usually at least one Cornishman among the chapter; and in the later fourteenth and early fifteenth centuries this rose to three or four, reaching a peak of five in the 1420s. Within the archdeaconry the canons were fairly evenly spread. Five canons came from north and east Cornwall, and twelve from west of Bodmin, two of these from as far west as the Lizard peninsular. A further five are known to be Cornish, either by attribution or in the case of Henry and John Bloyou by their surnames, but their precise location in the archdeaconry is unknown. Over half the Cornishmen later became resident at Exeter, but only three of them became archdeacons of Cornwall, and these three only held office for twenty-three years between them. However two Cornishmen – Ralph Tregrisiou from St Creed and John Cobethorn from Launceston – occupied the deanery for seventy years, in 1384–1415 and 1419–58 respectively.[10] The archdeaconry of Totnes was the largest of the three in Devon but it contained the extremes of sparsely populated Dartmoor and the most fertile land in fourteenth century Devon, in the South Hams. Twenty-three canons are known to have originated in this archdeaconry, eleven of them from the fertile valleys of the South Hams. In contrast the archdeaconry of Barnstaple, similar to the archdeaconry of Totnes in containing both moorland and the fertile valleys of the Taw and Torridge but smaller in area, is known to have produced only eleven canons. Most of these came from a coastal strip from Hartland to Ilfracombe. A less extensive survey of the Lincoln chapter suggests that in such a large diocese the influence of the cathedral waned at its southern extremities. Within the diocese canons from Lincolnshire, the archdeaconries of Lincoln and Stow, predominated, a total of seventy-three spread evenly across the county. The archdeaconries of Northampton and Leicester produced twenty-nine and twenty-one canons respectively. Fewer came from the more southerly archdeaconries, twelve from Oxford, ten from Buckingham, five from Bedford and only one from Huntingdon. In large parts of these four archdeaconries Lincoln would have seemed distant. In contrast much of north-east Nottinghamshire was within

---

[10] BRUO iii, 1893 (Tregrisiou); Reg. Stafford Exeter 62, 286, 460, and Reg. Lacy Exeter iii, 246 (Cobethorn).

twenty miles of the city and six canons are known to have originated from this region. With the exception of larger towns, such as cathedral cities, it is unusual to find one place producing several canons unless they were from the same family. However, the village of Ugborough on the southern edge of Dartmoor was the birthplace of three Exeter canons.[11]

Social Origins

The social origins of the higher clergy are much more difficult to establish than the geographical. The major problem is lack of evidence; a canon's social status unlike his geographical origins is rarely given in the sources. Studies at Exeter and Lincoln have identified the social origins of about a third of each chapter. Consequently it is not possible to do more than indicate the range of social backgrounds of canons. The obscurity of most origins, however, should not be taken as an indication of humble status. Despite the opacity in the evidence, it is clear that most came from landholding families, though there was considerable variation in their status and wealth ranging from the yeomanry to the peerage. Relatively few were born into the lower levels of medieval society. Only to this limited extent were the higher ranks of the Church open to talent. The structure of late medieval society is best understood, for our purposes, if a broad distinction is made between those who formed the aristocracy and those who were outside it.[12] The aristocracy can be divided into two groups: the greater aristocracy, those who gradually emerged as the parliamentary peerage, and the lesser aristocracy, which by 1500 was subdivided into knights, esquires, and gentlemen. The prominence of the greater aristocracy and our knowledge of their pedigrees makes it possible to be reasonably certain about their numbers among canons, something that cannot be ascertained for any other social group. Baronial and peerage families never dominated English cathedrals, either in numbers or influence. Members of these families can be found in all chapters forming a small but constant presence up to the Reformation. A handful of canons were of royal birth, albeit illegitimate; James Hispania, the son of Alfonso X of Castile and nephew of Queen Eleanor, held six prebends and Henry Beaufort, John of Gaunt's son, three.[13] Such prominent families as Berkeley, Clare, Neville, Percy and Stafford were represented in several cathedrals.[14] At both Exeter and Lincoln

---

11 BRUO i, 215–16 (Bolter), ii, 735–6 (Fylham), i, 282–3 (Browning).
12 The social structure of later medieval England is discussed in C. Dyer, *Standards of Living in the Later Middle Ages: Social Change in England 1200–1520*, Cambridge, 1989, Chapter 1; M. Keen, *English Society in the Later Middle Ages 1348–1500*, Harmondsworth, 1990; F. R. H. du Boulay, *An Age of Ambition*, 1970. The most recent work on the aristocracy is C. Given-Wilson, *The English Nobility in the Later Middle Ages: the Fourteenth-Century Political Community*, 1987.
13 BRUO iii, 1736–38 (Hispania), i, 139–42 (Beaufort).
14 James Berkeley (*BRUO* i, 174–5), Richard Clare (*CPL ii*, 12), Robert Neville (*BRUO*

baronial families formed less than 5 per cent of the chapter, at the former amounting to only nineteen canons out of 474 and at the latter forty out of 1127. Though a small number their impact was wider because most held several canonries. Lionel Woodville held prebends at Lincoln, Salisbury, Exeter and St Paul's.[15] Birth and family influence undoubtedly helped those of this rank who wanted to become canons, though direct evidence rarely survives. Few of them took up residence as their interests usually lay elsewhere. They were more likely to be promoted to the bench of bishops than those from other social groups. At Exeter over half of the canons from baronial and peerage families were raised to the episcopate, four of them to Exeter, and five to archbishoprics.[16] At some cathedrals local baronial families were particularly evident, though rarely over long periods. Three members of the Fitzalan family, earls of Arundel, were canons of Chichester in the early fourteenth century.[17] A little later no less than five members of the Charlton family, lords of Powys, four of them brothers, were canons of Hereford between 1317 and 1385.[18] Their influence in the chapter was limited by the fact that none were resident or held dignities. A far greater influence was open to the family when two of them, Lewis and Thomas, became bishop. The Courtenays differed in several respects from most other baronial families, partly because they had a continuous if chequered existence through the period 1300–1539, and partly because their wealth and power were concentrated in the diocese. They seem to have regarded the chapter as one of their interests. Four members of the family were canons or dignitaries, one of them, Peter Courtenay, rising to be dean in 1477–78 and bishop from 1478 to 1487, and a further fifty-seven canons had some connection with the family. The Courtenays' position in the diocese was strengthened by the absence of any other baronial families of comparable influence for much of the period.[19] Alongside the native nobility were a smaller group of foreign nobles the majority of whom owed their canonries to papal connections. During the first two-thirds of the fourteenth century most chapters included a handful of French or Italian nobles, often members of the Roman aristocracy or relatives of the Avignon popes who might already be cardinals. Typical of these is Manuel de Fieschi a member of the Genoese aristocracy who was a canon of York, Salisbury and Lincoln before becoming bishop of Vercelli in 1343.[20] Even more than their English counter-

---

ii, 1350), Thomas Percy (*BRUO* iii, 1462) and Edmund Stafford (*BRUO* iii, 1749–50).

15 *BRUO* iii, 2083–4.

16 Lepine, 'Origins and Careers', 95–6.

17 Richard Arundel (d. 1305), John Arundel (d.1331) and Thomas Arundel (fl. 1372) (*Chichester Fasti*, 48, 23, 59).

18 Thomas Charlton 1317, Lewis Charlton 1336–61, Griffin Charlton 1345–81, William Charlton 1366, and Humphrey Charlton ?–1371 (*Hereford Fasti* 17, 50, 40, 14, 48).

19 The relationship between the Courtenays and Exeter Cathedral is the subject of Lepine, 'Courtenays and Exeter Cathedral'.

20 Chew, *Hemingby's Register*, 198–9.

parts they were absentees from their cathedrals, and a source of resentment and complaint about papal provisions.

The much larger lesser aristocracy came to be differentiated during the late fourteenth and fifteenth centuries into knights, esquires, and gentlemen and ranked in that order. The greater knights were often important landowners with substantial political influence. Canons born into knightly families form a larger group those from the peerage. Some were members of such prominent, wealthy, and politically active families as Braybroke, Burghersh, Calverlegh, Loring and Molyens.[21] Others came from less prominent families with regional or county influence such as John Metham, a canon of Lincoln, the son of Sir Thomas Metham of Yorkshire.[22] Local families were often members of a chapter. At Exeter West-Country knightly families were particularly well represented. A list of them reads like a roll call of the county families of Devon and Cornwall and includes the names of Arundel, Bodrigan, Botriaux, Carew, Cary, Cergeaux, Chambernoun, Edgecombe, Ferrers, Fulford, Grenville, Hals, Lercedekne, Pollard, Speke and Willoughby.[23] Among the county families providing canons of Lincoln were the Ayremynnes, Beks, Daubeneys, Eyncourts, Husseys, Sheffields and Wimbushes, though local families do not form such a large group here as they do at Exeter.[24] The Church was used by these families to provide a career for their younger or illegitimate sons. Canons from this rank started off with considerable advantages: family money to provide a good education, family benefices to

[21] Nicholas and Robert Braybroke (BRUO i, 253–5; CCR 1374–77, 352–3; Reg. Arundel Canterbury i, fo. 165); Henry Burghersh (BRUO iii, 2157–8); David Calverley (BRUO i, 341); William Loring (BRUO ii, 1163); Adam Moleyns (BRUO ii, 1289–91).

[22] CPL iii, 292.

[23] John Arundel (BRUO i, 50–1); William Bodrigan (J. Maclean, The Parochial and Family History of the Deanery of Trigg Minor, 3 vols, 1873–75, i, 55); Walter Botriaux (CPR 1327–30, 529; CPR 1345–48, 227); George Carew (BRUO 1500–1540 101–3); Thomas Cary (CFR 1383–91, 244); Michael Cergeaux (BRUO i, 377–8); Reginald Chambernoun, who was rector of the family benefice of Ilfracombe from 1297 till his death in 1333 (Reg. Stapeldon Exeter 93–4); John Eggecombe (BRUO i, 630;D&C 1183); Hugh Ferrers (CPP 221); William Fulford (CPL viii, 534); Richard Grenville (Reg. Stafford Exeter 275); John and Richard Hals (BRUO ii, 856–7); Martin and Michael Lercedekne (BRUO ii, 1133–4); John Pollard (PRO PCC 23 Mellershe); John Speke (Somerset Medieval Wills 1501–30 132–4); Edward Willoughby (BRUO iii, 2051; Vivian, Visitation of Devon, 790).

[24] Richard and William Ayremynne (Chew, Hemingby's Register, 174–5); Anthony and Thomas Bek (BRUO i, 153–4); John and Philip Daubeny; the latter was in the service of Sir John Daubeny of Broughton and both held two benefices successively, the recory of Watton-on-Stone and the archdeaconry of Bedford (LAO Reg. V (Reg. Burghersh) fos 35r, 461r; LAO Reg. IV (Reg. Burghersh) fo. 372r; Lincoln Fasti, 16); Oliver d'Eyncourt (BRUO i, 576–7; Inq. Post Mortem, vi, no. 746); Peter Huse (BRUO ii, 989–90; Inq. Post Mortem Hen VII i, no. 883); William Sheffield (BRUC 521–2); Nicholas and Robert Wymbush; their wills show them to be connected to the Lincolnshire family from Nocton (LAO D&C A/2/35 fos 87v–88v; A/2/36 fos 90v–91r).

occupy, and family influence to secure other benefices and patronage. Several rose to the episcopate but not as readily as those from baronial families. For the unambitious there was the prospect of a comfortable and independent life as a pluralist, with few commitments and a good income. A small miscellaneous group of canons are referred to in ecclesiastical sources as being of noble birth, but their families, and therefore their precise social status, are not known. It is unlikely that they came from prominent baronial or knightly families but the title can be taken to indicate gentle birth.

The remaining armigerous ranks, esquire and gentleman, were less well defined. Although the lesser aristocracy had these three ranks, regional studies have found that it is more meaningful to divide them into two groups based on differences in wealth: the greater or county gentry, consisting of knights and esquires, and the lesser or parish gentry, consisting of the poorer esquires and gentlemen.[25] It is quite rare to find canons or their families defined with a precise rank as esquire or gentleman though many must have existed. However, examples can be found: George Trevilian, a sixteenth century canon of Chichester and Exeter was the fourth son of John Trevilian esquire of Yarnscombe, Devon, and John Bolter, a kinsman of Roger Bolter precentor of Exeter, was styled gentleman.[26] Often more is known of their landholdings than their precise rank; Thomas Fincham, a canon of Lincoln in the late fifteenth century, held lands in Fincham Norfolk but his status is not known.[27] By the end of the fifteenth century priests were sometimes considered gentlemen by virtue of their office and called spiritual gentlemen, a reflection of their status in the early middle ages as members of the first estate. The Book of St Albans of 1486 lists nine types of gentlemen, the ninth being spiritual gentlemen: 'There is a gentleman, a churl's son, a priest to be made, and that is a spiritual gentleman to God and not of blood'.[28] Canons, as senior churchmen, would have been considered of this rank by virtue of their office if they were not already by birth. In 1510 Robert Spencer, a canon of Lincoln, was styled 'clerk or gentleman'.[29]

The stratification of the greater and lesser aristocracy was accompanied by and partly achieved through the use of heraldry.[30] In 1300 the possession of a coat of arms was confined to baronial and knightly families. Esquires were allowed arms from the middle of the fourteenth century. From the mid fifteenth century gentlemen were also allowed coats of arms, though this process had probably started earlier. By the end of the fifteenth century possession of a coat of arms

---

25 See note 12 and D. A. L. Morgan, 'The Individual Style of the English Gentleman', in Gentry and Lesser Nobility in Late Medieval Europe, ed. M. Jones, Gloucester, 1986, 15–35.

26 J. L. Vivian, Visitation of Devon, Exeter, 1895, 736 (Trevilian); DRO MCR 10–11 Hen VI (Bolter).

27 PRO PROB 11/ 19 fos 38v–40r.

28 W. Blades, ed., The Book of St Albans, 1889.

29 LPFD, i part 1, no. 438 4 m 21.

30 A. Wagner, English Genealogy, 1978, 119–24.

established gentle birth, though this was not enforced until the heralds' visitations under Henry VIII. Several Exeter canons are known to have come from armigerous families because their coats of arms were displayed in the cathedral or city guildhall. Among them in the fifteenth century were Roger Bolter, John Cockworthy, John Druell, Roger Keyes, Baldwin and John Shillingford, and John Stevens.[31] None of these canons' families are known to have been landowners on a large scale. Occasionally the details of a grant of arms are known. William Franklin, a canon of York and Lincoln, who served Wolsey and the king in the north, received his in 1530 as a reward for the recovery of Norham castle from the Scots.[32] At about the same time as the Book of St Albans gave all priests the status of spiritual gentlemen, the offices of the four principal dignities of the cathedral at Exeter, dean, precentor, chancellor, and treasurer, acquired armigerous status, which they conferred on their occupants by virtue of their office. Two of these arms, those of the dean and treasurer, appear in the early sixteenth century on the Speke chantry of c.1518–19, though the creation of the arms predates this slightly. The precentor's arms are known from 1496, and possibly from before 1477.[33] Dignities in the other cathedrals, with the exception of the dean at Hereford, do not seem to have become armigerous. The distinctions between greater and lesser aristocracy were in part based on status rather than way of life and wealth. Status differed widely between a baronial and gentlemanly family, whereas they shared principles of lifestyle and the reputation for being 'noble' or 'gentle'.

The non-aristocratic groups from which canons came included small landholders, franklins and yeomen as they were later called, and leading urban families.[34] Two Exeter canons had yeoman connections in the earlier use of the term to denote service in a great household: Henry Somersete, whose brother, John, was butler to Henry III, and Hugh Bridham (d.1392) who was probably descended from Baldwin Bryggham, a receiver-general of the Courtenay family.[35] Like the lesser aristocracy there are few recorded examples of franklin connections and it is difficult to do more than describe the lands they held. Undoubtedly there were several in all chapters. Two sixteenth century Lincoln canons, William Blencow and Thomas Lillylowe, are known to have had kinsmen styled as yeomen.[36] This was almost certainly the family background of Walter

---

[31] F. Colby, 'Heraldry in Exeter', *Archaeological Journal* xxxi, 245–60.

[32] *Heraldic Visitations of the Northern Counties in 1530, by Thomas Tonge, Norroy King of Arms*, W. H. D. Longstaffe, SS, xli, 1863, 31.

[33] The arms of the dean and treasurer can be found on the Speke chantry of c.1518–19 in Exeter Cathedral; the precentor's arms can be found on a fireplace now in the deanery (M. Wood, *The English Medieval House*, 1965, 271–2).

[34] See note 12 and M. Campbell, *The English Yeoman under Elizabeth and the Early Stuarts*, New Haven, Conn., 1942, Appendix I.

[35] BRUO iii, 1727 (Somersete); R. Dunning, 'Patronage and Promotion in the Late-Medieval Church', in R. A. Griffiths, ed., *Patronage, The Crown and the Provinces in Later Medieval England*, Gloucester, 1981, 167–80, 169 (Bridham).

[36] BRUO 1500–1540 687, A. R. Maddison, *Lincolnshire Wills 1500–1600*, Lincoln, 1888,

Stapeldon, a canon and future bishop of Exeter, and that of Richard Tyttesbury another Exeter canon, whose brother held half a knight's fee in Woolfardisworthy with two others.[37] Canons from this background needed the support of a greater patron to make a successful career. In the case of John Druell from a family of small landholders near Higham Ferrers in Northamptonshire this was the future archbishop Henry Chichele, a native of Higham Ferrers.[38] Urban, like rural society, had wide divisions of status. Towns were dominated by wealthy merchants forming a ruling oligarchy whose status was often effectively that of gentlemen. Below the merchants were the master craftsmen and shopkeepers, many of whom might be freemen.[39] Canons from the upper ranks of urban society can be found in small numbers in all cathedrals. Ralph Shaa, a residentiary of St Paul's in the late fifteenth century, came from the apex; his brother Sir Edmund was lord mayor of London.[40] John Shirwode, a non-resident canon of York, came from the same rank at York where his father was town clerk.[41] Three Exeter canons came from families of slightly lower rank. Richard Gabriel's father was a barge owner from Dartmouth, and John Rowe left money to a smith and a dyer, craftsmen, who shared his name, and were presumably his relatives.[42] John Burneby's father was a freeman of Exeter.[43] None of the Lincoln or Exeter canons are known to have come from the lower levels of urban society, journeymen and unskilled labourers. Exeter was exceptional in the closeness of the relationship between the city and the cathedral. The families of Bosoun, Crudge, Germeyn, and Shillingford were canons as well as freemen and mayors. Two Shillingfords and a Bosoun were canons between 1371 and 1418, reflecting the close though not always harmonious relations between them.[44] This common membership of the city elite and chapter is not found at Lincoln.

Few canons are known to have come from humble backgrounds, that is from non-landholding rural families or the lower levels of urban society. There is one unreliable assertion (it comes from a much later hostile source) that John Hody's father was 'a bondeman to my Lorde of Awdeley and heywarde of Woolavington',

35 (Lillylowe); BRUO 1500–1540 51 (Blencow). He was presented to Marston St Lawrence in 1541 by Thomas and John Blencow, yeomen (LAO Reg. XXVII (Reg. Longland) fo. 143v).
37 M. Buck, Politics, Finance and the Church in the reign of Edward II: Walter Stapeldon, Treasurer of England, Cambridge, 1983, Chapter 1; Feudal Aids i, 460 (Tyttesbury).
38 BRUO i, 595; CPL ix, 62.
39 See note 15, especially Keen, English Society, 97–101.
40 Brooke, 'St Paul's Cathedral', 93–4.
41 BRUO iii, 1692–93.
42 CPR 1422–29, 218, CCR 1399–1402, 446 (Gabriel); DRO Chanter Ms 12 part 1 (Reg. Neville Exeter) fos 139v–140.
43 M. M. Rowe and A. M. Jackson, Exeter Freemen 1266–1967, DCRS, Exeter, 1973, 46.
44 Exeter Fasti, 23, 30, 39, 40, 54, 65; Mayors of Exeter, Exeter, 1964, 6–10. Relations between the city and cathedral are discussed in M. Curtis, Some Disputes between the City and Cathedral Authorities of Exeter, Manchester, 1932.

but otherwise references to humble origins are best thought of in relative terms.[45] The clearest evidence of modest origins comes from the late fifteenth and early sixteenth centuries. Winchester College educated the sons of a number of its tenants some of whom were probably of yeoman stock. This was the background of Thomas Bedyll and Thomas Wellys who held six canonries between them.[46] Some clerics are described as being of humble birth or poor scholars. It is probable that both terms indicate modest landholding family backgrounds rather than anything lower. Two Exeter canons, William Polmorva and William Nassington, were described as poor scholars in the early stages of their career when they were at university, but nothing is known of their social origins.[47] For a handful of individuals it is possible to infer relatively humble birth from the details of their early careers. In some chapters isolated individuals can be seen beginning as vicars choral; examples are known from Wells, Exeter and Lincoln.[48] Thomas Lillylowe, of yeoman stock, started as a chantry priest at Lincoln, served as clerk of the common fund for nearly twenty years and became a canon in 1531.[49] The long hours and poor stipends of vicars made them relatively undesirable posts in the Church which the well born or well connected would have avoided. Those starting in this way probably came from small landholding families. Though it was common for unfree villeins to be manumitted, freed, and then ordained there are no examples from the Exeter and Lincoln chapters, a total of some 1,500 individuals. This suggests that it is reasonable to conclude that the vast majority of canons came from property owning families of various ranks, and were relatively well born.

Educational Origins

All canons, whether university graduates or not, would have started their education with a grounding in reading, Latin and grammar. However, direct evidence of this for individuals is hard to find. We know nothing of the pre-university training of the vast majority of canons. There were various places for gaining a schooling; a noble household, a religious house, a school, or private tuition. The well born were educated in their own and other noble households by tutors. Roger Stanford was described as the 'special companion, teacher, and governor' of Canon Philip Beauchamp in 1361, a position he had held for ten years, ever since Beauchamp was thirteen.[50] He presumably prepared him for

45 Orme, *Education in the West of England*, 108–9.
46 BRUO i, 148–9 (Bedyll), iii, 2008–9 (Wellys).
47 *Reg. Stapeldon Exeter* 577, BRUO iii, 1492–93 (Polmorva); ib ii, 1339 (Nassington).
48 BRUO ii, 1405–06 (Orum); Orme, *Minor Clergy of Exeter Cathedral*, 91, 60 (Parys).
49 He appears as a chantry priest in 1510 and clerk of the chapter's common fund in 1511 (LAO D&C A/3/4 fo. 32v; A/2/4/ fo. 24r). Both offices were held for over a decade. He resigned as a chantry priest in 1521 and occurs as clerk of the common fund from 1520–28 (Cole, *Lincoln Chapter Acts 1520–36*, 14, xviii). For his later career see BRUO 1500–1540 687.
50 CPP 374.

university and may even have accompanied him there in 1357, when Beauchamp is known to have been at Oxford. Stanford himself was a law graduate of Oxford and a small-scale pluralist thanks to his Beauchamp connections.[51] In contrast family tradition later related that James Berkeley, another canon of baronial rank, was educated at a local religious house, Kingswood Abbey near Bristol.[52] Hugh Hickeling, a canon of Wells and Exeter, may have been educated at Haltemprice Priory in Yorkshire under the supervision of a relative, Robert Hickeling, who was prior in the 1360s. In his will he left instructions for the return of two books the priory had lent him in his youth.[53] Reginald Pole, a future cardinal and archbishop of Canterbury, is known to have been educated at the grammar school of the Charterhouse at Sheen.[54] Unfortunately few medieval schools have left details of the individuals who passed through them, Eton and Winchester being notable but rare exceptions. Consequently these are the ones canons are known to have attended. In the century and a half before 1541 all chapters had some canons who had been educated there; at Lincoln thirteen had been to Eton and thirty-seven to Winchester. One, William Cosyn a future dean of Wells, was a chorister at King's College Cambridge in 1482–83 before going on to Eton.[55] Occasionally a canon is known to have attended another school; John Longland, a canon and later bishop of Lincoln, was educated at Henley school.[56] It is probable that some canons of a modest background went to a local grammar school where one existed. According to one local and probably biased tradition, John Hody was educated by a mere chantry priest at Woolavington in Somerset.[57] On a more speculative note it is possible that some were educated in a bishop's or canon's household, as both are known to have brought up boys. Unfortunately there is rarely direct evidence of this for individual canons because so little is known of their childhoods. They usually first appear on the threshold of manhood in their late teens in the early stages of ordination or beginning their university studies. However stray scraps of information allow some modest speculation. Several canons are known to have been in episcopal service very early in their careers, between the ages of seventeen and twenty as calculated from ordination details. Though this does not establish their boyhood in a bishop's household, it points to the possibility. The strongest evidence of a canon's boyhood being spent in the household of a resident canon at Exeter is found in the early career of James Carslegh (d.1438). He occurs as the clerk of John Lydford in 1406, when his benefactor bequeathed him £10 for his study, the year that he was ordained acolyte.[58] If this was done at the minimum age of

---

51 *BRUO* iii, 1759–60.
52 *BRUO* i, 174–5.
53 *Reg. Stafford Exeter* 410–11.
54 *BRUO 1500–1540* 453–5.
55 *BRUC* 162.
56 *BRUO* ii, 1160–62.
57 See note 45.
58 *Reg. Stafford Exeter* 389.

fifteen he was born around 1391, and was in his mid teens when in Lydford's household. This is consistent with his later ordination to the priesthood in 1419, for which the minimum age was twenty-four, and with his later education.[59]

Evidence of canons' university education is comparatively abundant and sufficient to produce statistical analysis. By the fifteenth century a university education was almost essential for a successful ecclesiastical career. Graduates came to dominate the higher offices of the Church and its administration. Nowhere is this more clearly demonstrated than in the chapters of the secular cathedrals where by 1500 they held a virtual monopoly of canonries and dignities. The proportion of graduates rose steadily from the beginning of the fourteenth century to the Reformation. Not only were more canons university educated during this period but they were more highly educated as an increasing number held higher degrees. In recognition of this Oxford University wrote to four chapters, Exeter, Lincoln, Salisbury and Wells, in 1426 appealing for funds to help complete the new lecture rooms 'because many of your members were educated at Oxford'.[60] But a university education was expensive and required considerable application and determination to complete, putting it beyond the reach of the average cleric. Many attended for a few years without ever graduating. There were three principal methods of financing a university education: possession of a benefice, financial support from family or a patron, and charitable support.[61] Canons, with their comparatively well born origins, tended to have their access to university eased by the first two of these. At Exeter about sixty-five of the 371 canons who went to university are known to have started their studies after receiving their first benefice, and in a further sixty cases this is likely but not certain. However, this leaves most graduates, about 250, who had begun, or in a few cases, completed their first degree before acquiring their first benefice. At least sixty of these came from prominent baronial and knightly families who could finance their studies. Those from more modest landowning family backgrounds might either be supported by their families, or wait until they were beneficed. Those without family resources or a benefice had to rely on charitable bequests and patronage, which were uncertain at the best of times, though educational bequests were a common theme in clerical wills of the later middle ages. Some made elaborate arrangements to provide money or books, the most expensive part of a university education. In many cases some sort of patronage was involved, with connections either with the testator or his executors.[62] William Doune, archdeacon of Leicester from 1354 to 1361, made detailed arrangements for the education of his nephew Robert Bosoun, a future chancellor of Exeter, leaving him £17 and the use of his library of law books.[63] Such precise

---

[59] BRUO i, 363.

[60] Epistolae Academicae Oxon, ed., H. Anstey, 2 vols, OHS, xxxv–vi, 1898–99, i, 25–6.

[61] For a fuller discussion of this see Aston et al, 'Medieval Alumni of Cambridge'.

[62] The educational patronage of residentiary canons is discussed in Chapter 8.

[63] A. H. Thompson, 'The Will of William Doune', Archaeological Journal, lxxii, 1915, 233–48.

TABLE 7. PERCENTAGE OF CANONS AND DIGNITARIES WITH UNIVERSITY STUDY
AT FIVE SECULAR CATHEDRALS, 1301–1500

	CANONS ONLY			CANONS AND DIGNITARIES	
	Lichfield	St Paul's	York	Exeter	Lincoln
1301–25	52	63	28	66	63
1326–50	61	57	43	72	51
1351–75	43	33	43	58	47
1376–1400	42	42	39	55	56
1401–25	64	60	60	78	60
1426–50	65	71	83	77	73
1451–75	77	91	83	93	93
1476–1500	88	95	83	95	95

provisions for individuals who later became canons are rare; only four others are known. Poor scholars from the diocese of Exeter were better off than most, as Exeter College, as Stapeldon Hall later became known, was one of the few Oxford colleges of the period open to undergraduates. College fellowships were usually reserved for higher study. From the mid fifteenth century it was common for canons to have financed higher degrees in this way.

Detailed studies of five of the nine secular chapters, Exeter, Lichfield, Lincoln, London and York, set out in Table 7, show the steady rise of graduates in canonries and dignities.[64] Despite individual variations clear patterns can be seen. At the beginning of the fourteenth century, with the exception of York, graduates formed a majority, and at three formed over 60 per cent. Their numbers tended to increase, though unevenly, in the second quarter of the century. All but York suffered a notable decline after the Black Death in the third quarter of the century with numbers dropping by 10 per cent or more to below half the chapter except at Exeter. This lower figure of 40–50 per cent remained until the fifteenth century though at Lincoln and London there was some recovery in the last quarter of the

---

[64] Table 7 has been drawn up in the following way: only those who became canons have been included, excluding those who had ineffective provisions. Each canon has only been included once with his highest or latest degree. Information about degrees has been taken from BRUC, BRUO, BRUO 1500–1540, the Fasti for each diocese and occasionally from episcopal registers. The principal studies of the English medieval universities are Aston, 'Oxford's Medieval Alumni'; Aston et al, 'Medieval Alumni of Cambridge'; Cobban, The Medieval English Universities, Aldershot, 1988; W. J. Courtenay, Schools and Scholars in Fourteenth-Century England, Princeton, 1987; Catto, History of the University of Oxford, vol. I; Catto and Evans, History of the University of Oxford, Vol II; D. Leader, A History of the University of Cambridge, Vol. I: The University to 1546, Cambridge, 1988.

fourteenth century. By 1400 graduates formed 60 per cent in all five chapters. The proportion rose reaching 75 per cent by mid century and 90 per cent by the last quarter except at Lichfield and York. At Exeter and Lincoln the proportion remained at over 90 per cent up to 1541, suggesting that the high levels elsewhere were sustained in the first half of the sixteenth century. The overall figures are impressive; in the period 1300 to 1541 over three-quarters of Exeter canons (78 per cent) had studied at university and at Lincoln over two-thirds (70 per cent). It was unusual for a cleric to become a canon before completing his studies, including a higher degree. It was even rarer for an undergraduate to be appointed a canon. John Northwode was exceptional, becoming a canon of Lincoln in 1328 when he first went to Oxford. He owed his promotion to his uncle, Bishop Grandisson of Exeter, whom he succeeded as prebendary of Stoke.[65] John Ward obtained his canonry at Exeter in 1442 while studying canon law, becoming a B.Cn.L. in 1450. Like Northwode he was something of an exception, and went on to gain a doctorate in 1458.[66] Some canons seem to have gone to university a long time after being collated. John Cheyne, on the other hand, was a fellow of King's Hall Cambridge from 1355 to 1362, long enough to earn the title *magister*, but is not called this until 1373 by which time he had prebends at Salisbury and Exeter.[67] It was more common, though still unusual, for an individual to become a canon before completing his higher degree. John Lydford, a noted canon lawyer and prebendary of Exeter, gained his doctorate six years after his canonry.[68]

Canon and civil law were the most popular subjects studied by canons. This is not surprising given their obvious practical value. Law was the best qualification for an ambitious cleric, and there was plenty of scope for the legal graduate in diocesan administration. Many rose to their canonry in this way and examples from all chapters are plentiful. At Exeter John Lydford, John Shillingford, and Ralph Tregrisiou, all doctors of civil law, were part of a notable group of West-Country lawyers beginning their careers in the 1370s.[69] On the eve of the Reformation the diocesan administration at Chichester was in the hands of canons with law degrees the most notable of whom were John Worthial and William Fleshmonger.[70] Tables 8 and 9 show that at Lincoln and Exeter between 1300 and 1541 an average of 50 per cent studied either or both laws.[71] At their height, in the first half of the fifteenth century, lawyers make up 60 per cent of graduates. Despite their differences in wealth and prestige the number of lawyers in the two chapter was broadly similar. The balance between canon and civil law was uneven. Civil law predominated forming 45 per cent at Exeter and 51 per

---

[65] *BRUO* ii, 1371–2.
[66] *BRUO* iii, 1980.
[67] *BRUC* 134–5.
[68] *BRUO* ii, 1184.
[69] *BRUO* ii, 1184, iii, 1689–90, 1893.
[70] Kitch, 'Chichester Cathedral', 284–5.
[71] Tables 8 and 9 have been drawn up in the same way as Table 7; see note 64.

cent at Lincoln compared with 23 per cent and 32 per cent respectively studying canon law, and a significant proportion studying both, 26 per cent at Exeter and 17 per cent at Lincoln. This reflects the balance at Oxford with civilians outnumbering canonists by 31 per cent in the medieval period, where the majority of both chapters were educated. However, the balance was reversed among the residentiaries of York in the last quarter of the fifteenth century when there was an influx of canonists from Cambridge.[72]

Arts graduates tended to outnumber lawyers at the beginning of the fourteenth century when at both Exeter and Lincoln they formed the largest group, 43 per cent at the former and as many as two-thirds at the latter. During the fifteenth century their numbers declined as the number of lawyers grew. At both chapters they formed a quarter or less in that century, numbering 12 per cent at their lowest, a pattern confirmed by the residentiaries at York. At Exeter and to a lesser extent at Lincoln arts graduates increased in the early sixteenth century, particularly after 1525 when they returned to the level of the early fourteenth century. At both Exeter and Lincoln there is a parallel reduction in the number of law graduates. Theologians were always a relatively small group among canons. Only four (12 per cent) of the thirty-four canons resident at York in the fifteenth century had theology degrees.[73] The proportion at Exeter and Lincoln over the period 1300 to 1541 was a little higher at 16 per cent and 20 per cent of all graduate canons respectively. A similar proportion were appointed to prebends in Lichfield, London and York between 1301 and 1500.[74] The number of theologians in a chapter partly reflects the interests of the bishop. Under Bishop Lacy at Exeter, himself a theologian, the proportion increased to form nearly a quarter in 1426–50, a trend continued by his successor Bishop Neville resulting in a further increase to 39 per cent in 1451–75. Archbishop Rotherham, another theologian, also had a policy of promoting theologians at York, appointing twelve between 1480 and 1500.[75] All but two cathedrals, Chichester and Hereford, expected the chancellor to lecture on theology or sometimes canon law. At four, Exeter, Lincoln, St Paul's and York the majority of chancellors were theology graduates, but at Lichfield and Wells and to a lesser extent Salisbury they were the exception.[76] All but two of the chancellors of York between 1290 and 1496 held doctorates of theology. Fifteen of the twenty-one chancellors of Exeter between 1294 and 1492 were theologians, twelve of them doctors, the most distinguished of whom was Thomas Buckingham.[77] There is some evidence that he lectured at Exeter, which is supported by the fact that he was briefly resident

---

[72] Aston et al., 'Medieval Alumni of Cambridge', 72 (Table).

[73] Dobson, 'Residentiary Canons', 157.

[74] Aston et al., 'Medieval Alumni of Cambridge', 75.

[75] Ibid.

[76] *Exeter Fasti* 8–10; *Lincoln Fasti* 23–4; *St Paul's Fasti* 18–19; *York Fasti* 9–10; *Lichfield Fasti* 9–10; *Wells Fasti* 7–9; *Salisbury Fasti* 16–19.

[77] *Exeter Fasti* 8–10; *York Fasti* 9–10.

TABLE 8. ANALYSIS OF THE SUBJECTS OF THE ACADEMIC QUALIFICATIONS OF EXETER CANONS AND DIGNITARIES, 1301–1541

	Total Degrees	BA, MA, Magister University Study	Lic and B Canon and/or Civil Law	Lic, B or Sch Theology	B Medicine	D Medicine	D Theology	D Canon and/or Civil Law	D Music
1301–25	28	12 (43%)	2 (7%)	0	0	1 (14%)	4 (3.5%)	9 (32%)	0
1326–50	37	12 (32%)	11 (30%)	0	0	0	6 (16%)	8 (21%)	0
1351–75	29	10 (34%)	7 (24%)	0	1 (3%)	0	4 (14%)	7 (24%)	0
1376–1400	34	12 (35%)	10 (29%)	0	0	0	2 (6%)	10 (29%)	0
1401–25	40	8 (20%)	16 (40%)	4 (10%)	0	2 (5%)	3 (7%)	7 (17%)	0
1426–50	31	4 (12%)	14 (45%)	1 (3%)	0	1 (3%)	6 (20%)	5 (16%)	0
1451–75	36	5 (14%)	5 (14%)	5 (14%)	0	0	9 (25%)	11 (31%)	1 (3%)
1476–1500	51	12 (24%)	16 (31%)	5 (10%)	0	0	3 (6%)	15 (29%)	0
1501–25	44	11 (25%)	9 (20%)	0	0	4 (9%)	6 (14%)	14 (32%)	0
1526–41	26	12 (46%)	2 (8%)	1 (4%)	0	0	6 (23%)	5 (19%)	0
TOTAL	356	98 (27.5%)	92 (25.8%)	16 (4.4%)	1 (0.28%)	8 (2.2%)	49 (13.7%)	91 (25.5%)	1 (0.28%)

TABLE 9 ANALYSIS OF THE SUBJECTS OF THE ACADEMIC QUALIFICATIONS OF LINCOLN CANONS AND DIGNITARIES, 1301–1541

	Total Degrees	BA, MA, Magister, University Study	Lic and B Canon and/or Civil Law	Lic, B or Sch Theology	B Medicine	D Medicine	D Theology	D Canon and/or Civil Law	D Music
1301–25	60	41 (68%)	3 (5%)	0	0	0	8 (13%)	8 (13%)	0
1326–50	69	36 (52%)	6 (9%)	4 (6%)	1 (1%)	0	5 (7%)	17 (25%)	0
1351–75	49	18 (37%)	10 (20%)	0	0	0	2 (4%)	19 (39%)	0
1376–1400	68	21 (31%)	27 (38%)	1 (1%)	0	0	3 (4%)	16 (24%)	0
1401–25	79	20 (25%)	22 (28%)	7 (9%)	0	0	11 (14%)	19 (24%)	0
1426–50	74	9 (12%)	25 (34%)	6 (8%)	1 (1%)	2 (3%)	7 (9%)	24 (32%)	0
1451–75	105	26 (25%)	18 (17%)	11 (10%)	3 (3%)	1 (1%)	21 (20%)	24 (23%)	1 (1%)
1476–1500	93	18 (19%)	25 (27%)	4 (4%)	1 (1%)	4 (4%)	10 (10%)	31 (33%)	0
1501–25	99	25 (25%)	12 (12%)	12 (12%)	0	1 (1%)	22 (22%)	27 (27%)	0
1526–41	59	14 (24%)	9 (15%)	4 (7%)	0	1 (2%)	15 (25%)	16 (27%)	0
TOTAL	755	228 (30%)	157 (21%)	49 (6%)	6 (0.7%)	9 (1%)	104 (14%)	201 (27%)	1 (0.1%)

in 1348.[78] Medicine was even more of a minority subject than theology, and Tables 8 and 9 show that only 2.5 per cent at Exeter and 1.7 per cent at Lincoln studied it, a reflection of its position at Oxford and Cambridge. The Exeter evidence suggests this is probably a slight under-representation. Two more canons studied medicine but are not included in the table because they also studied theology, either at a higher level or a later date. Three other canons are known to have had some medical skill. Two of these were described in a visitation of the cathedral by Archbishop Courtenay in 1384 as *in arte phisica eruditos*; the same description was given to Henry Whitfeld who was a bachelor of medicine.[79] Robert Cisterna was physician to Edward II but is only recorded as *magister*. He may have studied medicine but not taken a degree, though he is known to have written a medical treatise.[80] Even so only fourteen Exeter canons are known to have had any medical skills. Scarcer still were those who had studied music. Thomas St Just, a canon of Hereford, St Paul's, Exeter and Lincoln, who gained a doctorate, is one of the few known, though a handful of others were musicians.[81]

Most canons, therefore, did not finish with an arts degree but went on to a higher degree, as bachelor, licentiate, scholar, or doctor of one of the higher faculties. They formed 70 per cent of all those with degrees in the period 1300 to 1541 at Lincoln and Exeter, though at the latter the number fell to 54 per cent in the second quarter of the sixteenth century. Not only were more canons educated at university through these two and a half centuries but they were more highly educated. Over 40 per cent of these two chapters had doctorates. Law predominated among doctorates, as it did among all degrees. Few graduates studied long enough to qualify in more than one subject. Not surprisingly doctors of both laws were extremely rare; only eighteen canons of Exeter achieved this distinction, among them William Lyndwood, the noted canonist, and Walter Stapeldon.[82] Even fewer, just seven, graduated in two subjects other than the two laws. Four of these combined theology and medicine, and only one, William Exeter, was a doctor in both subjects.[83] Nicholas Wootton was exceptional in holding doctorates in three subjects, both laws and theology.[84]

The balance of Oxford and Cambridge men in a chapter reflects the regional character of the universities with the former recruiting from the west and also the north and the latter from the east and north.[85] Local recruitment patterns by individual colleges are less clear. Oxford was larger and more influential than Cambridge until the late fifteenth century. As a result Oxford men were generally

[78] Pantin, *English Church*, 113–15, DRO D&C 3766 fo. 2v.

[79] *Metropolitical Visitations of William Courtenay 1378–86*, ed. J. H. Dahmus, Illinois Studies in Social Sciences, xxii, 1950, 102.

[80] C. Talbot and E. Hammond, *The Medical Practicioners of Medieval England*, 1967, 302–3.

[81] BRUC 503.

[82] BRUO ii, 1191–3 (Lyndwood), iii, 1764–5 (Stapeldon).

[83] BRUO i, 659–60.

[84] DNB lxiii, 57–61.

[85] See note 64 for recent studies of the English medieval universities.

more numerous than Cambridge graduates, though this might be altered by a deliberate episcopal policy. In the three cathedrals of Lichfield, St Paul's and York over the two centuries from 1300 to 1500 Oxford alumni formed the majority of graduate canons, 56 per cent compared with 18 per cent from Cambridge, though this masks a steady increase in Cambridge graduates after 1450.[86] At Lincoln Oxford men formed the same proportion, 56 per cent but there were more from Cambridge, 24 per cent, whereas at Exeter the imbalance was greater with 63 per cent from the former and only 12 per cent from the latter. The Oxford dominance at Exeter is not surprising given its location in the western heartlands of the university's recruitment base. The trend was reinforced by a succession of Oxford educated bishops and the chapter's close links with one college in particular Stapeldon Hall. Among the York canons an Oxford bias was lessened at the end of the fifteenth century by the deliberate appointment of Cambridge graduates by Archbishop Rotherham who had been educated there and was chancellor of the university.[87] Graduates from foreign universities were much thinner on the ground; few could afford the extra expense of travelling abroad. They form less than 10 per cent of graduates at Lincoln and Exeter. The foreign universities attended by Englishmen tended to reflect their changing academic reputations. In the early fourteenth century Paris was the most popular but by the late fifteenth century it was more common to study in Italy. Some had already studied at Oxford before going abroad. A considerable number of graduates have left no trace of where they studied. This is particularly true of Lichfield canons.

Close links between chapters and individual colleges are more difficult to establish reflecting the relatively small part colleges played in university life for much of the later middle ages, being generally reserved for postgraduate study. The Lincoln evidence suggests that alumni from the larger and more established colleges were, as might be expected, most numerous in the chapter. Most colleges at both universities had a handful of alumni who became canons. At Oxford New College had the largest number, thirty, followed by Merton College with twenty-six and at Cambridge King's College twenty-one and King's Hall seventeen. Lincoln College Oxford did not have special ties with Lincoln Cathedral. Exeter is exceptional in this respect in its connections with Stapeldon Hall, later known as Exeter College, Oxford. Twenty-three of its alumni were canons, most of them in the fifteenth century. The college statutes stipulated that its original twelve fellows should come from the diocese of Exeter, four of them from the archdeaconry of Cornwall.[88] The other colleges of both universities had between four and six of their alumni among the chapter. The exception to this pattern is Merton College Oxford which provided twelve canons. A remarkable group of contemporaries at Merton during the later 1330s and early 1340s became dignitaries at Exeter between 1346 and 1352. The most senior and outstanding

86 See note 72.
87 Dobson, 'Residentiary Canons', 158.
88 Buck, *Politics, Finance and the Church*, Chapter 5.

of these was the theologian Thomas Buckingham who became chancellor in 1346. His successor in 1349 was another Mertonian, John Wyliet. Robert Middelond was appointed treasurer in 1351 and Hugh Monyton archdeacon of Barnstaple in 1352. All four were doctors of Theology. Buckingham was at Merton from 1324 until 1340, and Middelond from 1330 to 1347. Monyton and Wyliet were from a younger generation, but were at Merton in the closing years of Buckingham's time, from 1338 and 1339.[89] All these men were appointed by Bishop Grandisson at a time when Merton was the largest and most flourishing Oxford college and had produced scholars with a European reputation. They are one of many examples of Grandisson's interest in and knowledge about the academic life of his day.

Many canons, while at university, combined academic study with administrative duties. The most outstanding became chancellors of the university and a much larger number held other university offices such as proctor. With the growth of colleges in number and importance in the universities in the fifteenth century it became increasingly common for canons to have held offices in them as rectors, principals, provosts, or as bursars or other functionaries. Examples in all chapters abound. Typical of these is John Selot, archdeacon of Cornwall, who was a fellow of New College Oxford from 1437 to 1444 and third bursar from 1443 to 1445.[90] Thomas Hawkins, a canon of Lichfield as well as archdeacon of Stafford and precentor of Salisbury, was principal of St Peter's Hall Oxford in 1445 before holding office in Oriel College of which he was provost from 1475 to 1479.[91] It was not unusual to move from college to college. In most cases these activities formed only a part, usually the earlier part, of a wider and longer career. It was at university that they first acquired administrative experience often in the course of higher studies which might last ten or fifteen years. A small group of canons can be said to have had careers as scholars, in that their reputation and advancement was based on their learning, in contrast to those whose progress had come through secular or episcopal service. Such scholars spent many years at university and often combined higher study with either university or collegiate office. Many of them rose to be doctors of theology (lawyers were likely to find secular or ecclesiastical employment), and spent at least fifteen years at university. Robert Rygge, a canon of Wells and Exeter, was at Oxford for over twenty years, first as a fellow of Exeter College in 1362–72, and later as a fellow and bursar at Merton in 1374–75. A doctor of theology by 1380, he was chancellor of the university four times between 1381–82 and 1391.[92] For many of these scholars becoming resident at a cathedral marked their retirement from academic life. Their learning enriched the life of the close where they contributed by preaching, or, as chancellors, lecturing, or as benefactors of the library, as well as in the running of the cathedral. A smaller more eminent group of scholars can

[89] BRUO i, 298–9 (Buckingham), ii, 1274 (Middelond), 1299 (Monyton), iii, (Wyliet).
[90] BRUO iii, 1667.
[91] BRUO ii, 891–2.
[92] BRUO iii, 1616–17.

also be identified whose learning gave them a national reputation; Thomas Buckingham has already been noticed. The theologians Thomas Bradwardine, Walter Burley, and Richard FitzRalph, and the humanist scholars John Colet, William Grocyn, and John Shirwode all held canonries and often dignities in cathedrals, though they rarely had close connections with them.[93] By the early sixteenth century canons had become associated with the newly emerging educational institutions of the professions. As many as twenty-five Exeter canons and thirty-nine from Lincoln were members of the College of Advocates between 1500 and 1541.[94] Both John Chamber, who held canonries and dignities in four cathedrals, and Nicholas Halswell, a canon of York, Lincoln, Wells and Exeter, were leading figures in the foundation of medical bodies, the former as the first president of the Barber Surgeon's Guild in 1541, and the latter as a foundation fellow of the Royal College of Physicians in 1518.[95]

[93] BRUO i, 244–6 (Bradwardine), 312–13 (Burley), ii, 692–4 (FitzRalph), i, 462–4 (Colet), ii, 827–30 (Grocyn), iii, 1692–93 (Shirwood).
[94] G. D. Sqibb, *Doctor's Commons*, Oxford, 1977, 121–46.
[95] BRUO i, 385–6 (Chamber), ii, 858 (Halswell).

4

CANONS' CAREERS

When William of Wykeham became bishop of Winchester in 1366 he was a pluralist on an extensive scale, holding four cathedral canonries, an archdeaconry, six prebends in collegiate churches and a rectory. He had been in royal service a decade, and had risen to be keeper of the privy seal in 1364.[1] Though amongst the most successful of his class, he is in many respects typical of those who rose to be canons, the majority of whom, like him, were mature and experienced men when they achieved this and already held several benefices (ecclesiastical livings such as rectories or vicarages). Most, like Wykeham, had been engaged in royal or diocesan service and had held a number of rectories or canonries in collegiate churches before acquiring cathedral prebends. Even so, like all aspiring clerics of the medieval period, whether of noble or humble birth, he had to possess several qualifications to be ordained priest and to occupy benefices.[2] Clerics were required to be of legitimate and free birth, not physically deformed. Those born illegitimate or unfree needed dispensations, from the bishop for minor orders and from the pope for major orders. Candidates also had to have reached a minimum age, fifteen for acolyte, seventeen for subdeacon, nineteen for deacon, and twenty-four for priest, though a few were ordained under age, particularly if they were scholars. A candidate not being ordained by his diocesan bishop had to produce letters dimissory from the diocesan before another bishop would ordain him. On proceeding to major orders a title, a financial guarantee, was required. Some clerics were ordained to the title of a benefice they already held, or if they possessed adequate personal means (an income of at least five marks a year) to the title of their own patrimony, but most were ordained to the title of a religious house. A few were ordained to the title of a named individual, a magnate or bishop. This was more common before 1350

---

[1] A. H. Thompson, 'Pluralism in the Medieval Church: with Notes on the Pluralists in the Diocese of Lincoln in 1366', *AASRP*, xxxvi, 1921–2, 31–4.

[2] The most recent discussion of clerical careers and the requirements for the priesthood is Swanson, *Church and Society*, Chapter 2. See also Heath, *Parish Clergy*, Chapter 1 and Bowker, *Secular Clergy*, Chapters 1 and 2. Patterns of ordination are also considered in R. N. Swanson, 'Titles to Orders in Medieval English Episcopal Registers', in H. Mayr-Harting and R. I. Moore eds, *Studies in Medieval History Presented to R. H. C. Davies*, 1985, 233–45.

but is occasionally found in the fifteenth century. Prior to ordination candidates were examined for their educational and moral suitability which included the ability to read and sing. Possession of a benefice did not require priestly status, but canon law stated that beneficed clergy should be capable of proceeding to the priesthood within a year. This seems to have been observed more strictly for vicars than rectors. Many held benefices while only in minor orders, putting off further ordination for several years, sometimes with a papal dispensation. Canon law also required candidates for benefices to be formally instituted to them. Suitability for institution was defined as being at least twenty-four and having a reputation for learning and an upright and moral way of life. The bishop could refuse to institute an unsuitable candidate, though this was rare. To acquire a benefice a cleric had to be presented by the patron: the king, bishop, religious house, or a member of the lay aristocracy. This was by no means a straightforward matter. A study of the clergy in the late fifteenth century has concluded that 'influence, vigilance, and pertinacity were essential for a clerk in search of a benefice'.[3] The unbeneficed clergy substantially outnumbered the beneficed, by as much as four to one in the diocese of York in the early fourteenth century.[4] Many had to wait several years before receiving a rectory or vicarage, and far more had to be content to be part of the clerical proletariat as parochial chaplains or chantry priests. As a result for the majority of clergy ordination preceded possession of a benefice. As members of the privileged higher clergy, the *sublimes and litterati* as they were called, cathedral canons avoided many of these delays and uncertainties. Most of them began with the advantages of being comparatively well born and well educated and started their careers with a benefice after which they were ordained, reversing the usual sequence.

Early Careers, First Benefices, and Ordination.

Most canons acquired a benefice early in their careers and in doing so started at a level that most clerics never reached. Though the pre-ordination and pre-benefice stages of clerical careers are notoriously obscure many canons can be traced before their institution to a benefice is recorded.[5] They can be seen starting to make the connections with influential patrons that would launch a successful career. Little survives showing just how these were made but sometimes there is enough evidence for reasonable speculation. Richard Ovingham of Lincoln's modest career culminated in his appointment as a canon in 1396, six months before his death that year.[6] Over the preceding twenty years he had held two

---

3   Heath, *Parish Clergy*, 28.
4   D. Robinson, *Beneficed Clergy in Cleveland and the East Riding 1306–40*, Borthwick Papers no. 37, York, 1969, 8.
5   For a general consideration of this topic see Swanson, *Church and Society*, Chapters 1 and 2.
6   The following convention will be used to identify which cathedral individuals were

Lincolnshire rectories Aswardby and Iwardby. His career was based on magnate service, first by 1381 to Gilbert Umfraville earl of Angus and later to Henry Percy earl of Northumberland. Ovingham in Northumberland was an Umfraville estate before passing to the Percys. It is likely that Ovingham was born there and where he came to the notice of his future patron. Through his service to the Umfravilles he acquired his benefices in Lincolnshire where they held important estates including Aswardby.[7] Countless aspiring clerics followed a route similar to Richard's but generally the results can only be observed as they entered royal or ecclesiastical service. In 1367, five years before he became a fellow of King's Hall Cambridge and eleven years before he became a canon, Adam Davenport of Lincoln had travelled to Spain in the service of John of Gaunt's daughter Philippa.[8] William Percehay of Lincoln followed a similar course but in episcopal service, first appearing as the bishop of Lincoln's commissary in 1352, three years before he acquired a benefice and eight years before he became a canon.[9] One or two started in the service of a magnate, such as John Blake of Lincoln, the earl of Warwick's treasurer.[10] Those beginning at this level with a powerful patron were the most fortunate. Humbler service was more common, though examples are scarce. Before a successful career in the service of Edward II and Edward III and three bishops, which brought him five canonries, Thomas Astley of Exeter began in 1306 as the proctor of Henry de la Wyle – a scholarly cleric and future chancellor of Salisbury.[11] Roger Bolter of Exeter (d.1436) was employed on minor financial duties by the dean and chapter at Exeter in 1391–92, ten years before his first known benefice.[12] Sometimes service was more formal. John Dalton of Lincoln was active as the archdeacon of Richmond's vicar general in 1390 and only twenty years later did he hold his first benefice.[13] Some sought a future in ecclesiastical administration, either as notaries or working in a diocesan consistory court. This sort of service and experience could be an important form of advancement for those whose families did not possess the right to present to benefices or have connections with those that did. Many of those who began engaged in service could expect to gain a benefice within a few years, often, in the case of the king or a bishop, in the patronage of their employer, though other types of service were less likely to have this advantage. Alongside service many canons first appear studying at university before acquiring a benefice. This also

canons of: Richard Ovingham of Lincoln. Where canons held several the first one they acquired or the place they entered residence will be used.

7   M. H. Dods, A History of Northumberland, vol. xii, 1926, 98–104; CPR 1381–5, 313; CCR 1377–81, 433, 496; LAO Reg. XI (Reg. Buckingham) fo. 76r.

8   BRUC 178.

9   LAO Reg. VIII (Reg. Gynwell) fos 24r, 77r; Fasti Lincoln, 101.

10   CPP 410.

11   Chew, Hemingby's Register, 172–4; A. Watkin, The Great Cartulary of Glastonbury Abbey, SRS, vol. lix, 1947, 161.

12   DRO D&C 3773 (Extraordinary Accounts) fo. 18v.

13   BRUO i, 536–7.

was an important opportunity to make connections with influential patrons that could lead to benefices or service.

Just how clerics learnt of vacancies and made contact with patrons remains obscure. It is quite possible that some canons made numerous unsuccessful attempts to gain benefices without leaving any traces. Even though they were amongst the most successful of the clergy there are enough scraps of evidence to suggest that some canons faced difficulties. Some were ordained to the title of a religious house which may indicate some delay in finding a benefice compared with those who were ordained to the title of a benefice. Occasionally a cleric was granted a pension rather than a benefice as requested, usually a temporary measure until one was available. These requests were normally made by an influential patron; even so they were not always successful. Others attempted a short cut. For much of the fourteenth century the papacy offered a route to a benefice. Some canons began their careers by securing papal provisions to a benefice which they were unable to effect. Two types of cleric used this method. At one extreme were members of the nobility who received provisions at the request of their powerful and influential families: Sir Nigel Loring petitioned the pope in 1345 for a benefice for his seventeen year old brother John of Lincoln.[14] Though their first provisions were ineffective high birth ensured ready alternatives. At the other were the poor clerics and graduates listed in university petitions to the pope. The more astute made several requests. Richard Thormerton of Salisbury held reservations for benefices in the gift of the bishop of Worcester and St Mary's Abbey Winchester.[15] Sometimes the difficulties are more clearly visible as the early careers of two Exeter canons demonstrate. In 1368 Ralph Pylaton was required to resign his expectation of a benefice in the gift of Plympton Priory on being provided to the rectory of Croydon. He was still trying to effect his provision to Croydon in 1370 and is not known to have gained possession.[16] John Seys of Exeter had greater difficulties, despite having two powerful patrons, Sir Guy Brian and the king. In January 1345 the king presented him to the living of Tenby, but this was disputed and remained so until at least June 1352. In August 1345 the king made alternative arrangements for Seys, sending him to Goldcliffe Priory to be 'maintained'. He was still unbeneficed in March 1347, by which time he was a clerk of Sir Guy Brian, when he was granted a benefice in the gift of Pembroke Priory, which also remained ineffective. Finally, in December 1347, he successfully gained the rectory of Shaldfleet in the Isle of Wight on the king's presentation.[17] Whatever the difficulties they may have had to overcome in gaining their first benefice, canons began their beneficed careers at a higher level than the majority of clerics. It was rare to begin in a relatively humble way with a benefice that required residence. Among this small group were the handful who rose from the ranks of a cathedral's minor

[14] CPP 102
[15] CPL ii, 317.
[16] CPL iv, 74; CPR 1370–4, 349.
[17] CPR 1343–5, 375; CPR 1345–8, 347, 259, 332; CCR 1343–6, 644.

clergy to become canons and a few who started as parochial vicars or chaplains.[18] William Wagott is exceptional among the canons of Exeter in serving as a parochial chaplain in Tawstock in 1454 some twenty years before gaining his prebend.[19] The majority of canons' first known benefice was a rectory. Those with influence could secure lucrative benefices: Thomas Nassington of Exeter was provided to Yaxley, valued at £35 6s 8d at the petition of the king and Thomas of Lancaster.[20] The most privileged, at both Lincoln and Exeter about 15 per cent of the chapter, began with canonries or even dignitaries, a reflection of high birth or, less frequently, service. Noble birth ensured that Edmund Audley, Richard Graystock and John Ufford began their careers with a cathedral canonry, whereas Henry Carnbull's prebend at Lincoln was a reward from Bishop Rotherham whom he served for nearly twenty years.[21]

Unlike the majority of lesser clerics who needed ordination to practice as parish chaplains or chantry priests, few canons were ordained beyond minor orders before acquiring their first benefice, and many postponed it for several years. Only at Exeter did the cathedral statutes require all canons to be in priests orders; at Salisbury there were three groups of prebendaries according to their rank, subdeacon, deacon and priest.[22] The requirement of priestly status at Exeter seems generally to have been observed and enforced.[23] The ordination of many canons is recorded but often sketchily and rarely in a sequence of three or more orders. However, enough evidence exists to indicate some alternative patterns of ordination. The little evidence that there is about ordination to minor orders, first tonsure and acolyte, suggests that many future canons went no further than this until they were beneficed, thus delaying any irrevocable commitment to the Church at the minimum canonical age. The age at which canons received their first tonsure is very hard to gauge because so few examples are known and most of these are uncertain. They indicate contradictory practice. William Pencrich of Exeter received the rectory of Blaketon in 1420 but was not tonsured until 1421 which was canonically illegal, though the record of his institution describes him as a clerk and therefore at least tonsured. The suggestion of irregularity here may account for the questioning of the validity of his orders in 1428.[24] In contrast Robert Middelond of Exeter (d.1367) was probably tonsured as a boy in 1317 and perhaps intended for the church from an early age. Unfortunately there is no evidence of his later ordination, but he did not hold a benefice until the 1340s,

18 See Chapter 3 for examples of this. At Wells John Menyman was a vicar choral before becoming a canon in 1493 (*Wells HMC* ii, 103; *Fasti Wells*, 43). Several of the minor clergy at Lincoln rose to be canons after serving in the important administrative post of chapter clerk (Major, 'The Office of Chapter Clerk at Lincoln').
19 *Reg. Lacy Exeter*, iii, 194.
20 *CPL* ii, 183; *Taxatio*, 36.
21 *BRUO* i, 75–6 (Audley); *Fasti Lincoln*, 124, *CPL* xi, 664 (Graystock); *BRUC* 603 (Ufford); *Beverley Fasti*, 32–3 (Carnbull).
22 Edwards, *Secular Cathedrals*, 34–5.
23 Lepine, *Canons of Exeter Cathedral*, 94.
24 *Reg. Bubwith Wells* ii, 395,401; DRO D&C 3550 (Chapter Act Book) fo. 137v.

and is known to have been at Oxford in the 1330s.[25] The evidence of ordination as acolyte indicates that few took this step until they were beneficed, when they quickly proceeded through major orders within a year or two. A few, usually the well connected, held benefices for a number of years before becoming acolytes. It was quite common for some clerics to spend several years in minor orders as they established themselves in the service of the church. Martin Dyer of Exeter, a notary and therefore at least twenty-five in 1439, was not ordained acolyte until 1442.[26]

Most canons seem to have taken major orders quickly on institution to their first benefice, many taking all three within a year, as canon law required. Some, however, remained in minor orders for several years, perhaps five or six. Papal dispensations were granted allowing clerics to delay ordination for five or seven years and remain subdeacons. A minority of canons completed their ordination before acquiring a benefice; at both Exeter and Lincoln they form about 10 per cent of the chapter.[27] For some this probably indicates a delay and element of difficulty in gaining one. Those without a benefice needed a title to proceed through major orders. These titles shed further light on the early careers of canons. Many combined ordination with university study being ordained to the title of a college fellowship or a religious house in Oxford or Cambridge. The abbeys of Oseney and St Frideswide's in Oxford frequently granted titles to students.[28] The lucky few might be ordained to the title of their own patrimony or that of a patron. Bishop Stafford of Exeter was unusual in granting titles to rising clerics in the early fifteenth century.[29] The overwhelming majority of titles were provided by religious houses and these are the most likely to indicate some difficulty in gaining a benefice generally lacking the element of patronage found in other titles. Individuals with titles from religious houses are not known to have come from aristocratic families or to have been in royal or ecclesiastical service at this stage of their careers. These titles are often a useful indication of a canon's geographical origins. Ordination records can also provide some insight into the mobility of canons as they began their careers. Letters dimissory were required by a cleric who wished to be ordained outside his diocese (this was not necessarily his native diocese). As many as seventy-four Exeter canons were granted them, though not all were used. Richard Gabriel received letters dimissory from Bishop Stafford of Exeter in 1399, was ordained acolyte in London in 1406, and priest

---

[25] *Reg. Stapeldon Exeter*, 512; *BRUO* ii, 1274.

[26] *Reg. Lacy Exeter* ii, 148; iv, 186.

[27] This figure is taken from the available evidence on ordination which is at best sketchy. For a fuller discussion of what has survived and the difficulties in using it see Lepine, *Canons of Exeter Cathedral*, 92–4. The same method has been used for the Lincoln material.

[28] For example Peter Partrich of Lincoln was granted one by St Frideswide's Abbey (*BRUO* iii, 1430) and Simon Green of Lincoln received his from Oseney Abbey (*BRUO* ii, 702–3).

[29] John Schute of Exeter received one from his diocesan, Bishop Stafford (*Reg. Stafford Exeter*, 449, 456, 465).

at Wells in 1409.[30] The whole process can be illustrated by the career of Henry Webber, a canon of Wells and dean of Exeter, about whom a good deal of evidence survives. He may have been born in north Devon around 1392 if he was the Henry Webber tonsured at Holsworthy in 1400.[31] On this assumption his ordination as acolyte in 1413 would have been at the age of 21. Six years later, in 1419, he was certainly ordained subdeacon and priest to the title of the dean and chapter of Exeter.[32] By this time he had been taken up by Richard Penels, archdeacon of Cornwall, who bequeathed him fourteen marks on condition that he became a priest within three years of his death, which he duly did. Penels also left him 20s for his ordination expenses and the use of his books for study.[33] Webber studied at Oxford, gaining a B.Cn.L. in 1422, the year that the chapter granted him his first benefice. He rose rapidly in the service of Bishop Lacy, becoming a canon in 1436, and was elected dean in 1458, dying at an advanced age in 1477.[34]

Patterns of Benefice Holding

Just how successful canons were among the secular clergy is revealed by an analysis of the benefices they held. All but three of the twenty-four richest clerics listed in the pluralist returns for the province of Canterbury in 1366 were canons or dignitaries.[35] Canons were usually mature and experienced men by the time they acquired their prebends as their careers and what little is known of their age confirms. Michael Tregury of Exeter was forty-six when he became archdeacon of Barnstaple in 1445, and Christopher Urswick thirty-nine on his appointment to a prebend in St Paul's.[36] Only the nobility tended to gain canonries at a significantly younger age, often around twenty. If the pattern at Exeter between 1300 and 1541 is typical only 20 per cent gained a canonry within five years of their first known benefice. A similar proportion acquired one within ten years but a gap of between eleven and twenty years was more usual, accounting for 35 per cent. As many as a fifth waited over twenty years, some as long as thirty. Virtually all canons held a succession of rectories, commonly three or four, both before and after their prebend. After the anti-pluralism legislation of the thirteenth and early fourteenth centuries even the multiple holders of rectories rarely held more than two simultaneously. John Leach of Lincoln, an eminent and successful canon lawyer, though he held nine rectories, rarely held more than

---

30 *Reg. Stafford Exeter*, 469; *Reg. Clifford Worcester*, 129; *Reg. Bubwith Wells* ii, 491.
31 *Reg. Stafford Exeter*, 438.
32 Ibid., 450, 466.
33 Ibid., 421.
34 *BRUO* iii, 2005.
35 C. J. Godfrey, 'Pluralists in the Province of Canterbury in 1366', *JEH*, vol. xi, 1960, 23–40.
36 *BRUO* iii, 1894–5 (Tregury); 1935–6 (Urswick).

two at once.[37] It was usual to exchange or resign them as the opportunity arose. In many cases the motive was advancement, with the second benefice being more valuable than the first. Peter Stukeley of Wells resigned his rectory of Walsoken, valued at £26 13s 4d, on being instituted to Stokenham, worth £33 6s 8d, in 1431.[38] Access to more lucrative rectories often came through service. But not all canons were motivated by financial gain or even greed. In a lot of cases it is far from clear why a canon progressed through several rectories and no doubt there are many hidden motives we know nothing about. John Burneby of Exeter, in holding a series of seven poor rectories in the diocese before becoming a canon there, seems to have made some curious decisions. In 1437 he resigned the rectory of Shobrooke, worth £6 13s 4d, on his institution to St Breoke, worth only £4 6s 8d. His new benefice had the further disadvantage of being in Cornwall, whereas Shobrooke was close to Exeter and the bishop, in whose service Burneby seems to have been at this time, hence his ability to acquire new benefices rapidly as he heard of vacancies.[39]

Prebends in collegiate churches were accumulated by canons nearly as readily as rectories, if often for short periods. The patronage of these churches lay mainly with the king or bishops who used them to reward and retain their servants. Many a king's clerk held a canonry in St Stephen's Westminster, St Martin le Grand London or St George's Windsor. Though these were often not very valuable they did have the advantage of being without cure of souls which meant they could be held in plurality without infringing canon law or requiring a dispensation. Their income could be enjoyed with few responsibilities. Wardenships and masterships of hospitals were commonly used in the same way as collegiate prebends, but were not as numerous. A great many canons could expect to acquire a second or third prebend in the course of their careers; half the canons of Lincoln achieved this in the period 1300 to 1541.[40] Almost as many, 45 per cent, also acquired a dignity. It was more usual to reach this rank after rather than before becoming a canon. Dignities were deemed to be with cure of souls and rarely held in plurality. Once gained cathedral canonries and dignities were usually retained for life, with the prospect of a comfortable retirement in residence in the close. The unlucky few were ejected by rivals after temporary possession. This was more likely in the richer cathedrals of Lincoln, Salisbury and York where there was more competition for the more valuable prebends and during the fourteenth century when the competing authority of pope; king and bishop to appoint canons provided opportunities for rival claimants.[41] The majority who gave up their prebends did so willingly: as part of an exchange of

37 BRUO ii, 1118–19.
38 BRUC 555–6; Taxatio, 80, 156.
39 Reg. Lacy Exeter I, 217; Taxatio, 144, 145.
40 These figures are taken from the major biographical sources BRUO, BRUO 1500–1540, BRUC, and the twelve volumes of Fasti 1300–1541.
41 A cursory glance at the Fasti volumes for Lincoln, Salisbury and York reveals the extent of the rivalry. For examples see Chapter 2.

benefices; on promotion to the episcopate; or by resignation. In the sixteenth century the turbulence of the Reformation resulted in a number of deprivations.[42] These were mainly isolated events affecting individuals rather than damaging chapters. Some were unable to accept Henry VIII's divorce or the royal supremacy in the 1530s. Others were deprived during the Marian reaction and a few were deprived as a result of the Elizabethan settlement in the 1560s. While at most cathedrals only two or three canons were removed Lincoln suffered more heavily losing twelve between 1534 and 1560.[43]

The Exeter evidence suggests that it was usual to hold prebends for ten years or longer; this was true of about half the chapter and as many as a quarter held them for twenty years or more. Quick exchanges or death account for most of those holding their canonries for short periods. The longest serving was William Leveson of Exeter; appointed by his uncle Bishop Veysey in 1528 he lived through the upheavals of the Reformation and died fifty-four years later in 1582.[44] Such individuals can be found in most chapters. Some, a significant minority, acquired no further benefices after their canonry or had to be content with a rectory or collegiate prebend. For the majority a second or third canonry and perhaps a dignity was the summit of their career. With just seventeen sees in England and four in Wales, some of them held by regulars, only the elite rose to the episcopate; at both Lincoln and Exeter almost one in ten of the chapter. These were some of the most distinguished clergy of their day: Richard Bury, Robert Hallum, and Thomas Rotherham.[45] In the late medieval period bishops were usually political appointees chosen by the king and often being rewarded for service in high office. Almost without exception, unless they were monks, they had held canonries before reaching the episcopate; about half appointed between 1300 and 1541 had held a canonry in the cathedral before their elevation. This was frequently only a nominal connection and very few had been residentiaries. Though a dean might rise to the episcopate only nine became bishops in the same cathedral. John Chandler was exceptional in this respect having been continuously resident at Salisbury from his election as dean in 1404 to his election as bishop in 1417.[46] A century later John Veysey occupied a similar position at Exeter.[47] Like their English counterparts foreign canons rose to the

---

[42] Little has been written on this subject. An account of the events at Salisbury can be found in Edwards, 'Salisbury Cathedral', 183–6.

[43] The twelve at Lincoln were Anthony Draycott (*Fasti Lincoln*, 34); Francis Gascoigne (Ibid., 113); Henry Litherland (Ibid., 23); John London (*BRUO 1500–1540*, 359–60); James Mallet (*Lincoln Fasti*, 65); Christopher Plummar (Ibid., 122); Edward Powell (Ibid., 115); Thomas Robertson (*BRUO 1500–1540*, 487–8); William Tresham (*Lincoln Fasti*, 30); Edward Whalley (Ibid., 75); Henry Williams (*BRUO 1500–1540*, 629–30); and Nicholas Wilson (*DNB* vol. lxii, 119–20).

[44] *Exeter Fasti*, 64.

[45] *BRUO* i, 323–6 (Bury); *BRUO* ii, 854–5 (Hallum); *BRUO* iii, 1593–6 (Rotherham).

[46] *BRUO* i 397–8; Salisbury D&C Reg. Draper fo. 14v passim, Reg. Vyring fo. 1r passim, Reg. Pountney fo. 1 passim, Communars' Accounts nos 20–35.

[47] *BRUO* iii, 1947–8; DRO D&C 3707 (Refections Accounts) s. a. 1506/7–1513/14.

episcopate in their native lands. Many had already achieved this and become cardinals before acquiring their English canonries. On appointment bishops were required to resign all their benefices but elevation to the cardinalate enabled them to acquire new ones, often with papal provisions. Only a small handful of Englishmen became cardinals and this was usually long after they had been canons.

Patronage and Career Patterns

> In these days pastors and prelates of the Church tire and sweat to obtain church dignities, one in the king's kitchen, another in a bishop's court, and a third in the service of a temporal lord; ... And when, after long toil, they obtain a church through such occupations, they cease not to labour, but must be prebendaries, then archdeacons and then bishops.

So wrote Alexander Carpenter, an obscure fifteenth-century moralist, in his *Destructorium Viciorum* of 1429.[48] The career patterns of successful clerics in the later middle ages were well understood and sometimes criticised by contemporaries. It was standard and widely accepted practice in the fourteenth and fifteenth centuries for popes, kings, bishops, and magnates to use the benefices in their patronage as rewards for service. Cathedral canonries were virtually reserved for administrators in Church, state, and noble households, or for the well born, who together form the higher or privileged clergy. Family influence was closely bound up with patronage and service, a reflection of how powerful a force in medieval society family and lineage were. Birth gave some canons considerable advantages. Those born into armigerous families, particularly the baronage and knightage, could expect the path to advancement to be eased by presentation to family benefices, access to other patrons, and an education. The luckiest could draw on family patronage for much of their career. William Caple, after being ordained to the title of his own patrimony, was presented to the family benefice of How Caple in Herefordshire by his brother Sir Walter in 1278, before becoming a canon of Hereford in 1303.[49] High birth almost certainly accounts for the presence of a number of canons not involved in service to a patron, the majority of whom were members of prominent local families in the diocese. Bishops and other ecclesiastics were the most zealous in promoting their families, partly because they had the greatest opportunities. There were few bishops who did not promote their relatives to a canonry or rectory in their diocese. Bishop Chedworth of Lincoln appointed three of his kinsmen to prebends in his cathedral, including his young nephew John who required a papal dispensation because of his age.[50] Thanks to his uncle's patronage he held a succession of

---

48 G. R. Owst, *The* Destructorium Viciorum *of Alexander Carpenter*, 1927, 15.
49 *Reg. Cantilupe Hereford*, 185.
50 BRUC 133 (John Chedworth); the bishop's other kinsmen were Nicholas Chedworth

prebends culminating, in 1465, in Sutton-cum-Buckingham the wealthiest in the cathedral as well as the premier archdeaconry of the diocese, the archdeaconry of Lincoln.[51] Other ecclesiastics can be seen presenting their relatives to benefices. Hugh Monyton of Exeter gained two benefices in the gift of Glastonbury Abbey while his brother was its abbot.[52]

In this way family networks of clerics were built up. Typical is the one around John Wynwyk a successful Lancashire clerk who rose high in royal service to be keeper of the privy seal from 1355 until his death in 1360. For this he was well rewarded, receiving prebends in six cathedrals. His brother Richard held prebends in two of them, Lincoln and York. Both brothers helped advance members of a neighbouring gentry family the Ashtons into which their sister Emma had married. Matthew Ashton senior followed John into royal service in the privy seal and was overseer of his will.[53] Richard used his influence as a clerk of the bishop of Lincoln to assist William Ashton's early career, obtaining for him a licence to study and farm his benefice in 1380.[54] He did the same for the next generation in 1394 helping Matthew Ashton junior secure a licence of non residence from his rectory of Slapton where he had succeeded his kinsman Matthew senior.[55] Better known and more successful were the Booths of Barton from further north in the county, four of whom reached the episcopate.[56] At their strongest these family links could become clerical dynasties. One of the most remarkable was founded at Exeter by William Kilkenny, a distinguished servant of Henry III and bishop of Ely. It lasted more than a century and spanned at least three generations. William had briefly been a canon of Exeter in the 1250s. His kinsman Andrew Kilkenny became a canon in 1282 and dean two years later. On his death in 1302 another William became a canon. He died in 1329, but not before, as Dean Andrew's executor, educating the next generation, Philip Kilkenny, at Oxford and founding the family obit at Exeter.[57] All chapters contained canons who were related; at Lincoln thirteen pairs of brothers and nineteen uncles and nephews can be identified and a further eighty were more distantly related. Thomas Winter, the son of Cardinal Wolsey, has the dubious distinction of being granted a prebend in his father's cathedral, but perhaps he was not unique in this, at least among papal 'nephews'.[58] Not all such family

(*Lincoln Fasti*, 60, 93) and William Chedworth (Ibid., 93). The family relationship is indicated in John Chedworth's will (C. W. Foster, 'Lincolnshire Wills Proved in the Prerogative Court of Canterbury 1471–90', *AASRP* xli, 1933, 179–218, 184).

[51] *Lincoln Fasti*, 114.

[52] BRUO ii, 1299.

[53] F. Crooks, 'John de Winwick and his chantry in Huyton Church', *Transactions of the Historic Society of Lancashire and Cheshire*, lxxv, 1926, 26–38.

[54] LAO Reg. XII (Reg. Buckingham) fo. 190v.

[55] Ibid. fo. 411r.

[56] Swanson, *Church and Society*, 79.

[57] BRUO ii, 1048–9; iii, 2186; DRO D&C 1927 (Miscellaneous Deeds).

[58] A. F. Leach, *Memorials of Beverley Minster. The Chapter Act-Book of the Collegiate*

relationships were among the higher clergy. Thomas Estbroke, subdean of Exeter from 1417 until his death in 1441, was the kinsman of Richard Estbroke the vicar of Okehampton.[59]

Magnate Service

When the *Black Book of Edward IV*, a fifteenth-century treatise on the royal household, advised dukes and marquesses to 'reward their . . . chaplains with . . . deaneries, prebends, free chapels, parsonages, pensions or such other.' it was setting out a practice widely followed by the nobility in the later middle ages.[60] Recent studies have confirmed that noble households usually had individual complements of clergy as chaplains or officers.[61] While not as widespread as royal or episcopal employment, magnate service was common among canons, though the scarcity of household records makes it difficult to quantify. Canons served lords of wide ranging rank from the greatest in the kingdom, such families as Beauchamp, Holland, Mortimer, Mowbray and Percy, to those of regional and local importance. Magnates of regional importance with strong interests in a diocese tended to have closest links with canons of their local cathedrals. This is particularly clear at Exeter where the leading Devon families of Cergeaux, Courtenay, Dabernon, Daumarle, Ferrers, Fulford, and Hankford all employed canons, occasionally as office holders but more often on a part-time basis.[62] The Courtenays' links with Exeter cathedral were unusually strong.[63] In Lincolnshire the Cromwell, Tailboys, Umfraville and Willoughby families had similar links with the canons of Lincoln.[64] Chapters looked to these families for 'good lordship' in return. Further research would probably confirm this pattern at other cathedrals. The most powerful magnates might retain several canons. Sir Guy Brian, a leading figure at the court of Edward III and one of the first knights of the garter, sought prebends for as many as seventeen of his clerks between 1350 and 1361.[65] Some canons were in the service of their families; Humphrey Hastanges, of Lichfield, joined his brother Ralph Lord Stafford to found an obit in 1344 and

Church of St John of Beverley, A. D. 1286–1347, with Illustrative Documents and an Introduction, 2 vols, SS 98, 108, 1898, 1903, ii, xcv–xcix.

59 CPL ix, 261; *Reg. Stafford Exeter*, 403.

60 Pantin, *English Church*, 32.

61 K. Mertes, *The English Noble Household*, 71–2, and Chapter 5.

62 Lepine, *Canons of Exeter Cathedral*, 113–17.

63 Lepine, 'Courtenays and Exeter Cathedral'.

64 Robert Beaumont was an executor of Ralph Lord Cromwell (*Test Ebor* ii, 198); John Gygur was a feoffee of Robert Tailboys in 1495 (*Inq. Post Mortem Hen VII*, i nos 1043, 1045); Richard Ovingham was a feoffee of Gilbert Umfraville in 1381 (*CCR 1377–81*, 433, 496); and John Derby was an executor and feoffee of Robert Willoughby, Lord Eresby in 1452 (*Early Lincoln Wills*, 173, 192).

65 CPP 205, 220–1, 224, 227, 234, 268, 279–80, 369–70.

four years later acted as his feoffee.[66] It is difficult to assess how long canons' service lasted as it is often only known from isolated references. However, there is evidence to suggest that some served for long if not continuous periods. William Dalton had been a canon of Lincoln for two years in 1351 when he entered the service of Sir Guy Brian and ten years later was described as his 'most special friend'.[67] Canons undertook a wide variety of duties for their patrons though most are described simply as the clerks of or in the service of a magnate. There are examples of them holding many of the offices found in larger households, attorney general, chancellor, treasurer, receiver, secretary and surveyor, as well as those with religious functions; almoner and chaplain. Thomas Duncan of Lincoln was physician to the fourth earl of March and Richard Manchester of Exeter served as chaplain to Sir John Russell, later earl of Bedford, in 1534.[68] There are occasional glimpses of these officials at work. Philip Leipyate, of Lincoln and York, emerges in the *Paston Letters* as a forceful agent of the duke of Suffolk pressing his master's claim to the manor of Drayton in Norfolk in 1465. According to John Paston he had a 'rytous and evyll dysposicyon' and caused an affray.[69] One or two canons seem to have specialised in magnate service and are known to have served several nobles.[70]

All office holders and many with less formal connections would have been liveried by their lords. The dearth of surviving livery rolls and household accounts makes examples rare. The earl of Devon liveried eight clerics in 1384–85, two of whom were Exeter canons, and one, his kinsman Richard Courtenay though an infant of two at the time, a future dean of Wells.[71] Rather more canons had a less formal relationship with the nobility. They were frequently chosen to act as feoffees in property transactions, normally on a one-off or occasional basis, but sometimes regularly over several years, and as their executors or supervisors of their wills. Both were positions of trust and responsibility and reflect the status and high regard in which they were held. Early in the sixteenth century three Yorkshire gentry thought it advantageous to appoint Brian Higden, dean of York, as supervisor of their wills.[72] A further reflection of their status and experience can be seen in membership of baronial councils. Magnates could derive considerable benefits from their links with canons beyond the direct results of service and the social prestige of having ecclesiastical retainers. John Abraham, a residentiary at Hereford, gave the Hastings family,

[66] CPR 1343–5, 316, 321.
[67] BRUO i, 538–9.
[68] BRUO i, 605 (Duncan); LPFD, vii, 1084 (Manchester).
[69] J. Gairdner, *The Paston Letters*, Gloucester, 1986, vol. iv, 132, 137–9, 142, 146, 157, 160.
[70] For an example of this see Robert Vaggescombe of Exeter whose career is discussed in Lepine, 'Origins and Careers', 114.
[71] M. Cherry, 'The Liveried Personnel of Edward Courtenay, earl of Devon, in 1385', part iii, *Devon and Cornwall Notes and Queries*, vol. 220.
[72] *Test Ebor* v, 85 (Henry Pudsey); Ibid., 229 (Thomas Ryther); *North Country Wills* i, 111 (Sir Richard Rokeby).

earls of Pembroke, faithful service through a time of crisis that included the capture and ransoming of one earl and the long minority of his infant son, and played an important part in preserving and managing the family estates. He was active on their behalf for over twenty years from 1369 until the early 1390s and his connection with the family dates back to 1353 when he received the living of Brunstead in their patronage.[73] Some risked treason like John Kynardessey of Lichfield on behalf of Thomas of Lancaster in 1322 and John Cheyne of Exeter in 1400 in the abortive uprising of the earl of Huntingdon.[74] Ecclesiastical retainers could provide spiritual benefits and were entrusted with the founding of obits and chantries. In 1463 Humphrey Stafford, earl of Devon, asked in his will that Nicholas Gosse of Exeter should preach a series of sermons for the sake of his soul.[75] Even thirty years after his death the duke of Exeter was remembered by his former chaplain John Ward of Exeter, when he came to establish his obit in the cathedral in 1478.[76]

Ecclesiastical Service

Canons were the mainstay of ecclesiastical administration in the later middle ages serving in the Church's bureaucracy at many levels from the papal camera to diocesan consistory courts. They were particularly important and numerous in episcopal service as diocesan administrators. Writing in 1540 Bishop Sampson of Chichester drew attention to the links between canons and diocesan administration noting that 'A buyshopp of a cathedrall chirche neyther having dignities prebends nor benefices at his disposition . . . without fayl schal neyther have lerned men with hym nor commissarie official or any other persen meate to serve his most humble desyrs.'[77] This was as true in 1300 as it was in 1540. Indeed canons had been closely involved in diocesan administration since the eleventh century when cathedral chapters originated in and evolved from bishops' households. During the thirteenth and fourteenth centuries diocesan administration developed becoming more complex as ad hoc commissions were replaced by routines carried out by officials, and being sufficiently autonomous to operate smoothly during long episcopal absences from the diocese. New bodies emerged, notably consistory courts, which existed in all dioceses by 1400, and higher courts of appeal, the most important of which was the Court of Arches, the principal court of the Province of Canterbury. This new bureaucracy tended to be staffed by graduates many of whom became or were canons.[78] As Bishop Sampson

---

[73] CPR 1374–7, 247; CCR 1385–9, 448.
[74] Kettle and Johnson, 'Lichfield Cathedral', 152 (Kynardessey); CCR 1399–1401, 552, Cal. Misc. Inq. 1399–1401 no. 65 (Cheyne).
[75] Somerset Medieval Wills 1383–1500, 201.
[76] DRO Chanter Ms 12 part 2 (Reg. Booth Exeter) fos 51v–52r.
[77] Kitch, 'Chichester Cathedral', 280.
[78] The development of diocesan adminsitration is set out in R. L. Storey, Diocesan

recognised cathedral prebends and dignities were a very important and often the most valuable part a bishop's patronage. They were habitually used to recruit, retain and reward officials. Episcopal and diocesan officials formed the core of all chapters in the late middle ages and were often among the first appointed by a bishop, though as many newly arrived diocesans found it was usually already full of his predecessor's men. The highly centralised bureaucracy of the see of York was dominated by a handful of resident canons during the fifteenth century who in the absence of the archbishop wielded considerable power.[79] In Bishop Sampson's own diocese the administration was in the hands of two senior dignitaries of the cathedral, chancellor Worthiall and dean Fleshmonger, for much of the early sixteenth century.[80] In the small chapter of Exeter as many as a quarter of canons were directly concerned with diocesan administration and a further 10 per cent were occasionally active.[81] As might be expected the proportion was smaller in the larger ones with twice the number of canons such as Lincoln where about 15 per cent were involved.

Canons tended to hold the more senior posts in both episcopal households and diocesan administration. In the former the offices of registrar and chancellor were often held by them or their occupants were soon rewarded with a prebend. They are known to have served bishops in many capacities, as receiver general, supervisor of manors, chaplain and cross bearer. At Wells in the fifteenth century the senior household offices were normally held by canons but it was unusual for lesser officials to hold prebends, indeed some were only minor clergy of the cathedral.[82] Episcopal households also contained a number of clerics simply described as clerks of the bishop of whom the most promising often rose to be canons some of whom may have been educated there. In diocesan administration the important offices of vicar general, official principal and commissary general were habitually held by canons from the fourteenth century to the Reformation. Canons also acted as sequestrators and regular commissaries. In the large diocese of Lincoln they often served as commissary in a particular archdeaconry. The diocese of Exeter in the second half of the fifteenth century illustrates well how important the role of canons was and the degree of reliance placed on them. This was a period of absentee bishops when it was more usual for the bishop to be away from the diocese than present. In the forty years 1456 to 1496 the bishop is only known to have been present for ten.[83] Dean Henry Webber virtually ran the diocese for twenty years during the frequent absences of Bishop Neville and

Administration in Fifteenth-Century England, Borthwick Publications, 16, 2nd edn, York, 1972. The subject is also considered in Thomson, *Early Tudor Church*, 60–73 and Chapter 5.

[79] Dobson, 'Residentiary Canons', 162–4.

[80] Kitch, 'Chichester Cathedral', 284–6.

[81] Lepine, *Canons of Exeter Cathedral*, 117–19.

[82] R. W. Dunning, 'The Households of the Bishops of Bath and Wells in the Later Middle Ages', *Proceedings of the Somersetshire Archaeological and Natural History Society*, cix, 1964–5, 24–39.

[83] This figure has been calculated from the episcopal registers DRO Chanter Ms 12 part

Bishop Bothe, acting as vicar general almost continuously from 1456 to 1476, the year before his death.[84] John Combe ran the diocese as vicar general at a dangerous time in 1483–85 during the treasonable absence of Bishop Courtenay. He had to face direct pressure from an angry Richard III.[85] It is difficult to say how long canons held their offices, especially in the early fourteenth century when diocesan administration was still evolving, because references to them are usually isolated. Some appointments were for limited periods, notably the office of vicar general, a temporary commission in the bishop's absence. Even so it is clear that many canons served for long periods working for successive bishops.

While a majority of those engaged in episcopal service worked in the diocese of their canonry many had experience in others. Some were deliberately recruited because of their experience and proven ability. Richard Morcestre had a career at Canterbury under Archbishop Winchelsey before moving to a canonry of Exeter and the service of Bishop Stapeldon.[86] Others followed the movements of their masters and patrons, none more loyally than John Hody a Somerset cleric who in the course of a successful career as an ecclesiastical lawyer acquired canonries at York, Salisbury, Exeter and Wells. Between 1420 and 1427 he moved from Hereford to Chichester and back to Worcester in the service of Thomas Polton, bishop of each diocese in turn, whom he had first served as official when Polton was archdeacon of Taunton. At the same time he maintained strong links with his native diocese and served successive bishops of Wells where he was resident.[87] Some of the most valuable experience had been gained in the provincial courts of appeal of Canterbury and York. Canons acted as advocates and officials of both, though experience in the larger province of Canterbury which contained all but one of the secular cathedrals and where there were two courts, the court of arches and the court of audience, was more common. The grant of a canonry was a useful way for bishops to make and retain contact with influential officials there who often represented them in appeals and also served as a reward. The chapter could also benefit. There are occasional glimpses of what must have been a common practice, the consultation of these successful lawyers. In 1381 the dean and chapter of Exeter wrote to John Shillingford, a former and future canon, and John Lydford asking for their opinion on the settlement of a vicarage appropriated to the cathedral.[88] The most able, invariably graduates, became eminent and widely consulted ecclesiastical lawyers who served several bishops during their careers; David Price was vicar general of Lincoln, London and Wells between 1413 and 1436 and also an advocate in the

1 (Reg. Neville Exeter) fo. 1 passim; Chanter Ms 12 part 2 (Reg. Booth, Courtenay, Fox, and King, Exeter) fo. 1r–173v.

[84] DRO Chanter Ms 12 part 1 (Reg. Neville Exeter) fos 4r–8v, 12v–29v; DRO Chanter Ms 12 part 2 (Reg. Booth) fos 4r, 7v, 15r–20v.

[85] Lepine, 'Courtenays and Exeter Cathedral', 51.

[86] Reg. Winchelsea Canterbury, 303, 892; Reg. Stapeldon Exeter, 124, 251, 489, 509.

[87] BRUO ii, 941–2.

[88] DRO D&C 3777 fo. 27v.

court of Canterbury. Within a year of each of his appointments as vicar general he had been granted a prebend in the cathedral.[89] Price is typical of this well rewarded small group of administrators found in all chapters who were amongst the most successful clergy of their day.

Papal service was much less common, particularly after 1400. During the fourteenth century papal provisions enabled French and Italian members of the papal civil service as well as cardinals to acquire canonries. Virtually all of these were absentees and had only a nominal connection with the cathedral which was merely a source of income to them. The exception were some financial officials, the papal collectors and sub-collectors, working in England who were often rewarded with canonries a few of whom made careers in the kingdom. All chapters had some papal servants among their members but the wealthier ones, principally Lincoln, Salisbury and York, and the richer prebends and dignities elsewhere attracted greater numbers. A few Englishmen did, however, find employment at the Curia in various administrative and spiritual capacities, as referendary, abbreviator of apostolic letters, or secretary and chaplain, which might last several years. Andrew Baret, of Lincoln and St Paul's, was a papal chaplain and auditor of causes in the papal palace from 1390 to 1395.[90] Another group was made up of those living or staying at the Curia who regularly acted as proctors for English clients, including the king, bishops, and religious houses. Both bishops and chapters found them useful contacts well worth a canonry. Many other canons paid brief visits perhaps combining business and a pilgrimage but did not stay to become involved. The scarcity of English cardinals probably accounts for the small number of canons serving the cardinalate. Of the handful known the majority were French or Italian beneficiaries of their masters' influence in securing provisions to English prebends. John Nans, a West-Country cleric from the diocese of Exeter, was exceptional. After studying at the university of Bologna he had joined the household of Cardinal Adrian di Castello by 1482 and later, in 1506, when Nans was a residentiary at Wells, served as his vicar general after the cardinal had become bishop.[91]

Episcopal administration accounts for most of the ecclesiastical service under-taken by canons but not all of it. They played a small role in two other spheres being employed by other dignitaries and religious houses. For those without patrons the position of official of an archdeacon could open up opportunities as well as provide useful experience and lead on to episcopal service. The office was a recognised route to a successful career and a number of canons started in this way. Though a significant proportion of canons relied on titles from them for their ordination or held benefices in their gift most seem to have had little connection with religious houses. Even for those requiring their titles the link seems to have been nominal. More formal contact was most likely when a religious house used their legal skills but this was not frequent, at least among

89 BRUO i 549–50.
90 BRUO iii, 2150.
91 BRUO ii, 1336–7; HMC Wells ii, 197.

the canons of Lincoln. The residentiaries of York were an exception to this being favoured agents of northern houses, particularly Durham.[92] William Hoper and Walter Sandwich, two contemporary canons of Lincoln in the 1440s, illustrate the range of connections. Hoper's was typical; he was employed as a legal advisor by Bicester Priory.[93] Sandwich was unusual in holding an office, being receiver general of Eynsham Abbey near Oxford for three years from 1438 to 1441, which he probably combined with his legal studies at the university.[94]

Royal Service

> ... the kingdom of England has always been governed principally and for the greater part by clerks, spaciously endowed with ecclesiastical benefices and honours ...

Though this statement was drawn up by royal clerks in 1279, it holds good throughout the middle ages.[95] From the late thirteenth century royal government expanded in size and complexity in response to the demands of diplomacy, war, taxation and the administration of France.[96] Until well into the fifteenth century it was largely staffed by clergy, the most readily available source of the literate and able men necessary to run it. Clergy had an additional advantage because they could be rewarded with Church benefices and were not a drain on the crown's resources. Cathedral canonries were one of the most sought after rewards and royal service was the surest route to one. King's clerks were numerous in the nine secular chapters, most commonly as absentee non-residents but also in retirement, resident in the close. Nearly two-thirds of the greater clerks of Edward III's chancery gained canonries.[97] At Lincoln during the two and a half centuries from 1300 to 1541 40 per cent of the chapter were engaged in royal service, a figure nearly matched at the much poorer chapter of Exeter where the proportion was 37 per cent over the same period.[98] This seems to have been the average in English chapters; at Lichfield in the fourteenth century the proportion was also 40 per cent.[99] At their peak in the mid fourteenth century they made up half the

---

92 Dobson, 'Residentiary Canons', 164–6.

93 BRUO ii, 958–9.

94 BRUO iii, 1640.

95 Pantin, English Church, 45–6.

96 For a general discussion of clerics in royal service see Heath, Church and Realm, 98–100, 349–50 and J. Dunbabin, 'Careers and Vocations', in J. L. Catto, A History of the University of Oxford, Vol 1, 581–93.

97 Wilkinson, The Chancery under Edward III, Manchester, 1929, 205–8.

98 These figures are taken from the major sources of information on royal service: BRUO, BRUO 1500–1540; BRUC; T. F. Tout, Chapters in the Administrative History of Medieval England, 6 vols, Manchester, 1923–35; J. C. Sainty, Officers of the Exchequer, Lists and Index Society, Special Series xviii, 1983; and the printed Calendars of Patent and Close Rolls.

99 Jenkins, Lichfield Cathedral, 206a.

appointments to prebends at Salisbury in the twenty years 1329–49.[100] Not surprisingly they form the largest service group among the chapter. There were particularly close links between the chapter and service to the crown at York under Archbishop Melton (1317–40) from whose household many were recruited into royal administration.[101] By the mid fifteenth century as the number of laymen in government increased there had been a corresponding decline in clergy, particularly in the junior and middle ranks. With the exception of the exchequer, clergy retained the principal offices until the Reformation and a presence in the majority of diplomatic missions abroad. This pattern is reflected at Lincoln where 70 per cent of canons in royal service were appointed before 1450 and only 29 per cent after. Such a decline brought pastoral advantages by decreasing non residence especially in parishes but it was offset by the loss of clerical influence in government administration and did not lead to an increase in residence at cathedrals.

There were few aspects of royal service not undertaken by canons who showed their versatility by serving in most government departments and many in the king's household. They were most numerous as envoys to the Curia and the courts of Europe, a role of increasing importance during the Hundred Years War, where their legal training was an asset in negotiation. Within the principal government departments chancery and exchequer clerks were commonly rewarded with cathedral canonries. The highest government offices, chancellor, keeper of the privy seal and to a lesser extent treasurer and many of the second rank positions, such as master of the rolls and keeper of the wardrobe, were usually held by bishops who had been canons or senior clerics who were cathedral dignitaries while in office. Humbler responsibilities entrusted to canons ranged from collecting taxes and surveying castles to auditing accounts. In the early fourteenth century they also held the offices of escheator and justice in eyre before generally being replaced by laymen. The more experienced acted as appeal judges in cases from the royal courts and some were members of the king's council. Canons' activities extended from royal administration in Gascony, Normandy and Ireland to local government in the English shires. In the fifteenth century some, usually senior dignitaries, were appointed justices of the peace alongside their episcopal colleagues and lay magnates. There is a similar variety in their roles in the royal household which included routine work in departments such as the kitchen and buttery and more personal service which might bring considerable influence. The office of king's secretary was frequently held by an able and rising cleric. Royal chaplains, confessors, physicians, almoners, the dean and many members of the chapel royal, all could expect to be rewarded with cathedral prebends. Much of this service was performed by clerics who held a specific office usually for some years. Another less formal type of service to the crown can be identified in which

---

[100] This analysis is based on Chew, *Hemingby's Register*, 171–260.

[101] J. L. Grassi, 'Royal Clerks from the Archdiocese of York in the Fourteenth Century', *Northern History*, v, 1970, 12–33.

occasional commissions were carried out, often by individuals styled 'king's clerk'. They were a large group of unspecialised clerks working on a temporary basis some of whom moved into full time service. Their title suggests some official status and access to crown patronage which secured them prebends. For some their title is all that is known about their activities. Service to the crown included employment in the households of the queen and royal dukes.[102] Isabella of France and Margaret of Anjou were no less vigorous in promoting their clerks to canonries than their husbands. Parallel to the king's administration were those of the Black Prince and John of Gaunt both of which contained many clerks some of whom went on to serve the crown. In the fifteenth century the ducal households of Humphrey of Gloucester, John of Bedford and Richard of Gloucester and that of the formidable Lady Margaret Beaufort offered similar opportunities though on a smaller scale. Though not unknown service to a foreign ruler was extremely rare; there are a handful of individuals in the fourteenth century working for the king of France.

Though we know few details about the work canons did beyond the names and general functions of the offices they held there are some fleeting glimpses of them engaged in royal business. In 1403 John Forster of Lincoln, a king's clerk, was caught up in the fighting at the battle of Shrewsbury and later sought a pardon from the pope for the injuries he caused while defending himself.[103] Occasionally they can be seen having a wider impact. Thomas Haxey of York risked his career as a chancery clerk in 1397 when he introduced a bill in parliament criticising the extravagance of Richard II's household. His precise role in the matter is unclear but was judged treasonable, though he was quickly pardoned.[104] Richard Layton of York emerges as a loyal but ambitious and ruthless agent of Thomas Cromwell and Henry VIII. During the 1530s he was closely involved in the accelerating rate of religious change, participating in the examination of Sir Thomas More and Bishop Fisher, the dissolution of the monasteries, the suppression of the Pilgrimage of Grace and the trial of Anne Boleyn.[105] Canons in royal service generally did not have what can be described as a political career. It was not until they rose to the episcopate, which they often combined with high office, that they could influence policy and decisions and played a political role in the government of the realm. The most able clerics were frequently in the service of several masters, either consecutively or simultaneously. In the medieval mind there was no clear distinction between ecclesiastical and secular administration. Many canons moved freely from one to another. William Loring of Salisbury's first experience was ecclesiastical, in the court of Canterbury in the early 1370s. By the end of the decade he was a king's clerk and had been appointed constable of Bordeaux.[106] Even within royal service

---

102 For some examples of this see Lepine, 'Origins and Careers', 118–19.
103 *BRUO* ii, 708–9.
104 *Reg. Chichele Canterbury* ii, 657–8.
105 *BRUO 1500–1540* 346.
106 *BRUO 1500–1540* 1163.

chaplains might be employed on government commissions as well as religious duties. Important contacts made while acting for one master often brought service and rewards from others. Civil servant bishops like William Melton and Nicholas Bubwith, both treasurers, recruited members of their episcopal administration into royal service.[107]

The wealth and status of canons were the rewards for this service. As the pluralists returns of 1366 show, most canons held several benefices, ranging from valuable rectories to prebends in collegiate churches and cathedrals and for the elite a seat on the bench of bishops. Their university education and administrative skill opened up lucrative careers and they became the backbone of ecclesiastical and royal bureaucracy. Prebends were a useful and cheap way for bishops and kings to reward their officials reinforcing the closeness of the relationship between cathedral chapters and service to Church and crown. This was an important, though not the principal function of cathedrals and one of the ways in which they demonstrated their usefulness to medieval society.

[107] *Handbook of British Chronology*, 80, 93 (Melton); *BRUO* i, 323 (Bubwith).

5

To the Praise, Honour and Glory of Almighty God: Canons' Residence at their Cathedrals

When Clement Denston asked to be admitted as a residentiary canon of St Paul's cathedral in 1447 he stated that it was for the 'praise, honour and glory of Almighty God'.[1] Although he was using a standard form of expression he was asserting a self-evident principle professed by all canons. For the primary purpose of cathedrals was to offer up a perpetual round of prayer and worship to God: in the words of Bishop Lacy of Exeter 'the singing, saying, and celebration of the divine service'.[2] This was done in the recitation of the eight daily offices, known as the *Opus Dei*. It was undoubtedly the intention of cathedral founders that canons should play a major part in this and keep residence in order to do so.[3] But by the twelfth and thirteenth centuries, if not earlier, the functions of canons were in practice complex and diverse. Literate and able clerics were required for episcopal, papal and royal administrations, and cathedral canonries, as we have seen, were widely used to reward them. As a result non-residence was already a serious problem in the twelfth century. It was compounded by the post-Conquest practice of dividing cathedrals' estates and revenues into individual prebends which, except at Exeter, were attached to each canonry. Not only would many canons be absent from their cathedrals on other duties but they would take with them a substantial proportion of its wealth. The twelfth-century reformers' reaction to pluralism and non-residence was often to view and condemn it simply as a moral failing. However, during the thirteenth century bishops and chapters came to terms with the problem and accepted it as a fact of life. Non-residence was dealt with by recognising two groups of canons: residents and non-residents, and rewarding them accordingly. A common fund of estates and revenues was retained by chapters after creating individual prebends as a reserve and to make daily payments to canons. This was used to encourage residence by ensuring that most of its income was divided only among residentiaries in daily and quarterly

---

[1] GL Ms 25,513 fo. 239v.
[2] BL Harl Ms 1027 fo. 73v.
[3] For a general discussion of this Edwards, *Secular Cathedrals*, 1–22 and chapter 1, especially, 35–8.

payments. Residence could in this way be made financially attractive by increasing the common fund. Indeed this was often the explicit aim of grants of lands or churches by bishops to their cathedrals. Greater specialisation within the cathedral with the development of the minor clergy also helped overcome the problem of non-residence. The vicars choral came to bear the brunt of the daily offices, deputising for the canons and allowing a high level of non-residence without a breakdown of the *Opus Dei*.

Regulations and Qualifications for Residence

The rules and regulations for residence varied widely among the nine secular cathedrals and evolved gradually over nearly three centuries from the late eleventh century to the mid fourteenth. Most, though not all, were set out in the cathedrals' statutes.[4] These are a miscellaneous collection of statements by successive bishops on various aspects of the rules by which their cathedrals were organised and run that gradually accumulated and were written down over the centuries. Unwritten custom alone was sufficient to organise chapters until the mid-twelfth century. The writing down of custom and practice on a somewhat ad hoc basis was a later development, a response to the increasing complexity of cathedral life and the need to have clear statements to resolve disputes. It also reflects the wider trend in government, the law and land tenure to use written records rather than memory.[5] The earliest statutes were not intended to innovate but to set out what already existed and throughout the period custom and statute were both regarded as valid. However, with the continued increase in the complexity of chapter life and business and changing circumstances, episcopal initiative resulted in new statutes that developed and altered the organisation of secular cathedrals. Statutes became more comprehensive and detailed in the thirteenth century as they responded to new problems and persistent abuses and were codified by bishops and deans. An episcopal visitation was often the prelude to new statutes to amend or improve existing practice. This process was largely complete by the end of the fourteenth century. Fifteenth-century and later statutes tended to be more narrowly focused or restatements of existing ones.

Statute making can be divided into three broad periods: the era of the first statutes in the late twelfth and early thirteenth centuries, the great codifications from the mid thirteenth to the mid fourteenth century, and later additions and revisions from the later fourteenth century to the Reformation. Statutes were made in all three periods at most cathedrals. The earliest known is St Osmund's *Institutio* for Salisbury, originally thought to date from 1091 but in fact gradually compiled over half a century between c.1146 and 1215.[6] At about the same time

4   Ibid. 22–8, 115–19.
5   For the wider context of using written records see M. T. Clanchy, *From Memory to Written Record*, 1979, part ii.
6   Wordsworth and Macleane, *Salisbury Statutes*, 26–38; D. Greenway, 'The False

the first known statutes were being made at Exeter (1133x1161), Lichfield (1189x1198), St Paul's (1192), Chichester (1197), Lincoln (1186x1200) and probably Wells; at York they followed in 1222.[7] The most important development in statute making was the process of expansion and codification during the century after 1240. Major statutes were made in the 1240s at three cathedrals: Wells in 1240 and 1259, Lichfield in 1241 and 1294, and Chichester in 1247 and 1251.[8] Hereford's statutes were compiled slightly later and completed by 1264 at about the time that Bishop Bronescombe codified Exeter's between 1268 and 1277.[9] Dean Baldock had completed a similar process at St Paul's by 1305. The three wealthiest cathedrals were the last to carry this out: Salisbury in Bishop Martival's great codification of 1319, York in 1325 and Lincoln in the *Liber Niger* of c.1330. The last phase of statute making was rarely innovatory and largely consisted of clarification of any remaining uncertainties and responses to any new problems or abuses. Many dealt with individual matters as they arose and often included a restatement of existing statutes. These later additions were issued with varying frequency according to circumstances from the mid fourteenth century onwards. There was a burst of activity at Wells between 1298 and 1338 when three were issued and one at Exeter between 1328 and 1363 – here the result of having a disciplinarian bishop, John Grandisson.[10] At Lichfield the main period of legislation took place in the mid-fifteenth century (1428, 1454 and 1465).[11] Elsewhere there were long gaps between sets of statutes; none were made at Chichester between 1251 and 1481 and at York and Hereford there were none after the great codifications until the Reformation. The pace of statute making declined during the fifteenth century and became rare in the sixteenth. Only at Exeter (1511 and 1519x41) and Lichfield (1526) were new ones issued, though Dean Colet tried unsuccessfully to introduce reform at St Paul's in 1518–19.[12] The initiative in statute making generally lay with bishops seeking

Institutio of St Osmund', in D. Greenway, C. Holdsworth, and J. Sayers, *Tradition and Change: Essays in Honour of Marjorie Chibnall*, Cambridge, 1985, 78, 91–4.

[7] Though many are printed, the statutes of the nine secular cathedrals are widely scattered. For Salisbury see Wordsworth and Macleane, *Salisbury Statutes*. The Exeter statutes are only partly printed; for a discussion of them and the main manuscript sources see Lepine, *Canons of Exeter Cathedral*, 141–55, and Oliver, *Lives*, 465–76. The Lichfield statutes are printed in Dugdale, *Monasticon*, vol. vi, part iii. For St Paul's see Sparrow Simpson, *Registrum Statutorum*; for Chichester see Swainson, *History and Constitution*; for Lincoln Bradshaw and Wordsworth, *Statutes of Lincoln*, which also contains an abstract of the York statutes, vol. ii, 44–85.

[8] The Wells statutes are contained in Reynolds, *Wells Cathedral*. There is also useful material and discussion in Watkins, *Dean Cosyn*, and Church, *Chapters in the Early History of the Church of Wells*, 273–5.

[9] The Hereford statutes are printed in Bradshaw and Wordsworth, *Statutes of Lincoln*, vol. ii, 44–61.

[10] Lepine, *Canons of Exeter Cathedral*, 149–52; Watkin, *Dean Cosyn*, 11–16, 20–1.

[11] Kettle and Johnson, 'Lichfield Cathedral', 160.

[12] Oliver, *Lives*, 465–76; Sparrow Simpson, *St Paul's Statutes*, 217–48.

to regulate and improve their cathedrals. They often worked with the coopera-
tion and consent of their chapters. Reforming deans were also active, most
notably Ralph Diceto and Ralph Baldock at St Paul's but also Edward de la Knolle
and John Godeley at Wells.

Though the details varied widely there were common general requirements
for residence at all cathedrals.[13] Custom and statute set out minimum periods of
time in residence, the services that had to be attended, duties in the choir and
enjoined the practice of hospitality, most of which were established by the end
of the thirteenth century. At five cathedrals a stricter probationary period was
enforced in which canons had to spend most of the year in residence with full
attendance at the daily offices sometimes with no payments. At Lincoln and
Hereford this lasted for three years but at Chichester for only one and at York
for just six months. The strictest probationary residence was at St Paul's which
imposed heavy duties of hospitality for much of the fourteenth century, requiring
the regular entertainment of several minor clergy and fellow canons and two
major banquets for the canons and city dignitaries.[14] Once qualified, residence
– usually called greater or major residence – was less exacting. The shortest
minimum periods of residence were at Lichfield and Salisbury where the requirements were two and three months respectively which could be undertaken at
any time in the year and did not have to be continuous. This practice evolved
from unsuccessful attempts at both cathedrals in the thirteenth century to ensure
that all canons resided for a quarter of the year and that there was always a quarter
of the chapter in residence. In both places the requirement on all canons to reside
broke down leaving a flexible and modest minimum period of residence, though
in practice most canons were much more assiduous. York and Lincoln also set
no limits on when in the year residence should be performed but required much
longer periods: twenty-four weeks at the former and thirty-four weeks and four
days at the latter. Elsewhere residence was more strictly defined by quarterly term
with annual totals of between six and nine months. St Paul's required twenty-four
weeks like York but did not allow a whole term's absence, the maximum being
twenty-seven days per quarter. The West Country cathedrals of Exeter and Wells
stipulated forty-six days residence each quarter, a total of six months a year. The
most rigorous were Hereford, where the total was thirty-six weeks but the sixteen
weeks absence could not be taken consecutively, and Chichester, where only
three weeks absence each quarter were allowed. Lincoln was unique in permitting
minor residence for a third of the year with reduced payments. Chichester
granted half residence for six months but this was a special dispensation from the
chapter rather than an entitlement. Dignities were widely expected to spend
longer in residence because their offices were deemed to have cure of souls. This
might be expressed generally as 'assiduous' or for the greater part of the year and
was defined as two-thirds of the year at Exeter and Wells. The dean of Lichfield

13 Edwards, *Secular Cathedrals*, 50–6.
14 Brooke, 'St Paul's Cathedral', 87.

was expected to be in continuous residence. In general the wealthiest cathedrals had the least rigorous rules for residence and the poorer the strictest.

Canons were not considered resident unless they worshipped in the cathedral regularly and attended the offices set out in the statutes.[15] Matins seems originally to have been regarded as the most important of the daily offices and remained the only requirement at Hereford and Lichfield. Most other cathedrals introduced an element of flexibility allowing a choice, Chichester permitted either matins or high mass, and this choice extended to vespers at Exeter and vespers and prime at St Paul's. Lincoln residentiaries could choose any one of the offices. Only York enforced attendance at more than one requiring its residents to be present at matins, high mass and vespers. This seems to have been relaxed to high mass only in 1350, but the relaxation may have been temporary as in Archbishop Lee's visitation in 1534 the original requirement was restated for visiting non-residents.[16] No details of the rules at Salisbury and Wells survive, probably because custom and practice were clear enough and the details did not need to be written down. It is likely that both cathedrals had the same practice, since the early Wells statutes were modelled on those at Salisbury. Most chapters allowed their residentiaries a 'quiet' night each week when they were excused attendance at services. All required them to act as 'hebdomadary canon' from time to time. This lasted for either one or two weeks when they took a leading part in the services, all of which they were expected to attend. As residentiaries canons were expected to keep hospitality for the minor clergy, visitors and the poor. Hospitality was an important and sometimes burdensome obligation that was regarded as one of the primary purposes of residence; it will be discussed more fully in a later chapter.[17] Once resident, canons were expected to attend chapter meetings regularly and help run the cathedral by taking their turn in holding chapter offices.

A canon's presence in the close and at cathedral services was not enough for him to become a residentiary. Some non-residents lived in the close and attended the daily offices but never formally entered residence. It was necessary to go through a formal process of entry and acceptance. This began with a canon protesting his residence, by asking at a chapter meeting to begin his residence at the start of the next term; at Lichfield forty days notice was required.[18] The chapter's consent was normally a formality but this was not always the case. In exceptional circumstances it might be refused or postponed according to the suitability of the individual or the economic health of the chapter. Once accepted, a canon began his probationary period of strict residence if that was required. This was a means of testing an individual's intentions and commitment to reside. He also had to provide an entry feast which fulfilled a similar function.

[15] Edwards, *Secular Cathedrals*, 56–9.
[16] York D&C H1/1 fo. 69r; 'Visitations in the Diocese of York holden by Archbishop Edward Lee', *YAJ*, vol. xvi, 1902, 433–5.
[17] See Chapter 6.
[18] Kettle and Johnson, 'Lichfield Cathedral', 152.

Little is known of these celebrations as no descriptions have survived but it was the custom at most cathedrals for a canon to mark the start of his residence with a feast for his fellow canons and the minor clergy.[19] At St Paul's and York the heavy obligation of hospitality lasted for the whole probationary period and might cost up to a thousand marks. Concern about the lavishness of entrance feasts led to their being replaced by fixed entry fines. During the fifteenth century St Paul's, Wells, Lichfield and Hereford set theirs at one hundred marks with only Salisbury expecting more, 107 marks 6s 8d for canons and 157 marks 6s 8d for dignitaries. Chichester had set an entry fine of fifty marks as early as 1251 but also required a feast and Exeter set a low fine of £40 though not until 1507. Chapters found entry fines a useful source of income which was put to various purposes according to need; a proportion was frequently diverted to the fabric, and the rest might be divided among the residentiaries or placed in the common fund.

The Financial Benefits of Residence

Residence at an English cathedral was an expensive undertaking, particularly the obligation of hospitality. In the twelfth and thirteenth centuries bishops sought to make it more attractive by instituting generous payments to residentiaries and building up the chapter's common fund to provide them.[20] There were four principal sources of income for resident canons: daily payments in both money and kind, annual or quarterly distributions of surplus income from the common fund, payments for attending obits in the cathedral and the profits that could be made by leasing chapter estates or farms. These were supplemented by a number of miscellaneous small payments from various sources such as cathedral offerings. By the fourteenth century the most generous cathedrals – Exeter, Lichfield, Lincoln and York – paid daily commons of 12d, known as *cotidiane*, to their residents. These were considerably enhanced on feast days, rising to 15d on minor feasts and 18d on major ones at Exeter. York was more generous still, paying 2s on minor feasts and 3s on double feasts of which there were nearly fifty a year.[21] Though the sum at Lichfield on these days was lower at 2s, it paid 10s on the four principal feasts of the year which included that of its patron St Chad.[22] The other five cathedrals were not as generous, offering less than half the 12d daily commons available elsewhere. Of these Wells paid 6d, Chichester 3d and St Paul's 12d per week. The main incentive to residence at Hereford was the payment of mass pence to canons attending the daily mass. Originally this was fixed at 4d per mass but by the second half of the fourteenth century this had been reduced to 1¼d as the income set aside for it fell. Salisbury was unique in

19 Edwards, *Secular Cathedrals*, 63–7.
20 Ibid., 39–49 for this and the next three paragraghs.
21 Dobson, 'Later Middle Ages', 60.
22 Dugdale, *Monasticon*, vol. vi, part iii, 1260.

not specifying daily payments. Instead by the early thirteenth century it had established a maximum sum payable each quarter for full residence: 53s 4d for the first; 49s 6d for the second; 52s 9d for the third; and 51s for the last. This averages out at about 6d per day.

The longer residence expected of dignitaries was reflected in enhanced payments at two cathedrals; they were entitled to double commons at Salisbury and Wells and at Lichfield the dean received the same enhancement. Commons received in kind, where they existed, had largely been replaced by monetary payments by 1300. Only three cathedrals retained them: Exeter, Hereford and St Paul's. At Exeter residentiaries received three loaves each day and weekly distributions of wine. These together with the daily payments of 12d made Exeter the most generous cathedral to its residents even though others made high payments on feast days. All canons of St Paul's were entitled to twenty-one loaves and thirty gallons of ale a week but these seem to have been discontinued by the residentiaries in the mid fourteenth century when they became a source of controversy and remained so as late as 1438.[23] Payments in kind at Hereford, known as little commons, consisted of a share of bread and grain as well as 20s a year and were available to all canons. Those present at matins were entitled to a further share of bread and grain whether resident or not.[24] Exeter residents received between £6 and £15 a term depending on how long they resided and on what days; an annual income of £50 could be expected.[25] Continuous residence at York yielded about half this, around £26–7 a year. In the late fifteenth century, payments ranged from £6 to £12 per half yearly term as few canons remained in residence for much longer than the statutory minimum of twenty-four weeks.[26] The maximum payments at Salisbury were fixed by statute at about £10 for canons and £20 for dignitaries and the fifteenth century accounts show this to be enforced up to the Reformation. The smallest sums were paid at Hereford. Those making full residence in 1290–91 received only £4–6 in mass pence and their counterparts in the 1450s had to make do with 20–30s a year.[27]

The annual or quarterly distributions of the surplus income from a chapter's common fund, the date of payment differed from chapter to chapter, were highly variable and always made in arrears, often in a series of complex accounting procedures over many years. They were particularly complex at Hereford where at least three different sets of accounts were used to make payments to residentiaries from different sources of income, mostly from churches. The main factors causing fluctuations in distributions were the number of canons in residence, who each received an equal share, and the economic health of the common fund. When the number of residentiaries was high the distributions were spread more thinly. In times of economic hardship or high expenditure there was little to

[23] Brooke, 'St Paul's Cathedral', 88.
[24] Bradshaw and Wordsworth, *Lincoln Statutes*, vol. ii, 52.
[25] Lepine, *Canons of Exeter Cathedral*, 158.
[26] For example York D&C E1/45–55 (Chamberlains Accounts 1471–88).
[27] HCA R381, R491–3.

distribute. Annual payments could be substantial sums that equalled and sometimes exceeded the totals of daily *cotidiane*. This was most clearly the case at York in the fifteenth century when the total annual surplus was between £200 and £170.[28] Even in the 1370s the sum distributed was over £30 divided among eight residents and in 1487–88 the three canons in residence received over £100 each.[29] York was exceptional in the value of its common fund and the small number of its residents. More typical were the distributions at Wells and Lincoln. In the fourteenth century at Lincoln they ranged from just below £10 to nearly £60, averaging at between £20 and £30.[30] The same average is found at Wells throughout the fourteenth and fifteenth centuries with the total rarely falling below £20 and rarely rising above £35.[31] At Exeter, with its generous *cotidiane* and high residence levels, the distributions were somewhat lower, only reaching the levels of Wells and Lincoln in good years. In the Michaelmas term 1306 the residentiaries received £6 12s 7d each but in the Easter term of 1400 only 14s.[32] Like Exeter, Salisbury paid its distributions quarterly and during the fourteenth century they matched those of Wells and Lincoln in good years with payments of £6–12 per term. In difficult years they might be £3 or £4 a quarter.[33]

Together, daily and quarterly or annual payments formed the bulk of a resident's income. Further small sums could be earned by regular attendance at obits in the cathedral. The most generous of these paid 2s or more to canons attending but it was more usual for payments of a few pence to be made. Obits established by resident canons tended to be among the more generous. By the fifteenth century there might be as many as a hundred celebrated each year in the majority of cathedrals. Though many were founded for a fixed number of years and others lapsed as their endowment income dried up, in general the rate of new foundations was sufficient to maintain a high number. If the Exeter evidence is typical the small income from obits, which in the 1360s was barely 20s a year, did not deter canons from attendance which generally remained at a high level.[34] Residentiaries could supplement their income from other small payments and distributions which varied according to the customs of the cathedral. At many they were entitled to a share of the public offerings such as those at Whitsuntide, known as pentecostals. Offerings at the high altar and the altar of the relics were distributed to the residents at Salisbury and at Wells there were special payments to those attended the procession on St Mark's day.[35] A winter fuel allowance of a hundred bundle of fagots was paid to residents at Exeter.[36] They also received a share of the porpoises occasionally washed up on the beach

28 Dobson, 'Later Middle Ages', 60–1.
29 Ibid.
30 Edwards, *Secular Cathedrals*, 45.
31 Colchester, *Wells Communars Accounts*, 5, 81, 165.
32 DRO D&C 2780, 2807.
33 Edwards, *Secular Cathedrals*, 46, 350–2, 354.
34 Exeter D&C 3766.
35 Chew, *Hemingby's Register*, 56; Colchester, *Wells Communars Accounts*, 106.
36 Exeter D&C 3550 fo. 23v.

at Dawlish, a chapter farm.[37] Their counterparts at Wells enjoyed occasional gifts of venison and sturgeon.[38]

Much more lucrative were the estates of the common fund, which were often farmed by residentiaries who paid a fixed rent and retained any surplus profits they made.[39] At York and Exeter this was originally a privilege of residence. The Salisbury statutes gave priority to residents but recognised it might be necessary to grant them to non-residents or laymen. Elsewhere laymen farmed estates alongside canons and sometimes they acted as sub-farmers to residents running the farms. Lay involvement in farms seems to have increased through the fifteenth century. Farms were undoubtedly profitable but this is very difficult to quantify; accounts are scarce and the economic history of most cathedrals has yet to be written. There is plenty of evidence of the rents paid but very little of the actual income the farmer received. The indirect evidence suggests that at its peak a canon's income from a group of farms may well have been greater than the daily and termly payments. This would account for the considerable competition to farm the most profitable, which led chapters to establish orders of precedence for them, usually based on seniority of residence. A great deal of time was spent discussing and dealing with farms at chapter meetings as claims were set out and disputes resolved. Some canons were prepared to go to considerable lengths to secure them, appealing to both king and pope. Bishops watched this scramble with concern, noting the evidence of negligence and debt. Farms, in particular the importance of proper accounting and prompt payment, were a regular and prominent theme in episcopal visitations and later statute making. At some cathedrals residentiaries were entitled to receive the daily payments normally due to them for a year after their deaths, with the intention that they should be put to pious uses in their wills.

Residence Levels, 1300–1541

Since the pioneering work of Kathleen Edwards the general levels of residence at cathedrals have been well known.[42] The following survey is intended to widen her detailed study of Lincoln and Salisbury to include the other seven cathedrals and to extend it to the Reformation. The archives of all but two of the nine secular cathedrals contain a great deal of material on residence, the most useful

---

[37] D&C 3773 fos 38v, 40r, 51r.
[38] Colchester, Wells Communars Accounts, 33, 179.
[39] For some discussion of this see Lepine, Canons of Exeter Cathedral, 159–60, and Chew, Hemingby's Register, 49–55.
[40] Henry Blakeborn, an Exeter Residentiary appealed to the king (DRO D&C 3498/6) and his colleague John Cheyne to Rome in 1376 (CPL iv, 224).
[41] This was the case at Exeter (BL Harl Ms 1027 fos 4v–5r) and Lichfield (LJRO D30/2/1/1 fos 93r–v). At Salisbury a share of the income from the prebend went to a deceased canon (Wordsworth and Macleane, Salisbury Statutes, 62–3).
[42] Edwards, Secular Cathedrals, 70–83.

of which are sets of accounts and chapter act books. Exeter, Hereford and Lincoln are outstanding in having long series of accounts with few gaps from the fourteenth to the mid sixteenth century. The sources at Salisbury, Wells and York, though considerable, have more serious gaps. At Lichfield virtually no accounts have survived and residence levels have to be compiled from the chapter act books. Only at St Paul's and Chichester is there almost no evidence, though at the former there is a fifteenth-century chapter act book. Appendix 1 sets out the major sources, their difficulties and the methods used to calculate residence levels for each cathedral. Appendix 2 sets out these findings and the following analysis is based on it.

Residence flourished in the first half of the fourteenth century. The number of canons resident in cathedral closes was high; there could be as many as fifteen at Exeter, Hereford, Lincoln and Wells and it was unusual for there to be fewer than ten. This lasted up to the Black Death when there was a noticeable decline. Though the accounts for 1347–49 are often missing, the numbers at Salisbury and Exeter fell below ten. The practice of residence was vigorous enough to recover from this set-back during the 1350s but at a varying pace: almost reaching pre-Black Death levels by the middle of the decade at Exeter and by the end of it at Hereford. It occurred slightly later at Lincoln in the early 1360s. The 1360s were a difficult time for residence when some of the recovery was lost and levels remained around ten in most cathedrals. From these relatively low levels numbers increased steadily through the 1370s. During the last twenty years residence levels were generally increasing, exceptionally so at Exeter where virtually the whole chapter of twenty-four canons were resident in the mid 1390s, exceeding the pre-Black Death levels. This reflected a golden age of residence between 1390 and 1410 at the three West-Country cathedrals, Salisbury, Wells and Exeter. Elsewhere the increases were smaller, reaching the level of the 1340s of around ten at Hereford in the 1380s and in the 1390s at Lincoln. Neither of these cathedrals reached their early fourteenth-century peak. Lichfield did not fully share this recovery and suffered a decline in the mid 1390s. The fifteenth century saw a steady but not dramatic decline in residence levels but they remained relatively high for much of its first quarter. The numbers ranged between five and ten at Lichfield, Lincoln and Hereford and between twelve and fifteen at Wells, Salisbury and Exeter. The levels started faltering during the 1420s: first at Hereford by 1421, with a decline becoming clear by the late 1430s and early 1440s. By this time there were often only five or six residentiaries at Lichfield and Hereford, and about the same number as York which generally had a low level of residence. Exeter, Salisbury and Wells shared this decline with numbers falling to around twelve. The decline was partly reversed during the late 1440s – a trend which lasted to the early 1460s when there was a trough from 1462/3 to 1465/6 at Hereford, Lincoln, Exeter and Salisbury. Some recovery had been made by 1470. Thereafter residence levels remained remarkably stable up to 1541 with only minor fluctuations. These levels were generally lower than those of the beginning of the century with totals of nine to twelve at Exeter and four to nine elsewhere. There was no crisis of residence in the years leading up to the

Reformation. York remained exceptional in rarely having more than two or three residentiaries throughout the fifteenth and early sixteenth centuries. There was no sudden decline as a result of the religious uncertainty of the 1530s.

From this general survey it is clear that residence levels could vary considerably from cathedral to cathedral. This becomes clearer still when the levels of residence at individual cathedrals are analysed in detail. The highest level was at Exeter because of its unique arrangement of equal prebends.[43] For the first three decades of the fourteenth century an average of fourteen canons resided. This rose to fifteen in the 1330s but fell back to the earlier level in the mid 1340s. The Black Death brought a dramatic decline to eight or nine in 1348–50. By 1355 there had been a recovery to pre-plague numbers but the return of the plague in 1361–62 caused a further setback to the level of 1348–50. A lasting recovery was underway during the 1370s which led to the zenith of residence at Exeter in the late fourteenth century; in the 1380s and 1390s between eighteen and twenty were resident. At its peak in 1397 and 1399 twenty-three of the twenty-four canons were in residence. Though numbers remained relatively high, these levels were not repeated. There was a slow decline in the first half of the fifteenth century with totals falling to around thirteen in the second decade and around twelve in the early 1440s, despite a temporary recovery to fifteen in the 1420s. By the 1450s the level of the early fourteenth century of thirteen or fourteen was being equalled. Apart from temporary blips down, such as 1462–65 and 1477, this was maintained until the mid 1480s. In 1485 there was a sudden drop from fifteen to eleven residents which lasted until the end of the century. There was a high degree of stability at a slightly higher level of between eleven and thirteen in the first quarter of the sixteenth century. It was followed buoyant levels of around fourteen in the 1530s, double the number at most other cathedrals.

The levels of residence at Wells were almost as high as those at Exeter, often equalling and sometimes rising above them. High levels of fifteen or sixteen were maintained from the 1320s to the 1440s, though there is a forty year gap in the records from the 1350s to the 1380s. At their peak in the 1390s the numbers reached nineteen or twenty. After a fall to ten or eleven in the later 1440s there was a modest recovery to eleven or twelve by the mid 1450s. The number of residentiaries stayed at this level for the rest of the century. Unfortunately the sixteenth century accounts do not contain the numbers in residence, though isolated references give some clues. Eight canons were resident in 1512–13, and probably twelve in 1513. Though large numbers of canons were resident at Wells they were a relatively small proportion of a large chapter of over fifty prebendaries. At their height they formed less than half the total and more usually between a quarter and a third, a much smaller proportion than Exeter with similar numbers of residentiaries. Between eleven and thirteen canons were resident at Salisbury in the 1340s. The Black Death reduced this to seven in 1350 but there

---

[43] Lepine, *Canons of Exeter Cathedral*, 168–71, 361–6.

had been a recovery to earlier levels by the late 1360s. This was not sustained in the short term as numbers dipped to ten in the later 1370s but they had risen by the middle of the next decade to around thirteen. The 1390s and early 1400s were the high point of residence at Salisbury with frequently as many as fourteen or fifteen present. This level was maintained up to 1430 during which time the residentiaries were particularly distinguished churchmen.[44] For the rest of the fifteenth century the numbers fell, to between eight and eleven in the 1440s and further still to between five and eight after 1480 despite a slight recovery in the late 1450s and again in the early 1470s. Despite gaps in the evidence the late fifteenth century levels of six or seven seem to have lasted up to 1541. Residence was healthy in the 1530s with about eight canons in the close apart from a brief hiatus in 1535–36 when the number fell by half. Salisbury, like Wells a large chapter of over fifty prebends, rarely had a third of its canons resident. Up to 1430 there were usually nearly a quarter, but subsequently less than a seventh.

Residence at Hereford fluctuated widely. It reached its highest level in the late thirteenth century when up to twenty canons were present. This was not sustained in the early fourteenth century and the level fell back to eleven to thirteen rising to a peak of fifteen to sixteen in the mid 1330s. Even this level was not achieved again, probably because the chapter's income was falling. During the 1340s, around ten canons were resident. This fell to eight by the mid 1350s but had risen to twelve by the early 1360s, a similar total to the first years of the century. The number remained steady through the 1380s and 1390s and into the first years of the new century. By the 1420s, after a decade of decline, the total had fallen dramatically to four. A gradual recovery followed from the 1430s to the late 1450s when eight or nine were in residence. Despite a trough in the mid 1460s this level, of between six and nine, was maintained for most of the rest of the century. From the mid 1490s only four or five were resident. In the sixteenth century there was a small increase to six or seven by the mid 1520s. As the Reformation began, this increase continued reaching between seven and eight from the mid–1530s. Like Exeter Hereford was a small chapter with poor prebends and had a relatively high proportion of its canons resident. During the fourteenth century over a third of the chapter was resident and for much of the fifteenth and sixteenth an average of a quarter were. Even at its height, residence at Lincoln never matched the levels at Exeter and Wells or even Salisbury and Hereford, though it nearly equalled the latter two. At the beginning of the fourteenth century barely a fifth of the chapter were resident: around ten or eleven canons, rising to twelve or fourteen in the best years, the 1310s to the early 1320s and the later 1330s. No records survive for the period 1340–60 but during the 1360s the losses of the Black Death were replaced as the number rose from seven in 1360–61 to ten by the end of the decade having peaked at fourteen in 1364–65. Over the last two decades of the fourteenth century, residence increased steadily from between nine and eleven in the 1380s to between twelve

44 See Chapter 9.

and fourteen in the mid 1390s. This was not sustained. From the late 1390s to the mid 1420s an average of eight to ten were present. This steady decline continued for the rest of the fifteenth century reaching between five and seven by the 1450s and remaining at this level until the mid 1490s when it rose slightly. There were eight residentiaries in 1501–02. For the rest of the sixteenth century, up to 1541, the levels were virtually identical to those of the second half of the fifteenth century. By this time barely a tenth of the chapter were resident.

The residence figures for Lichfield need to be used with caution, being entirely based on the attendances at chapter meetings recorded in the chapter act book.[45] This is likely to lead to some under-representation. Evidence from other chapters suggests that canons did not always attend meetings though they were resident. The first indications of residence levels date from the mid 1340s when ten or eleven canons were present. A decade later in the late 1350s, the level was a little lower at eight or nine. It stayed at this total to the end of the fourteenth century with occasional peaks of ten or eleven. In the fifteenth century the numbers fell from seven or eight in the first decade to four or five in the 1430s. After a forty year gap in the sources the chapter act books resume in 1481 with a similar number of residentiaries. This rose to seven or eight in the later 1490s but fell back to five for much of the first decade of the sixteenth century. Six or seven canons were generally resident up to 1541. For much of the fourteenth century, between a third and a quarter of Lichfield's canons were resident but in the fifteenth the average was a sixth. York had one of the lowest residence levels of the secular cathedrals.[46] Even when residence elsewhere was at its height in the first half of the fourteenth century, it had significantly fewer: probably no more than five. In the 1340s this had risen to nine in 1343 and seven in 1346–47 but this was still the lowest. Residence levels were at their peak at York through the 1370s and up to the late 1380s when it fell to three or four. This lower level was sustained for the next fifty years rising slightly to four or five in the 1420s and 1430s. No figures survive for the 1440s but from the 1450s to the 1470s the number of residentiaries ranged between three and five. There was a serious decline at the end of the fifteenth century; only two resided in 1486–88 and just one in 1499 and again in 1505–06. Despite some recovery around 1510, levels remained low during the first half of the sixteenth century. During the 1520s and 1530s there were usually two resident canons at York, but in 1539–41 only one.

The only cathedral with similarly low rates of residence was St Paul's where at the end of the fourteenth century the number had sunk to one or two.[47] The loss of much of the chapter's records makes it impossible to trace the pattern of residence for most of the later middle ages and compare it with that of York. Fortunately a fifteenth-century act book has come down to us and enables some analysis to be carried out between 1411 and 1447. Residence levels had recovered

[45] See Appendix 1.
[46] Dobson, 'Residentiary Canons', 150.
[47] Brooke, 'St Paul's Cathedral', 88–9.

from the late fourteenth century nadir by the second decade of the fifteenth century, reaching five or six. Though this was the lowest at any of the cathedrals, except perhaps York, it was sustained until the end of the decade. The revival continued in the 1440s, the next and final period for which there are figures, when there were usually six and sometimes seven residents. There is even less evidence of residence levels at Chichester. Occasional lists can be found in the few episcopal registers that remain, but the surviving chapter act book, containing material from the late 1470s to the early 1540s, is much less systematic in recording canons' attendance at meetings. Nevertheless, from these scant sources some glimpses can be seen. In the late fourteenth century there seem to have been either four or five in residence and in 1403 there were eight. Towards the end of the fifteenth century, in the 1470s, between three and five are recorded as present at chapter meetings. In the first decade of the sixteenth century a recovery was taking place and there were often five or six present. Thereafter the records are silent.

From this survey three broad levels of residence can be identified at cathedrals. There were high levels at two, Exeter and Wells. At both there were clearly more canons resident through the whole period 1300–1541 than at the other seven. Four cathedrals, Hereford, Lichfield, Lincoln and Salisbury had moderate levels of residence. At their peak they might equal the levels at Exeter and Wells but these were not sustained over the two and a half centuries. Salisbury generally had higher levels than the others which were very similar, though of these three Lincoln tended to have the most residents and Hereford the least up to the mid fifteenth century. In the sixteenth century the level at all four cathedrals was very similar. York and St Paul's had low levels of residence. Even at their lowest the numbers at the four with moderate residence rarely fell to these levels. The higher levels at York and St Paul's often only matched the lower levels at Hereford, Lichfield, Lincoln and Salisbury. Chichester has been excluded from this comparative survey because so little evidence survives.

The Nature of Canons' Residence

We know a great deal more about canons' residence than the numbers present at a cathedral; names are generally recorded and something is known of how long individuals resided and how often they were absent. From this, patterns of residence can be reconstructed and an impression formed of how conscientious canons were. Few took up residence, with its expensive entry requirements, without intending to make a long term commitment. The clearest demonstration of this is the large number of canons who spent many years in residence, providing a high level of continuity in their chapters. Detailed studies of Exeter and York have measured this. At the former in the period 1300 to 1455 nearly half resided for over ten years and 16 per cent for twenty years or more.[48] Their counterparts

48 Lepine, *Canons of Exeter Cathedral*, 173, Table 7.

at York in the fifteenth century were present for an average of 10.5 years and six of the thirty-four to enter residence remained for more than eighteen.[49] A smaller survey of the eleven canons of Lichfield who started residence between 1500 and 1539 reinforces this pattern; their average length of residence in this period was thirteen years and six remained in the Close for more than ten years, three of them for more than twenty.[50] Individual examples of longevity abound in all chapters. In January 1346, Richard Boule and Hugh Hopewas were beginning careers as residentiaries at Lichfield which were to last for a total of eighty years between them ending with Hugh's death in 1381 and Richard's in 1394.[51] A decade later, Edward Prentys entered residence at Salisbury on 7 September 1408 and stayed until his death nearly forty years later in 1446.[52] One of the most remarkable of these long serving residentiaries was William Leveson of Exeter who, when a young man, started his residence in 1537 as the pace of religious change quickened and lived through the upheavals of the Edwardian Reformation, the Marian Reaction and the Elizabethan Settlement. After forty-five years residence he died in 1582.[53]

Men like William Leveson and Edward Prentys not only spent many years in residence but spent most of each year at their cathedrals. Dean Stretton of Lichfield scarcely missed a chapter meeting from his election in 1390 until his death thirty-six years later in 1426.[54] Such exemplary commitment to residence as Stretton's was unusual but not unique. It was matched by some of his successors at Lichfield, notably Dean Heywood (d. 1492), and elsewhere by Dean Chandler at Salisbury.[55] The proportion of the year spent by residentiaries at their cathedrals was partly determined by the requirements of the statutes. At Exeter, residents had to spend part of each quarter at the cathedral and at Hereford the minimum length was thirty-six weeks with absences of no more than seven weeks. In contrast the residentiaries of Salisbury and Lichfield were required for less than three months. However, the majority of residents at these four cathedrals resided for substantially longer than the minimum requirement. On average nearly half of the residents at Exeter in 1300–1455 were present for more than eighty of the ninety-one days each quarter.[56] In the late fifteenth century many resident canons at Hereford attended over three hundred masses annually and early in Henry VIII's reign some were resident for over forty weeks a year.[57] Few canons at Lichfield and Salisbury took advantage of the statutes and spent only two or three months in residence. The fifteenth-century chapter act books at

[49] Dobson, 'Residentiary Canons', 153.
[50] LJRO D30/2/1/3–4.
[51] Bod Lib Ms Ashmole 794, s. a. 1347.
[52] Salisbury D&C Reg. Vyring fo. 9v; Reg. Burgh s. a. 1446.
[53] Exeter D&C 3707 s. a. 1537 et seq. to 1581.
[54] LJRO D30/2/1/1 fos 20r et seq. to fo. 111v.
[55] LJRO D30/2/1/2 fos 1r et seq. , D30/2/1/3 fos 1r–6r; Salisbury D&C Reg. Draper s. a. 1404–7, Reg. Vyring s. a. 1408–17.
[56] Lepine, *Canons of Exeter Cathedral*, 175, Table 8.
[57] HCA R501–25, R182–5.

Salisbury show about half the residentiaries in more or less continuous residence and the remainder absent for long periods of several weeks or months (though act books need to be used with caution as residents did not always attend meetings). During the golden age of residence at Salisbury in the early fifteenth century, six of the thirteen residentiaries in 1404 attended virtually all the chapter meetings that year; the precentor Adam Mottram missed only one.[58] His colleague William Loring is typical of those who broke their residence but still kept the minimum. He was absent for much of April that year and most of the late summer during August and September.[59] The pattern at Lichfield broadly follows that of Salisbury. Only at York did the canons spend little more than the minimum period of twenty-four weeks per year in residence. Most were present for between twenty-five and thirty weeks, most often from November to May, which enabled them to be involved in royal and diocesan administration.[60]

Two broad types of residence can be distinguished: assiduous, which can be subdivided into continuous and interrupted; and partial, which can be subdivided into occasional and short term. The great majority of residentiaries, probably as many as two-thirds or three-quarters, were assiduous. The most committed of these kept continuous residence, that is resided for at least the minimum period each year required by the statutes and often for much longer, as we have seen, over many years with only occasional breaks. This type of residence accounts for most residentiaries. Typical of these is Thomas Hendeman of Exeter whose nineteen years residence was broken by only one absence during the Easter term of 1425.[61] Though less demanding Thomas Walleworth's residence at York from 1386 to 1405 and probably to his death in 1409 was continuous.[62] Interrupted residence differed from continuous residence only in the frequency and length of the breaks but could still total many years of residence. During his fifteen years residence at Lincoln Thomas Clifford was absent twice, in 1310–11 and 1312–13.[63] Richard Delves, a canon of Lichfield from 1485 to 1527, delayed entering residence until 1502 but remained in the Close for the next fourteen years. He was absent from 1518 to the autumn of 1520 and fully resident again from 1522 until his death in November 1527.[64] Clifford and Delves were part of a relatively small group whose residence was interrupted. A systematic survey of Exeter in the century and a half 1300–1455 has identified less than a fifth of the residentiaries practicing this type of residence.[65] Those who made partial residence were a slightly larger group but still a minority. As with continuous residence it is helpful to distinguish between

58 Salisbury D&C Reg. Draper s. a. 1404.
59 Ibid.
60 Dobson, 'Residentiary Canons', 150.
61 Lepine, Canons of Exeter Cathedral, 178.
62 York D&C E1/8–38 (Chamberlains Accounts).
63 Edwards, Secular Cathedrals, 330–5.
64 LJRO D30/2/1/3 s. a. 1502–27.
65 Lepine, Canons of Exeter Cathedral, 179.

two types of partial residence. Occasional residence is typified by Richard Tischo at Lichfield. Though a canon for over thirty years from 1366 to 1398 he was resident for only eight, widely scattered over this period. He was at Lichfield from 1369 to 1371, 1375–77 and again for two isolated years 1381 and 1393.[66] The same pattern of short periods of residence scattered over several years is found in John Seys' residence at Exeter. Between 1361 and 1373 he was resident for nine quarterly terms and only twice for three consecutive terms.[67] Short term residence differs from occasional residence in its continuity generally lasting a few years but not spread over a long period. Many of these canons seem to have made a serious attempt at continuous residence but for a variety of reasons gave it up. William Kingscote's motive was frustrated ambition. He was resident at Exeter for three terms in 1309 when he was elected dean but left when Bishop Bytton declared the election void.[68] John Home resided at Hereford briefly in 1466–68 and again in 1472–73, the year of his death.[69] Some busy ecclesiastical administrators made brief periods of residence; Richard Thormerton spent two years at Salisbury in 1346–47 and moved to Exeter the following year but his career ranged much wider encompassing several visits to the Curia.[70] Canons making partial residence played a much smaller part in the life of the cathedral and their careers and interests lay elsewhere.

This generally favourable impression of canons' residence needs to be treated with a degree of caution. The numbers actually present at a cathedral was often slightly lower than the total in residence that year or term since residentiaries, particularly those holding offices, went about chapter business or visited their prebendal estates. It was a constant preoccupation of canons to ensure that their absences on cathedral matters were accepted as legitimate and entitled them to receive the payments they would be entitled to had they been present. This is a major theme of surviving chapter act books which record the close attention paid to such decisions. Those absent on genuine chapter business were granted their entitlements. On rare occasions a chapter was prepared to make a more generous concession. In 1393 the Lichfield chapter allowed Richard Conningston to receive the benefits of residence though he was absent in the bishop's service acting as his Official. This was carefully recorded as a special case that was not to set a precedent which others might claim. It was made because the chapter recognised the value of his influence and usefulness at the bishop's court.[71] An equally exceptional concession was made by the Lincoln chapter in 1501 when it granted the privileges of residence to Geoffrey Simeon and John

---

[66] Bod. Lib. Ms Ashmole 794, s. a. 1369–70, 1371, 1375–81.

[67] See note 65.

[68] Lepine, *Canons of Exeter Cathedral*, 180.

[69] HCA R503–4, R509.

[70] Edwards, *Secular Cathedrals*, 350; Lepine, *Canons of Exeter Cathedral*, 366; for his wider career see Chew, *Hemingby's Register*, 236–9.

[71] LJRO D30/2/1/1 fo. 37v.

Walles while they were absent in the service of Henry VII.[72] Judging by their scarcity in the chapter records, such grants were infrequent. Two cathedrals, Hereford and St Paul's, operated complex systems of dispensations which reduced the time residentiaries were required to be present. In the first half of the fifteenth century the stagiaries, as the resident canons of St Paul's were known, regularly asked for and received dispensations for absence. These usually lasted for a few days or sometimes up to a month. In Walter Sherrington's case it was nearly three months in 1440 to allow him to carry out his duties as a royal clerk.[73] Such absence on royal or episcopal business was common in the 1420s and 1430s and reflects a long standing willingness at St Paul's to condone this practice. Indeed, so regular were these dispensations that on occasion chapter business had to be delegated to a non-resident canon as happened in September 1423 and October 1439.[74] Stagiaries' attendance at chapter meetings improved in the early 1440s. At Hereford there was a complex arrangement whereby canons could have extended absences of up to three months if they resigned their residence, which could later be resumed.[75] This system was still in operation in the early sixteenth century. By this date residentiaries were entitled to two years study leave during which they received some but not all the emoluments of residence.[76] This privilege continued to be granted up to the Reformation, though some did not take it up. Hereford and St Paul's were exceptional in the degree to which they allowed dispensations from residence. A more general problem faced by all cathedrals was false residence by canons who did not meet the requirements set out in custom and statute. Bishops in their disciplinary visitations complained of this but rarely in detailed terms.[77] Canons were almost as vigilant lest one of their colleagues gain an advantage; scrutiny of an individual's residence was a regular occurrence in chapter meetings. It is difficult to measure the frequency and seriousness of such lapses which undoubtedly happened but they do not seem to have been a major abuse. The records of visitations and chapter meetings show most to have been relatively minor infringements. Despite these caveats it is reasonable to conclude that at most cathedrals, except St Paul's and York, there was a vigorous if sometimes small community of canons committed to residence in the later middle ages.

---

[72] LAO D&C A/3/1 fos 184r–185r.
[73] GL Ms 25,513 fo. 182.
[74] Ibid. fos 94r, 175v.
[75] Edwards, *Secular Cathedrals*, 52.
[76] HCA Baylis, i, fo. 46.
[77] For a typical example see Bishop Beauchamp's visitation of Salisbury in 1468 when he found three canons not carrying out strict residence (Salisbury D&C Reg. Machon fo. 101v).

Factors Determining Residence

Residence was undoubtedly attractive to some canons; at its peak in the first half of the fourteenth century, an average of eighty to a hundred were resident at the nine cathedrals and even in periods of low residence there were fifty or sixty. The decision to enter residence was a major career move and generally marked a commitment to the cathedral for the rest of a canon's life. A mixture of motives lay behind the decision. Most canons probably had some sort of religious vocation, though this is hard to define, and attended cathedral services out of a sense of religious duty or habit. For the successful cleric who could afford the burdens of hospitality and the initial cost of entry, residence in the close offered a comfortable existence; it was sufficiently attractive to draw many members of the leading gentry families of a diocese. At a few cathedrals, notably York, the resident canons could expect to enjoy a substantial income. In addition they gained considerable status as residentiaries, something their wills and tombstones reveal them to have been highly conscious of. The greater cathedrals, York, St Paul's and Salisbury which had a national standing and reputation, conferred significant prestige on their canons, and this was shared on a regional and diocesan scale at the remaining six.[78] Residence for many canons marked their retirement from active royal or diocesan administration whether after many years service or after a few brief commissions. The majority were experienced and middle aged by the time they came to live in the Close. It was also possible to combine residence with administrative duties. The diocese of York for much of the fifteenth century was run from the Minster by resident canons.[79] At Lincoln, which in this respect was more typical, only a minority combined residence with simultaneous diocesan duties; peripatetic service with the bishop was not always compatible with a regular presence at the cathedral. Residentiaries were most often used by the bishop to carry out occasional commissions rather than to hold offices. Those who held office tended to become resident on their retirement.

However, the attractions of residence failed to appeal to all canons, the majority of whom did not take it up. This used to be explained as a deliberate policy by resident chapters to limit their size by deterring residence with high entrance fines. They have been portrayed as closed self-perpetuating oligarchies unwilling to increase their numbers to avoid spreading their income more thinly among a larger body of resident canons.[80] There is little direct evidence to suggest that new residentiaries were discouraged or blocked for this reason. It was difficult to prevent a canon's entry provided he went through the correct formal procedures of application and completed his probationary period. While it is true that the costs of entry fines and hospitality could be considerable and might put off

---

[78] The prestige and status of cathedrals and residentiaries is considered in chapters 1, 7 and 9.

[79] Dobson, 'Residentiary Canons', 163–4.

[80] Milman, *Annals of St Paul's*, 83, 139–40.

some canons this does not seem to have been a major factor in deterring residence. The fixing and reduction of entry fines that took place at most cathedrals in the fifteenth century did not restore levels to their fourteenth century peaks. Only at St Paul's was the trend reversed, following a significant reduction in the burdens of hospitality, which were unusually heavy, at the end of the fourteenth century.[81] As we shall see, it was a chapter's poverty rather than wealth that was more likely to limit residence. However, one resident chapter, York, has been described by its leading historian as 'an exclusive and distinctive circle' and a 'self-perpetuating corporation'.[82] Its members were few in number and amongst the most able and successful clerics of their day. For most canons, residence placed too many restrictions on their careers in royal and ecclesiastical service. Many received their prebends in mid-career when they were busy elsewhere and often travelling a good deal. They held canonries in distant cathedrals remote from their centres of activity and found it easier to take the income from their prebends with the minimum of contact. Others preferred to live on their prebendal estate or at a favourite parish church and carry out their pastoral duties rather than live in a cathedral close.

Poverty restricted residence in at least three cathedrals in the later middle ages: Lichfield, Hereford and Chichester which were the poorest in the valuation of clerical property in 1535.[83] The first to face this problem was Lichfield. As early as 1300, the meagreness of the common fund which mainly came from appropriated churches was causing concern as the number of residentiaries rose.[84] Steps were taken to discourage residence to prevent the costs of residence payments exceeding the income of the common fund. An ordinance of 1301 required prospective residentiaries to give forty days notice of their intentions to allow the chapter to consider their application. They were also required to pay an entry fine of £40. Isolated accounts from this period confirm the financial difficulties of the common fund: its surplus in 1293 had been over £300 but had fallen to £40 in 1327. In 1322 the chapter decided to try and raise money by imposing a levy on non-residents though this ultimately failed. Matters had not improved by 1396 when the entry fine was fixed at 100 marks and residents were expected to spend an equivalent sum each year. The cathedral's economic health grew worse. After borrowing heavily from other accounts, the chapter was forced in 1429 to grant residents 40 days absence each quarter to save the cost of their daily payments. A century later it was still grappling with the same problem. At the chapter meeting on 8 April 1528 it was stated that its resources were insufficient to allow an increase in residence.[85] Despite this Richard Strete was allowed to begin his in recognition of his efforts on the cathedral's behalf. Others had to wait: Ralph Whitehead for nine months and Richard Sneyd for two years

81 Brooke, 'St Paul's Cathedral', 87–9.
82 Dobson, 'Residentiary Canons', 146, 152.
83 Lehmberg, Reformation of Cathedrals, 27, Table 1.2.
84 Kettle and Johnson, 'Lichfield Cathedral', 152–3, 159–60.
85 LJRO D30/2/1/4 fo. 53r.

from 1529 to 1531 until there was a vacancy following the death of Ralph Cantrell.[86] Financial hardship struck at Hereford in the mid-fourteenth century and forced a dramatic cut in mass pence, one of the main daily payments made to residents; they were reduced from 4d to 1¼d.[87] From one of the highest residence levels of around twenty in the late thirteenth century numbers fell to around ten or fewer. As at Lichfield, the late 1520s and early 1530s were a difficult time at Hereford. In 1532 the chapter, facing falling revenues, decreed that for the next five years canons could have an extra twelve weeks absence free from hospitality.[88] The 1530s had seen a modest revival in the numbers of residents which rose to seven or eight in some years. Though we know very little about the practice of residence at Chichester, it is clear it faced even more acute problems. The cathedral's common fund seems to have been on the verge of collapse at the beginning of the fifteenth century. It was so desperate that in 1408 Dean Maidenhith bequeathed £40 so that daily payments could continue being made. As his will went on to explain, each year the resident canons had to lend the common fund £40 until the rents due were received so that the canons and minor clergy could be paid.[89] Unfortunately no details have survived to show what effect this had on residence levels.

Bishops and deans had some, though limited, opportunities to influence residence levels. Both could have an impact on those already in residence but it was much harder to persuade canons to begin; neither could enforce residence. Their task was made harder by the highly developed sense of corporate identity all chapters shared, which was at its strongest when they felt their privileges were being encroached on. Bishops had two principal means of influence: encouragement and discipline. The former mainly consisted of exhortation and making residence as financially attractive as possible by endowing the common fund generously. It was reinforced by the bishop's predominant role in statute making which clarified the requirements and emoluments of residence. At four cathedrals – Hereford, Lichfield, Wells and Chichester – he also had some control over the conferring of canons' houses in the close.[90] Episcopal discipline was exercised through visitations of the cathedral. Though these ranged widely over all aspects of cathedral life, most included some correction of infringements and lapses in residence. Absentee civil-servant bishops rarely took much interest in residence at their cathedrals and left the canons to themselves, though even a notorious absentee like Bishop Oliver King of Wells was concerned enough to try and find a resident precentor to direct cathedral worship.[91] However, there

86 Ibid. fos 61r, 64r, 66v, 67, 71v–72r.
87 Capes, *Hereford Charters*, ix–x.
88 HCA Baylis, i, fo. 68v.
89 Swainson, *Chichester Statutes*, 79–80.
90 Edwards, *Secular Cathedrals*, 124.
91 J. A. Robinson, 'The Correspondence of Bishop Oliver King and Sir Reginald Bray', *Proceedings of the Somerset Archaeological and Natural History Society*, lx part ii, 1914, 1–10.

were some bishops who sought to promote residence. Bishop Braybrooke of London battled for most of his episcopate to increase the number of stagiaries at St Paul's which had fallen to just one before he succeeded in beginning a revival.[92] His colleague at Exeter, Bishop Grandisson, was a noted disciplinarian who tried to uphold high standards of residence by regular visitations. An alternative method was tried by Bishop Longland at Lincoln following his visitation of the cathedral in 1525.[93] Having concluded that there were too few residentiaries for the 'maintenance of the honour of God' he deliberately appointed new canons on the understanding that they would reside and intervened directly to ensure the appointment of a resident dean in 1528. His desire to see all the dignitaries resident proved too ambitious and overall Longland was not able to increase the size of the residentiary body though he did prevent any reduction. Longland's concerns about the paucity of residents was shared by his contemporary Archbishop Lee of York.[94] A bishop's ability to gain an undertaking of residence before appointing a canon was probably his most effective way of increasing the number of residentiaries; there is some evidence from Exeter of these being sought and given.[95] But as Longland found at Lincoln, a canon might go back on undertaking and resign his residence. Exeter also illustrates the limits of episcopal influence. The highest levels of residence were reached during the episcopate of Edmund Stafford, before his only known visitation in 1400. Yet as bishop he is not known to have tried to encourage residence and he made no new statutes or endowments to the common fund.

Deans generally had fewer opportunities to influence residence than bishops. Their responsibilities, which varied from cathedral to cathedral, were primarily pastoral and as Kathleen Edwards has noted they had little chance 'to develop autocratic tendencies'.[96] The impact some deans had came through leading by example, particularly when the bishop was frequently absent. Men like William Mancetter at Lichfield and John Godeley at Wells were involved in statute making. The greatest influence came from deans who resided and took an active interest in their cathedrals; Lichfield was especially fortunate in having an almost unbroken succession from 1390 to 1533. This was nearly matched by several other cathedrals in the fifteenth century including Salisbury, Hereford and Exeter. Many were also generous benefactors. At Salisbury Thomas Montagu, the first resident dean of the fourteenth century, did much to reform and reinvigorate cathedral life in the 1390s.[97] His contemporary and fellow residentiary at Salisbury John Maidenhith tried to apply the same standards at Chichester when he became dean in 1397. Their counterparts at St Paul's were Thomas Lisieux (d.1456), a respected administrator who revised the statutes,

---

[92] Brooke, 'The Earliest Times to 1485', 88–9.
[93] Bowker, Henrician Reformation, 31.
[94] See note 16.
[95] Lepine, Canons of Exeter Cathedral, 187.
[96] For a general discussion on the role of deans see Edwards, Secular Cathedrals, 137–48.
[97] Edwards, 'Salisbury Cathedral', 176.

and the humanist scholar and reformer John Colet.[98] Colet was scathing about the standards of residence he found, concluding that '. . . residence in the Cathedral is nothing less than seeking one's own advantage . . .', and '. . . the residentiaries . . . need reformation . . .'. To this end he compiled a new set of statutes based on those of his predecessors Baldock and Lisieux. The chapter, set in their comfortable ways, refused to accept the new statutes and secured the support of the bishop. Even with Cardinal Wolsey's backing, Colet was unable to effect any reform and died soon after in 1519.[99] A dean's influence could also be negative. For over thirty years Dean Mackworth of Lincoln was in dispute with various members of the residentiary chapter that drove at least one, Peter Partrich, from the Close to his parish church.[100]

Individual circumstances at cathedrals influenced residence levels. The status and location of St Paul's contributed to its lack of stagiaries and the poor quality of their residence, since many of them were preoccupied with royal duties in the capital and even abroad. At Easter 1432, Thomas Damet confessed he had been continuously absent overseas for six months on the king's business. The chapter allowed him to resume his residence.[101] In contrast the highest levels of residence in the country at Exeter were the product of its unique arrangement of prebends. All twenty-four of its prebends were equally small, worth just six marks. An Exeter canonry was worth little without the financial benefits of residence. These were relatively generous and widely available because the bulk of the chapter's resources were concentrated in the common fund. Only £96 of its revenue of £1,276 6s 3d was allocated to prebends, leaving an income of £1,180 6s 3d for the common fund in 1535, the highest of all nine secular cathedrals.[102] It was the combination of poor prebends and wealthy common fund that resulted in high residence levels. Wells too combined poor prebends and a substantial common fund, though not to the same extent as Exeter. Nearly half of its prebends were of a similar value to Exeter's and its common fund was the second largest, valued at £729 3s 4d in 1535.[103] Hereford had generally poor prebends but lower residence levels than Exeter because its common fund was also poor with an income of just £423 17s 2d in 1535.[104]

The principal cause of short term fluctuations in residence levels was death. The overwhelming majority of canons remained in residence until they died. A harsh winter or local outbreak of plague might reduce the residentiary body by two or three which could be a significant proportion of the total. A minority left for other reasons as their careers developed. Roger Martival left Lincoln in 1315

---

98   Brooke, 'St Paul's Cathedral', 96.
99   Ibid., 113–4.
100 Thompson, *English Clergy*, 90–8.
101 GL Ms 25,513 fo. 138.
102 See note 83.
103 *Valor Ecclesiasticus*, i, 134–7, Lehmberg, *Reformation of Cathedrals*, 27, Table 1.2.
104 See note 83.

to become bishop of Salisbury.[105] He was one of a handful, including Simon Islip and William Booth, who had been residentiaries before reaching the episcopate.[106] An even smaller group reversed the usual pattern and went into active employment after residence. Richard Royston's career started in the service of his kinsman William Smith successively bishop of Lichfield and Lincoln. He followed his patron to Lincoln where he spent six years in residence from 1505 to 1511 when he resigned on account of 'bodily weakness', though he was well enough to enter the service of the new bishop as vicar general in 1515–17 and lived to 1525.[107] The statutes at Lincoln allowed canons to undertake a less onerous form of residence known as minor residence which required their presence for only a third of the year. Evidence from the sixteenth century suggests that this was a special privilege only available to long serving residentiaries. For much of the later middle ages it was not widely taken up, being most common in the mid fifteenth and early sixteenth centuries. Some Lincoln canons resigned major residence to take up minor residence. Individuals sometimes resigned to begin residence elsewhere. Robert Wolveden had been resident at Lichfield for three years in 1416–18 before transferring his loyalties to York in 1419 where he remained until his death in 1432. Not even his election as dean of Lichfield in 1426 could tempt him back for more than occasional visits.[108]

Multiple Residence

The practice of being resident at more than one cathedral was, naturally, rare. Cathedral statutes and chapter act books seldom refer to the matter, probably because it was infrequently encountered. The vast majority of residentiaries were committed to their cathedrals. The nearest a few came to multiplicity was to move from residence in one cathedral to another; some twenty have been identified. Richard Rotherham spent the first half of his career resident at Hereford from the 1430s to 1446–47 and moved south to Exeter in 1448, remaining there until his death in 1455.[109] In some cases promotion to a dignity prompted the change. On securing the deanery of Wells, Stephen Pempel gave up his residence at Exeter in 1363 to transfer to his new cathedral.[110] No doubt there were also personal motives now hidden. Simultaneous residence at two cathedrals was rarer still, though some examples can be found. The statutes of some cathedrals, particularly those that did not enforce long periods of residence or attendance each quarter such as Salisbury, York and Lichfield, would have

105   Edwards, *Secular Cathedrals*, 333.
106   William Booth at St Paul's in 1421–47 (GL Ms 25,513 fo. 77r passim) and Simon Islip at Lincoln in 1335–40 (Edwards, *Secular Cathedrals*, 338–40).
107   Jones, *Lincoln Houses*, iii, 107.
108   LJRO D30/2/1/1 s. a. 1416–18, 1426–32. York D&C E1/39/1–2.
109   Hereford D&C R477–85; Lepine, *Canons of Exeter Cathedral*, 365.
110   Lepine, *Canons of Exeter Cathedral*, 365.

enabled a canon to reside at two. However, the practical difficulties of distance and expense would have discouraged it. The only cathedral known to have responded to the problem was Hereford. In 1524 the chapter decreed that one of its residentiaries could not accept a similar appointment in another cathedral without forfeiting his residence at Hereford but immediately went on to grant an exemption; James Bromwich was allowed to reside at Hereford and Salisbury. This dispensation was granted as a favour to Bishop Audley a former bishop and benefactor of the chapter who had been translated to Salisbury in 1502 whose chaplain Bromwich had been.[111] The concession was short-lived; within three months Bromwich was dead and six years later the chapter annulled its decree.[112] Perhaps the most notorious case was John Barnyngham who combined simultaneous residence at York and St Paul's and briefly at Beverley Minster, a collegiate church where he held a canonry, for much of the period 1433 to 1441.[113] Thomas Ward was less flagrant, managing to be resident at Lincoln and St Paul's in 1442–44.[114] When John Maidenhith became dean of Chichester in 1397 he did not give up his residence at Salisbury but combined the two. He seems to have spent the last quarter of the year away from Salisbury, probably at Chichester, where, as we have seen, he was anxious to promote residence at his new cathedral.[115] The West-Country cathedrals of Exeter and Wells were an exception to this general pattern of isolated cases of multiple residence. In the century and a half before the Reformation a small core of seven canons resided at both. Robert Rygge entered residence at Wells in 1387 and Exeter in 1393. He was certainly resident at both in 1407–08, but seems to have spent most of his time at the latter. Twice the Wells chapter sent a messenger to him at Exeter. In 1400–01 it wished to fetch him from Exeter to Bridgwater to attend Wells chapter business there.[116] In the early sixteenth century three contemporaries – Thomas Austell, Peter Carslegh and Thomas Tomyow – were resident at both cathedrals.[117] It is not clear why this arose. Both places required attendance each quarter which made simultaneous residence difficult. William Fulford got round this problem in 1461–62 by being absent from Exeter for two separate terms that year while Thomas Gilbert rarely spent longer than the minimum forty-six days required each quarter.[118] The closeness of the two cathedrals made multiple residence easier but this did not encourage a similar pattern at Wells and

111 HCA Baylis, i, fo. 34r.
112 Ibid. fo. 66r.
113 Dobson, 'Residentiary Canons', 151.
114 GL Ms 25,513 s. a. 1442–7; LAO Lincoln D&C Bj/2/13–14.
115 Salisbury D&C Reg. Draper s. a. 1403–7.
116 Lepine, Canons of Exeter Cathedral, 190.
117 DRO D&C 3762 s. a. 1496–1501, 3707 s. a. 1506/7–13/14. HMC Wells, ii, 144 et seq.
118 For Fulford see Lepine, Canons of Exeter Cathedral, 364; for Gilbert DRO D&C 3762 s. a. 1495.

Salisbury or St Paul's and Chichester which are closer together than Exeter and Wells. The scarcity of multiple residence reinforces the commitment of residentiaries to their cathedrals.

The Non-Resident Canons

It would be wrong to assume that all non-residents were little better than drones drawing off the wealth of the cathedrals they held prebends in and giving little in return. Certainly, some never went near their cathedrals and merely sent their proctors or agents to collect the incomes due to them. Complaints about their negligence in maintaining prebendal estates and paying their vicars choral were a recurrent theme of chapter meetings and episcopal visitations. But these faults were as common among the residentiaries. Formally there was little to bring residents and non-residents together.[119] The non-residents were regularly summoned to chapters for the election of deans and bishops. Some responded by attending personally, most were represented by a proctor, and a few ignored the summons altogether. There was a similar response to citations for episcopal and decanal elections. Much rarer were the general chapters called at some cathedrals to discuss major issues such as the bishop's right of visitation or building campaigns. The general chapter held at Salisbury in 1387 lasted a week and dealt with three major items, relations with the bishop, the dangerous state of the tower and spire and the canonisation of their founder St Osmund. The meeting agreed to raise a tax of a seventh on all prebendal incomes.[120] Financial contributions from the non-residentiary body were infrequent and usually resisted. At Lichfield an attempt in 1325 to impose a tax of a fifth on prebends had to be abandoned in 1369 because it proved impossible to collect.[121] There was also resistance to a similar scheme at Salisbury.[122] These formal attempts to involve the non-residents as a body met with limited success. But as individuals non-residents were much more active and useful to their chapters. It was not only bishops but also chapters who cultivated and sought advice and help from the many leading ecclesiastical administrators and royal officials holding prebends in their cathedrals. There are occasional glimpses of what must have been a common practice, the consultation of these successful men. The Wells chapter was able to call on the services of John Offord, who as dean of arches was a leading official in the archbishop of Canterbury's administration, and one of their members. Writing in 1336 they thanked him for past help and sought further assistance.[123]

119 For a general discussion on the role of non-residents see Edwards, *Secular Cathedrals*, 83–96.
120 Ibid., 92.
121 Kettle and Johnson, 'Lichfield Cathedral', 153.
122 Edwards, *Secular Cathedrals*, 92. There was a tax of a seventh on the prebends of all non-residents at Lincoln in 1398 (*CPL*, vol. v, 169).
123 HMC *Wells*, i, 336.

Non-residents can be found acting as proctors at convocation and parliament for their chapters.[124] Even absentee foreign cardinals for all the resentment they aroused could be of use. When defending its rights at the Curia in 1333 the Salisbury chapter first wrote to its cardinal dignitaries the dean, Cardinal Raymond de Fargis, and the treasurer, Cardinal Arnold de Via, asking for their advice and support.[125] At York and St Paul's the scarcity of residentiaries on occasion led to the delegation of chapter business to non-residents. Robert Wellington took the place of the two residentiaries at York (Hugh Trotter and Martin Collins) who were both absent on convocation business in July 1499.[126] Such delegation was unusual but the presence of non-residents in the close on visits attending cathedral services or at chapter meetings was common enough if not regular. In his visitation of York in 1534 Archbishop Lee urged all canons visiting the city to attend the three principal daily services matins, high mass and vespers as well as any processions taking place.[127] Most of these visits were unrecorded but canons of Hereford and Salisbury were entitled to payments while at the cathedral which enables us to measure their frequency. The Salisbury communar's accounts reveal that in most quarters there were two or three non-residents visiting the cathedral. A similar picture emerges at Hereford where slightly more are recorded attending anything from five to thirty or forty masses a year, indicating that some stayed for several weeks. Some non-residents spent much longer and actually lived in the close without becoming resident. At St Paul's this practice seems to have been a protest at the high cost of hospitality which deterred some from becoming stagiaries.[128] As many as eight canons of Lincoln lived in the close without entering residence.[129] Towards the end of his life from 1378 to 1384 Richard Ravenser had a house in the Close in Lincoln where he had been a canon for nearly thirty years and archdeacon for nearly fifteen. Though his interests ranged across Lincolnshire and the East Riding from Beverley and Hull to York and despite his seniority in royal service as a master in chancery he retained close links with his native diocese and finally was buried in its mother church in 1386.[130] The majority of non-residents, as their wills and benefactions demonstrate, had some loyalty to and regard for the cathedrals that gave them income and status.

[124] J. H. Denton and J. P. Dooley, *Representation of the Lower Clergy in Parliament 1295–1340*, Woodbridge, 1987, 104–21.
[125] Chew, *Hemingby's Register*, 84–5.
[126] YML H2/3 fo. 216v.
[127] See note 16.
[128] Brooke, 'St Paul's Cathedral', 41.
[129] Jones, *Lincoln Houses*, i, 52, 75; ii, 17, 84; iii, 91.
[130] Ibid., ii, 84.

6

Canons' Houses, Households and Hospitality

When Dean Higden of York (d.1539) attended mass in the Minster on Christmas Day he was said to have been accompanied by fifty gentlemen in tawny livery with black velvet in front of him and followed by thirty yeomen in tawny livery with saffron velvet.[1] Though few matched the status of the dean of York, canons and dignitaries were men of rank and wealth in medieval society, both by virtue of their office in the Church and often also by birth, and their lifestyles were correspondingly grand and liberal. They lived in substantial houses with their households on a scale commensurate with their status, from which they dispensed hospitality freely. The setting for much of this was the cathedral close.[2] Unlike their continental counterparts, English cathedrals were surrounded by spacious precincts in which their clergy lived. Around the cathedral were grouped the bishop's palace, the houses of the dignitaries and canons and the corporations of the minor clergy – the vicars choral, chantry priests and choristers – who often lived a communal life. At most cathedrals the residentiaries were required to live in the close or in houses nearby authorised by the chapter. This was to enable them to fufil the requirements of residence properly: to attend the daily offices, to participate in chapter business and to dispense hospitality. Only at St Paul's were there several canonical houses outside the close but these were in neighbouring streets. At Wells two houses outside the close were used by residentiaries.[3]

By the early fourteenth century most closes had been enclosed with gates and walls. The first cathedral to do so was Lincoln in 1256, followed by York in 1285, Exeter and Wells in 1286 and Lichfield in 1299. Salisbury and Hereford were enclosed somewhat later, in 1327 and 1389 respectively. The construction of walls and gates was a response to the dangers in the close, especially at night when the clergy were vulnerable to attack as they went to matins in the cathedral. The brutal murder of the precentor, Walter Lechlade, on his way home from the cathedral after matins one night in 1283 led directly to the enclosure of Exeter

---

[1] C. Cross, *York Clergy Wills 1520–1600: I Minster Clergy*, Borthwick Texts and Calendars, Records of the Northern Province 10, York, 1984, 36.

[2] For a general discussion, on which this paragraph is based, see Thompson, *Cathedral Churches of England*, 157–8, and Edwards, 'Salisbury Close', 55–66.

[3] Bailey, *Canonical Houses of Wells*, 148, 157.

in 1286.[4] A rather lurid and perhaps exaggerated picture of the dangers emerges from the licence to enclose granted to the chapter of Hereford in 1389. It was to prevent 'thefts, secret burials, animals from grazing and digging up corpses from the cemetery and frequent immorality'.[5] Many of these fortifications were demolished in the nineteenth century but there are still impressive examples at Lincoln, Salisbury and Wells, none more so than the Exchequer Gate at Lincoln. Though a good deal of the medieval character of closes has been lost their topography survives at many cathedrals and some medieval buildings remain. The greatest loss has been at St Paul's where the Great Fire destroyed the close as well as the cathedral.[6] York has been extensively rebuilt but elsewhere there are survivals. Wells is the most complete with its bishop's palace, deanery, vicars close and walls and gates all of which are notable examples of their kind. Exeter retains several medieval houses and much of its original street plan.

Within the close houses were usually assigned to the four principal dignitaries and sometimes for the archdeacons. The number of canonical houses fluctuated according to demand and fashion, with some occasionally falling into ruin or being let to laymen and minor clergy. At the beginning of the fourteenth century there were fifteen canonical houses in the close at Exeter including those belonging to the dignitaries and a similar number have been identified at Wells.[7] There were slightly fewer at Salisbury where a survey of 1447 listed twelve and the deanery.[8] Canons' houses rarely survive in their medieval form, as closes have continued to be desirable places to live and they have regularly been modernised and rebuilt. Fortunately documentary and archaeological evidence allows us to reconstruct them. When John Leland travelled the country in the early sixteenth century he commented favourably on the canons' houses he found at Lichfield, Exeter and Wells describing them as 'very fair'.[9] This impression was deliberate, they were intended to display canons' status and wealth. In 1417 William Pelleson, a residentiary at York, asked for a house that was grand enough to reflect 'the honour of the Minster'.[10] When planning the close at Lichfield in the twelfth century Bishop Clinton set out the houses on a generous scale, assigning a frontage of 120 feet to the deanery and one of 60 feet for a canon's house.[11] Canonical houses were generally set out on a more extensive scale than was usual in towns because there was more space in the close than the crowded main street. In plan and size they are similar to the houses of the richest merchants in some towns and the wealthiest parsonage houses and small manor houses in the

---

4   Orme, *Exeter Cathedral*, 6–7.
5   CPR 1388–92, 160.
6   For a discussion of the close at St Paul's see Macleod, 'Topography of St Paul's', 1–14.
7   *Reg. Stapeldon Exeter*, 153–5; Bailey, *Canonical Houses of Wells*.
8   Edwards, 'Salisbury Close', 68.
9   John Leland, *Itinerary in England and Wales*, ed. L. T. Smith, 5 vols, 1964, i, 146, 228, ii, 102.
10 YML H2/1 fo. 26v.
11 Kettle and Johnson, 'Lichfield Cathedral', 57.

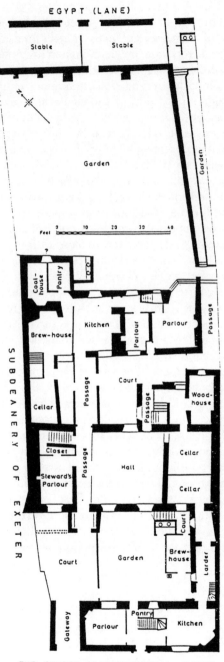

Figure 1. 7 The Close, Exeter.
An eighteenth-century plan
showing many medieval
features including the hall,
two courtyards, kitchen and
stables, and the gateway.

countryside.[12] The best surviving examples are at Exeter, Lincoln and Salisbury. Numbers 8–11 The Close at Exeter are among the closest to their original medieval appearance. Dating from the mid-fifteenth century they are two-storied stone houses built of the local red sandstone with white Salcombe stone for the window and door jambs.[13] The subdeanery and the Chancery at Lincoln also retain parts of their original appearance.[14] Canons' houses were usually arranged around a courtyard, a design that originated in important rural houses, with the principal rooms, hall, kitchen, chamber or solar and chapel on three or four sides. In the larger houses there might be a second courtyard as appears in Figure 1 of 7 The Close at Exeter and Figure 2, the reconstruction of the Chancery at Lincoln.[15] The entrance at both and in most canonical houses was through an imposing gateway high enough to allow entry on horseback. In many houses, even smaller ones, the gateway was part of a tower. At Lincoln Dean Fleming (1451–83) built a three-storied one.[16] Before the enclosure of closes these would have had a defensive function but by Fleming's time their purpose would have been display.

The hall, entered through a porch, was the centre of life in the house and its most important room, where hospitality was dispensed, feasts were given, guests received and entertained, and business transacted.[17] It was the largest room designed on an extensive scale. Archaeological investigation at Lincoln has identified five in canons' houses, the smallest at the subdeanery measuring 27 feet by 39 feet and the largest 50 feet by 20 feet at Atherton Place.[18] A particularly fine but slightly smaller hall (30 ft by 22 ft 9 ins) with an early fifteenth-century hammer beam roof decorated with lions and angels still exists in the former Law Library at Exeter.[19] The hall was complemented by the kitchen and its ancillery rooms needed to provide hospitality on an appropriate scale. At one end of the hall were the pantry and buttery, used respectively for storing bread and beer, and below it were the cellars. The pantry and buttery were likely to be hidden by a decorated screen. Kitchens were usually large with substantial fireplaces up to ten feet across. As well as a larder most houses would have had a separate bakehouse and the largest might, like that of Precentor Collins of York, also have a brewhouse to produce ale for the household and guests.[20] The most important private room in the house was the chamber or solar, usually situated behind the hall and on the first floor. It was smaller and more comfortable than the hall where a canon could enjoy more privacy. A major feature and source of comfort

---

12 M. Barley, *Houses and History*, 1986, 72–6, 141–4.
13 Portman, *Exeter Houses*, 66–70.
14 Jones, *Lincoln Houses*, i, 77–82.
15 Portman, *Exeter Houses*, fig. ix; Jones, *Lincoln Houses*, i, 56–65.
16 Jones, *Lincoln Houses*, iii, 29–31.
17 Much of what follows on the use of rooms is taken from M. Girouard, *Life in the English Country House*, Harmondsworth, 1978, chapter 3.
18 Jones, *Lincoln Houses*, i, 77–82, iii, 105–127.
19 Portman, *Exeter Houses*, 68 and Cherry and Pevsner, *Devon*, 410–17.
20 *Test Ebor*, iv, 288–9.

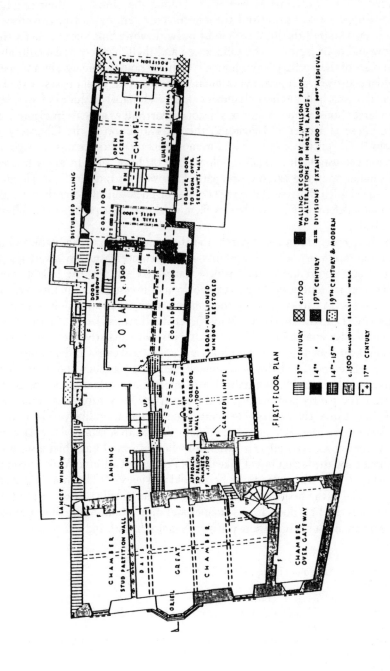

FIRST-FLOOR PLAN

LANCET WINDOW

CHAMBER

STUD PARTITION WALL

ORIEL

DAIS

GREAT CHAMBER

CHAMBER OVER GATEWAY

UP

UP

DN

LANDING

APPROACH TO RELIQUE CHAMBER c.1700?

LINE OF CORRIDOR WALL c.1700?

CARVED LINTEL

SOLAR

DOOR IN WINDOW SITE

CORRIDOR c.1300

CORRIDOR c.1800

BROAD MULLIONED WINDOW RESTORED

DISTURBED WALLING

CORRIDOR

OPEN SCREEN

CHAPEL

DN

STAIR TO ROOF LOFTS c.1800

AUMBRY

FORMER DOOR TO ROOM OVER SERVANTS' WALL

STAIR POSITION 1800

PISCINA

13TH CENTURY

14TH "

14TH-15TH "

c.1500 INCLUDING EARLIER WORK

17TH CENTURY

c.1700

19TH CENTURY

19TH CENTURY & MODERN

WALLING RECORDED BY E.J. WILLSON PRIOR TO ALTERATIONS IN NORTH RANGE

DIVISIONS EXTANT c.1800 PROB. POST MEDIEVAL

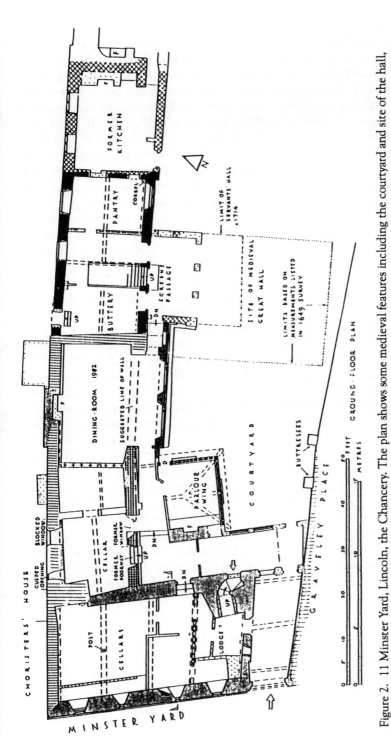

Figure 2. 11 Minster Yard, Lincoln, the Chancery. The plan shows some medieval features including the courtyard and site of the hall, and the late fifteenth-century parlour.

in the chamber was the fireplace which was often elaborately decorated with tracery and heraldry. In the fifteenth century a number of residentiaries at Lincoln rebuilt their chambers adding oriel windows.[21] A small house would probably have only one or two chambers but larger ones had several one of which was described as the principal chamber; a Lincoln inventory of Chancellor Thomas Cotte's house in 1384 lists four.[22] Another development towards privacy and comfort was the building of parlours. These were usually low ceilinged rooms on the ground floor. The deanery at Salisbury had an old and new parlour by 1440.[23] Geoffrey Simeon added a timber framed parlour wing to the chancery at Lincoln at the end of the fifteenth century.[24] The development of chambers and parlours was part of a trend in the later middle ages for the lord to withdraw gradually from the hall and the lesser household and to eat with his senior servants and intimates in the chamber or parlour. Whether this was so in the much smaller households of canons is difficult to determine, the only evidence being the rooms themselves. It is more likely to have begun in the larger houses of the more important dignitaries such as Dean Higden of York than more modest establishments. The archaeological evidence from Salisbury and Lincoln suggests that this was occurring in wealthier canons' houses by the mid fifteenth century.

A typical canonical house would have needed more than one private room or chamber so that important guests could be accomodated overnight. However, there is little evidence that they were set out on a large enough scale to have the separate ranges of lodgings that are found in the manor houses of bishops and lay magnates. Only at the unusually grand Atherstone Place at Lincoln has one with seven lodgings dating from the late thirteenth century been identified.[25] Most canons had their own private chapels. Although business was transacted in various rooms including the hall, parlour and chapel some houses had an office in the modern sense. The deanery at Exeter in the early fourteenth century had a 'parchment room'. In addition to a large supply of parchment it contained six tallies for accounts, several chests and two strong boxes and was probably used as a chancery and exchequer.[26] Thomas Cotte's house at Lincoln had a study which held his library.[27] At the back of the houses were storerooms for firewood and hay and the stables. Some are known to have had horsemills for grinding corn. There was enough space for households to supply some of their own produce, having dovecotes and poultry houses. Most had gardens in which fruit trees and herbs were cultivated and one at Lincoln had a vineyard.[28] Water was supplied either from a well in the courtyard or piped from a communal chapter

[21] For example Jones, *Lincoln Houses*, i, 58–61, 89.
[22] LAO D&C Dvi/14/1.
[23] RCHM, *Salisbury Houses*, 212.
[24] Jones, *Lincoln Houses*, i, 56–65.
[25] Ibid., iii, 117–19.
[26] DRO Exeter D&C 2846.
[27] See note 22.
[28] Jones, *Lincoln Houses*, iii, 67–85.

Plate 3. The Chancery at Lincoln, a fifteenth-century canon's house. The imposing front displays the wealth and status of late medieval residentiary canons. It was rebuilt in brick, a newly fashionable material, in the late fifteenth century. Oriel windows were also fashionable at this time and added to several other canonical houses at Lincoln.

Plate 4. The stone dresser dating from the early fourteenth century at the screens passage end of the hall at 2 Minster Yard, Lincoln. Originally brightly painted it was used for the silver bowls and fine towels canons provided for their guests to wash. It reveals the degree of luxury to be found in the lifestyles of wealthier residentiaries and the importance of hospitality among their functions.

conduit in the close. All houses had some form of sanitation, variously referred to as *cloaca* or latrine. Accomodation for servants is rarely mentioned. Generally they occupied some of the smaller rooms but the most important in larger households might have their own as at the deanery at Salisbury where in 1440 there was a chamber for the steward.[29] The same inventory also lists four 'upper chambers' for the household.

The decoration, furnishings and possessions of canons reinforced the status and wealth displayed in the scale and layout of their houses. The windows of the principal rooms might be glazed with coloured or heraldic glass; in 1441 John Morton bought gray and red glass for his house in Exeter.[30] Carved and painted roof bosses and corbels adorned the hall; images of kings and bishops have been found at Lincoln.[31] The hall of the house known as Aula le Stage at Salisbury had a fourteenth-century cornice with carvings of a Paschal lamb and a recumbent boar.[32] The walls of the principal rooms were painted. Traces of a dado with ochre colouring below a double band in red and red-line ashlaring have been found at the North Canonry at Salisbury and the deanery there also contains fragments of painted plaster.[33] The overall impression can be seen in the reconstruction of the thirteenth-century great chamber at the Leadenhall Salisbury which was originally built as a model canonical house by Elias of Dereham.[34] Floors might be tiled; those found in the deanery at Salisbury match ones found in the cathedral muniment room and date from the thirteenth century.[35] The hall as the focus of hospitality was the scene of most conspicuous display. Its walls were hung with tapestries: Chancellor Cotte of Lincoln had two, one showing the genealogy of Christ and the other the four Cardinal Virtues, and Nicholas Sturgeon, the precentor of St Paul's, had one depicting the Nine Worthies.[36] The tables were covered with fine imported cloths and the benches made more comfortable by coloured covers and cushions. At 2 Minster Yard Lincoln there is a fine early fourteenth-century carved stone dresser for the bowls and towels guests used to wash their hands, which was originally painted.[37] John Westcote, a canon of Exeter, provided Cornish towels.[38] Next to the high table was the cupboard, literally a board for cups, on which were placed the gilt and silver vessels, the main focus of display. All canons had at least a few pieces of silver and spoons, which are frequently mentioned in their wills. The inventories of the wealthiest list large amounts; Thomas Dalby, a York residentiary and

---

[29] See note 23.
[30] DRO ECA MCR 29–30 Hen VI.
[31] Jones, *Lincoln Houses*, i, 68.
[32] RCHM, *Salisbury Houses*, 118.
[33] Ibid., 196–9, 205.
[34] Ibid., 235.
[35] Ibid., 207.
[36] See note 22; Furnivall, *Earliest English Wills*, 131–4.
[37] Jones, *Lincoln Houses*, i, 27.
[38] *Reg. Stafford Exeter*, 418–19.

archdeacon of Richmond, owned plate valued at £60 at his death in 1400.[39] Such plate was elaborately decorated, often with heraldic devices or religious emblems. Canons also used high quality wooden vessels, called mazers, which were painted and gilded. Something of the ritual and splendour of the richer canons' halls emerges from the contents of Dean Kilkenny's at Exeter. His inventory lists twenty-three pieces of silver including thirteen cups, three jugs and a salt cellar, as well as thirty spoons. On arrival his guests washed their hands in silver basins before sitting to eat beneath canopies. The poor, too, were not forgotten at his meals; an alms dish was used to collect the part of the meal set aside for them.[40]

The luxury on display in the hall extended into the private chambers where there were also rich tapestries and fine cloths. Canons had feather beds with embroidered curtains; Thomas Morton's at York was made of red worsted and decorated with a pastoral scene of shepherds and sheep, and Nicholas Sturgeon's was finer still being made of green silk with red and white silk hangings.[41] Surviving inventories contain long lists of domestic linen from table cloths and napkins to sheets, blankets and curtains all of which were necessary to provide hospitality on the scale expected of residentiaries. Private chapels were often richly decorated with silver or gilt altar vessels and emroidered frontals and vestments. They were adorned with painted and gilded images of their patron saints and illuminated service books. Thomas Barton's chapel at Exeter contained enough cloth of gold to make a chasuble.[42] Occasionally a will lists a canon's more personal possessions. The same Thomas Barton (d. 1415) bequeathed a ring with a rotating head with a bluestone on one side and a doubleheaded eagle on the other, together with a precious silver bottle of balsam, a mirror and a coral rosary.[43] As might be expected canons' dress also reflected their status and wealth. On feast days and processions they wore magnificent copes and chasubles richly embroidered with religious images. For ordinary services they wore plainer black and white robes. Outside church they wore striking fur hooded scarlet gowns of the best materials lined with silk. Of course not all canons lived so opulently. Some lived modestly with a small household and few luxuries but the overwhelming impression of their wills, which survive in considerable numbers, is of an expansive and comfortable lifestyle enjoyed by men of substance.[44]

Canons' houses and possessions provide a general indication of their wealth but it is more difficult to measure this precisely. Few accounts survive, either of their households during their lifetimes or of their executors after their deaths. The fullest household accounts that have come down to us are those of Dean Worsley of St Paul's which cover eight years between 1479/80 and 1496/7. These

[39] Test Ebor iii, 9–22.
[40] See note 26.
[41] Test Ebor iii, 106–115; Furnivall, Earliest English Wills, 131–4.
[42] Reg. Stafford Exeter, 411–14.
[43] Ibid.
[44] Some Lichfield canons had small households which are discussed below.

show him to have been a wealthy dignitary with an annual income of between £300 and £800, though this included the income from several chapter estates, from which the farm owed to the dean and chaper was deducted; his net income was around £240 in an average year.[45] The York residentiaries were amongst the wealthiest of their class; both William Duffield and Martyn Collins had estates valued at over £1000 at their deaths and Thomas Greenwood's was worth nearly £900, though these and other valuations included debts.[46] Dignitaries at other cathedrals could be almost as wealthy; Dean Kilkenny of Exeter's estate was valued at £916 18s ¾d in 1311.[47] Such wealth was untypical of residentiaries as a whole, though it was not unusual for their estates to be worth several hundred pounds. The executors of Chancellor Cotte of Lincoln accounted for £659 3s.[48] Exeter canons were generally less wealthy; John Orum's estate was valued at £239 16s 9d in 1436.[49] Exeter also provides evidence of more modest means. Orum's contemporary Maior Parys left an estate of £116 15s 4¾d.[50] A significant proportion of this was held in cash; as much as £238 4s 3½d of Thomas Cotte's estate was in this form.[51] Even the least well off residentiaries were men of substance and lived accordingly.

Canons' Households

Like their houses, canons' households expressed their status in the Church and society. They were modelled on those of the lay nobility, in which many of them had been born or brought up, and shared a similar organisation and function.[52] During the later middle ages noble households tended to grow in size and the larger ones became more sophisticated in their organisation as servants became more specialised. The most important were the 'officers', the steward, chamberlain and treasurer who might be gentlemen and therefore of a similar social rank to their lord. Their function was to organise the household and to give advice for the lord. Other squires or gentlemen waited on him and provided company. The rest of the servants, the so called 'menials', whose job was to make life comfortable for the lord and his guests, were organised into the main departments of the household: kitchen, pantry, buttery, chamber, hall and stables. In smaller households these distinctions were rarer and offices were often combined. The size of a household, its conspicuous consumption, ritual and provision of

---

45 GL Ms 25,166/1–9 and Brooke, 'St Paul's Cathedral', 65.
46 Dobson, 'Residentiary Canons', 168.
47 See note 26.
48 See note 22.
49 *Reg. Lacy Exeter*, iv, 23–7.
50 Ibid. 33–4.
51 See note 22.
52 For the general background on which this discussion is based see Given-Wilson, *English Nobility*, chapter 4, Mertes, *English Noble Household*, chapters 1, 2, 5 and 6 and Girouard, *Country House*, chapter 2.

hospitality advertised a lord's status, which was an important part of its function. Though canons' households had much in common with their noble counterparts there were some significant differences which tended to make them smaller. Canons had no wives or legitimate children so their kindred played a smaller part in their households, though brothers, nephews and other relatives can be found in them. Nor did they have liveried retainers outside their households for political and military purposes in the way secular lords did. However, some are known to have retained leading members of the ruling oligarchies of their cities.[53] At most cathedrals canons had some responsibility for the minor clergy.

The size of canons' households, like those of the nobility, varied according to their social background, wealth and personal inclinations. Estimates for secular households in the mid fourteenth century range from ten to thirty for knights and esquires, and from fifty to a hundred for the baronage. Most canons' households ranged between six and ten, slightly fewer than might be found in the household of a modest knight or esquire. Dignitaries and wealthier canons, like many of the residentiaries at York, might have up to twenty or more and in exceptional cases like that of Dean Higden of York might equal those of the baronage. Some canons had even smaller households of one or two servants. Of the eight households at Lichfield listed in the poll tax return of 1379–80 only two were over four with the rest containing two or three and in Simon Malstange's case just one.[54] At Exeter such small households were considered unacceptable because they were deemed too small to carry out one of their major functions to dispense hospitality.[55] In 1532 a household of six servants was said to be a satisfactory minimum for this purpose.[56] The position at Lichfield in the later fourteenth century was unusual. The evidence of wills and inventories from the fourteenth and fifteenth centuries suggests between six and ten was more usual. Another Lichfield canon, Roger Nassington (d.1364) had a household of eight, as did Thomas Brandon (d.1390) at Lincoln, whereas a century later also at Lincoln William Skelton (d.1501) had nine.[57] Among the larger households were those of Thomas Dalby (d.1400) at York whose inventory listed fourteen.[58] Both Dean Kilkenny of Exeter (d.1302) and Archdeacon Smith of Lincoln (d.1528) had households of twenty-two but the treasurer of York in 1509, Martin Collins, had a larger one, twenty-six strong.[59] The most complete picture of the size of canons' households comes from an early sixteenth-century survey of Exeter. In 1522 the ten resident canons had between four and ten servants each,

53 These retainers are discussed below.
54 Boyd, 'The Poll Tax of A. D. 1379–81 for the Hundreds of Offlow and Cuttlestone', 168.
55 Reg. Brantingham Exeter, i, 470; Oliver, Lives, 468.
56 LPFD, v, 733–4.
57 Cox, Lichfield Muniments, 225–30; LAO Reg (Reg.Buckingham) xii fo. 378v; LAO A/3/2 fos 12v–15r.
58 See note 39.
59 DRO D&C 2846; Cole, Lincoln Act Book 1520–36, 91–4; Test Ebor iv, 277–307.

a total of sixty-six; five of the residentiaries had smaller households of four or five and the remaining five larger ones of six or ten.[60] All but the poorest had significantly larger households than those of the average parish clergy who had perhaps two or three servants, or large chantries with only one. Only the very wealthy matched those of the episcopate with over fifty members.

The organisation and distribution of offices in canons' households them varied as much as their size. Though relatively small in size, they were nonetheless carefully regulated. A rare glimpse of this can be seen in the ordinances drawn up by Humphrey Charlton, the archdeacon of Richmond and a residentiary at York, in 1379.[61] In eleven clauses it sets out how his servants should behave and what some of their duties were. Its main emphasis was on the prompt collection of income from rents and dues by officials as they travelled round Charlton's benefices and honesty by the servants in their business dealings for the household. The duties of the two principal offices, chancellor and steward, are set out as well as the use of the archdeacon's seal and the travelling expenses of servants. It is likely that most other households had similar practices even though they may not have been written down. Like secular lords, canons issued liveries or clothes to their servants according to their rank. Dean Worsley of St Paul's provided liveries of russet, mixed colours, 'fyne scarlet' and violet at Christmas 1480 and clothed his retinue in black for the funeral of Edward IV in 1483.[62] Thomas Cotte's robes were multi-coloured for his esquires and striped for valets.[63] Within the household there were generally three main ranks, esquires or gentlemen and clerks, valets and serving men or boys; the first two corresponding to the officers and the last to the menial servants. Larger households were run by a steward or perhaps a treasurer or chamberlain, the name of the office and its duties varied. In Humphrey Charlton's the office of steward was shared by two clerics who both had other responsibilities.[64] Stewards or their equivalent would have held the rank of esquire and been of 'gentle' rank. Larger households contained more than one esquire or gentleman and it is possible that one of them acted as steward even though they are not referred to by office. Others were liveried or retained. The precise nature of the relationship is unclear but there are occasional references to canons retaining senior members of the ruling oligarchies of cathedral cities. Robert Gare, a bailiff and sheriff of York, was retained by Thomas Haxey, a leading residentiary of the Minster, in 1400 and at Exeter Peter Soth, a steward of the city, was liveried by Roger Charlton, the archdeacon of Totnes in 1326.[65]

Canons usually employed a receiver to collect income, which might involve a good deal of travelling if his benefices were widely scattered. Some recievers

[60] M. Rowe, *Tudor Exeter: Tax Assessments 1485–1595*, DCRS, xxii, 1977, 30–3.
[61] YML P1 (2) ix.
[62] GL Ms 25,166/ 1 and 4.
[63] See note 22.
[64] See note 61.
[65] *Test Ebor* iii, 9–22; DRO ECA ED/M/276.

did not live with their masters but were based at a prebendal estate or benefice where they might act as bailiff, though they would be regular visitors to their masters houses. Canons who farmed chapter estates or held a number of rich parishes employed several bailiffs or reeves and might maintain households at the more important of their properties, particularly the prebendal estate where they were expected to reside for part of each year. The chamberlain, which some households are known to have contained, was responsible for looking after the lord's private rooms. Clerics, both cathedral minor clergy and local rectors, are frequently found in the service of canons. Some acted primarily in a spiritual capacity as chaplains serving in their master's chapels, though there is no evidence that these were elaborately staffed. Ecclesiastical households generally had more clergy than secular ones and most canons would have had at least two and probably more. Others did a variety of jobs and held some of the offices such as steward, butler or receiver. Being literate they also formed a secretariat for canons which was an important function in the household as many canons were actively engaged in diocesan administration. Some had qualified as notaries. At York Humphrey Charlton maintained a chancellor who was a cleric.[66] Occasionally secretarial work was done by laymen; William Pylton's household at Exeter contained a servant described as *homo litteratus*.[67] Among the lower ranks of servants cooks are mentioned most frequently in the sources, a reflection of the importance of hospitality and the kitchen in canons' houses. Even the smallest household would have had a cook. More specialised servants found in some households include butlers, who took charge of the buttery and sometimes the plate as well, and in at least one instance a cup-bearer.[68] Valets commonly occur but their duties are rarely specified. Like the rank and file serving men and boys they are usually defined by the department of the household they worked in such as kitchen, buttery, or chamber. Alongside the cook there would be a baker and a brewer in a larger establishment. All, whatever their size, had a number of serving boys and pages, who were cheap to employ. In a larger household there was a wide range of menial servants. Dean Kilkenny's at Exeter at the beginning of the fourteenth century included a doorkeeper, marshal, groom, baker and brewer as well as six boys.[69]

Though horsemanship, hunting and military skills had less importance in ecclesiastical households than secular ones, canons maintained stables and horses, occasionally on an extensive scale, and required grooms and stable boys. As Bishop Grandisson of Exeter noted with scorn in 1328 some residentiaries preferred to be out with the hawks and hounds than in the cathedral.[70] Men like Robert Vaggescombe (d.1380) at Exeter kept a pack of hounds.[71] But even a

[66] See note 61.
[67] DRO ECA MCR 6–7 Hen V.
[68] *Reg. Stafford Exeter* 410–11.
[69] See note 26.
[70] *Reg. Grandisson Exeter* i, 435.
[71] Reg. Courtenay Canterbury fo. 200.

critical commentator, like the Protestant Exeter historian John Hooker after the Reformation, found no incompatibility between the lifestyle of a country gen-tleman and that of a cathedral residentiary. He spoke highly of Canon Robert Tregonwell (d.1543) whom he described as 'very well learned' while noting that he delighted in keeping 'three or four good geldings in his stable and had pleasure in hawking and hunting with water spaniels'.[72] It is unlikely that Vaggescombe and Tregonwell were unique in their enjoyment of country sports. Female servants are occasionally mentioned, particularly washerwomen, but they were visitors who did not live in. The silence of the sources about women suggests that canons' households were almost exclusively male. However, an episcopal visitation of Salisbury in 1468 drew attention to the number of women frequent-ing canons' houses and bringing their children with them.[73] This aroused suspicion and the rumour was that a canon, William Osgodby, was the father of one of these children. The resident canons replied that the women were servants and had been coming to their houses for many years. Servants' wives were often remembered by canons in their wills and may have visited their houses and worked alongside their husbands.

Generally, little is known of the social and geographical background of the members of residentiaries' households. However, two remarkable examples from Exeter show the regard and high standing in which canons and their households were held in local society. At his death in 1436 Precentor Roger Bolter's contained four men of elevated rank: Robert Wilford and Nicholas Stoddon came from Exeter families prominent in the city's oligarchy and Richard Dobbe and Walter Buttokside were members of rising Devon gentry families.[75] It is possible that these men held senior offices such as steward or chamberlain in Bolter's household, but it is more likely that they were 'henchmen', younger sons or heirs awaiting their inheritances who had been sent to Bolter's household as part of their education. All seem to have been grown up and established by 1436 and making their careers in an ecclesiastical household of equivalent rank, the Bolters being a rising gentry family from South Devon. A similar picture emerges a century later in 1532 in the households of two residentiaries Nicholas Main-waring and John Gibbons.[76] Both contained men of rank, the most distinguished of whom, Baldwin Fulford, was a member of a leading Devon knightly family, and co-heir of his uncle Sir Philip.[77] Styled 'gentleman', he was a member of Nicholas Mainwaring's household. John Gibbons' household though it included two gentlemen did not have members of such a prominent family as the Fulfords;

---

[72] DRO ECA Exeter Book 51 fo. 346v.
[73] Salisbury D&C Reg. Machon fos 101v–107r.
[74] In 1448 the York residentiary Thomas Morton bequeathed a piece of plate to Joanna, the wife of his clerk Thomas Donn (*Test Ebor* iii, 106–7).
[75] PRO C47/7/6/1. For a fuller discussion of Bolter's household see Lepine, *Canons of Exeter Cathedral*, 303–4.
[76] PRO STAC 2 28/17.
[77] Vivian, *Visitation of Devon*, 378–9.

John Davels and Edward Drewe came from the lesser gentry of the county.[78] This may reflect the social backgrounds of the two canons themselves. The Mainwarings were an important gentry family from Cheshire whereas John Gibbons came from humbler Warwickshire gentry stock, though he was Bishop Veysey's nephew.[79] Isolated references from other cathedrals reinforce the impression from Exeter. In 1407 John Montague was described as the *famulus* of John Maidenith, a residentiary of Salisbury and dean of Chichester.[80] He was probably related to the former dean of Salisbury Thomas Montague (d.1404), a member of the baronial family, and perhaps the bastard son of Thomas earl of Salisbury (d.1428).[81]

Canons' kindred were often an important part of their households; six of the ten listed in the 1522 tax return at Exeter contained members of their families.[82] At Hereford in the 1460s the dean, John Barowe, employed his brother Thomas as a servant, as did another residentiary, John Asheby, his kinsman William Asheby.[83] Unfortunately nothing is known of their role and status in the household. Close-knit networks of kin can be found among the households of residentiaries. The same William Asheby spent fifty years in the close at Hereford.[84] He started, probably as a boy, in his kinsman John Asheby's in 1446 and remained for eighteen years. On his death in 1464 he moved to the service of John Baily staying for eight years and again outliving his master. After Baily's death in 1472 he transferred to Richard Jaquessone's household and was still there in 1495. A wider network was established at Exeter during the 1520s and 1530s by the Mainwarings, a leading knightly family from the North-West of England. The leading figure was Nicholas, a younger son, who, after entering the Church became a canon and residentiary of Exeter in 1525.[85] By this time his family was already established in the close. His brother Peter and cousin Oliver were members of the household of the subdean, Robert Weston, and another kinsman, Edward, had a place in the precentor's.[86] A fourth kinsman, Thomas, was a member of Nicholas's own household in 1532.[87] Oliver Mainwaring, who was styled gentleman, became a substantial figure in the city and retained his links with the Weston family.[88] Longevity of service, like that of William Asheby,

[78] Ibid., 273, 305.
[79] *Pedigrees made at the Visitation of Cheshire, 1613*, ed. G. Armytage and J. P. Rylands, Lancashire and Cheshire Record Society vii, 1909, 156–62; VCH *Warwickshire*, iv, 234.
[80] Reg. Arundel Canterbury, i, fos 240r–242r.
[81] BRUO, ii, 1296–7; DNB, vol. xxxviii, 208–11.
[82] See note 60.
[83] HCA 2957, 2958.
[84] HCA 2958.
[85] BRUO 1500–40, 690–1.
[86] See note 60.
[87] See note 76.
[88] E. L. Lega-Weekes, 'A History of St Katherine's Priory Polslo', part iii, TDA lxix, 1937, 464–5.

was not unusual. Roger Radcliff is known to have served continuously as steward of Dean Worsley's household at St Paul's from 1479/80 to 1496/7.[89]

Members of households were almost invariably recruited locally, from the diocese, the canon's place of origin or his centre of activity, particularly in the case of lesser servants but also among the senior ranks. At Lincoln Richard Chesterfield (d.1405) had servants from the neighbouring villages of Conningsby, Langwath and Launde if their surnames can be relied on.[90] John Pek, cook, steward and executor of Archdeacon Humphrey Charlton, came from Riccall in Yorkshire, which was his master's prebendal manor.[91] Even when servants came from greater distances, there was usually some direct connection. Precentor Colles of Exeter had a Gascon servant who had presumably entered his service when Colles was a royal official at Bordeaux.[92] Relations between canons and their servants could be close. Trusted servants were sometimes appointed as executors, a responsibility that would only be given to someone who had a man's confidence and with whom he had close personal relations. James Halap, the esquire of Dean Tregrisiou of Exeter, clearly had such a position, acting as his master's mainpernor in 1387 and his feoffee as well as his executor in 1415.[93] The lawsuit over Precentor Bolter's will in 1436 reveals glimpses of the intimacy that could develop.[94] On the morning of his death he dismissed his servants, confided his thoughts to Robert Wilford, a senior member of his household, and 'talked of many things'. The closeness of the ties between canons and their households is further reflected in their wills which often include provisions for servants' families. In a few cases canons had a number of servants from the same family.[95]

One of the functions of a noble household was to train the next generation in the noble way of life. This was being done by residentiary canons whose wills refer to *alumpni* or scholars. The executors of Chancellor Cotte of Lincoln made payments to three who had passed through his household one of whom had entered the Church and become a monk.[96] In 1432 Treasurer Wolvenden of York made bequests to six who were described as being of gentle birth and present in the household *causa eruditionis*, to be educated.[97] Two can be traced after leaving Wolvenden's household. The most certain is Andrew Terras who became a freeman of York in 1440–1, when he is styled yeoman. Robert Somer was probably the same man who became a freeman in 1438–9 and is described as a

[89] GL Ms 25,166/1–9.
[90] LAO D&C A/2/29 fos 13r–14v.
[91] Reg. Alexander Neville York fo. 88v.
[92] PRO E179/95/100.
[93] *Wells HMC* ii, no. 547; CCR 1385–9, 442; *Reg. Stafford Exeter*, 405–6.
[94] See note 92.
[95] PRO PROB 11/6 fo. 196v.
[96] See note 22.
[97] *Test Ebor* iii, 92.

tailor.[98] Of the ten canonical households at Exeter in 1522 half had scholars.[99] These were often members of their own families or those other residentiaries. A canon's household had sufficient status to attract the sons of local gentry as well as those of leading urban families. Edward Forde of Ford in Devon sent his son to the household of Nicholas Mainwaring a residentiary at Exeter where he 'hath meate and drink and gifts'.[100] Canons holding wardships may well have brought up their wards in their households.

Cathedral minor clergy were another important group who were often closely involved in canons' lives and in some cases can be regarded as part of their households, though this was very much a matter of the personal wishes of an individual canon; some made extensive use of them, others virtually none. The formal responsibilities of canons for minor clergy varied from cathedral to cathedral and according to the four ranks of vicar choral, chantry priest, secondary and chorister.[101] The vicars choral originated as canons' deputies and still remained closely dependent on them in the fourteenth century. At York they had rights of hospitality in canons' houses.[102] The vicars of Lichfield gave up similar rights in 1374 in return for increased incomes.[103] The closest links were at Salisbury where in the early fourteenth century most lived with the residentiaries and were regarded as members of their households.[104] In 1319 an episcopal injunction from Bishop Martival prevented vicars from carrying out secular services for their masters. During the later middle ages vicars gained greater independence as they developed into corporate bodies with a communal way of life, partly because there were too few residentiaries to maintain them. Chantry priests did not have formal links with canons because their chantries were private foundations. They acquired corporate status later than vicars, mainly in the fifteenth century. Up to this time they had to find their own accomodation and a few may have lived with canons. Secondaries, choir clerks and altarists who might also act as assistants to the chantry priests, are the most likely to have been members of canons' households. In 1532 Robert Johnson, a secondary at Exeter, was said to be 'under the governance of Master Gibbons', a residentiary.[105] Only at Lincoln did they have a common hall but they were also allowed to live with canons. Choristers lived communally at most cathedrals by the end of the fourteenth century but sometimes, as at Exeter, had dining rights with the canons. In the early sixteenth century the residents at Hereford were reminded by the chapter to make arrangements to 'board' their chorister with another

---

98   *Register of the Freemen of the City of York*, i, SS, xcvi, 1897, 159, 155.
99   See note 60.
100 PRO STAC 2 28/17 no. 15.
101 This paragraph is based on Edwards, *Secular Cathedrals*, 267–317 and Lehmberg, *Reformation of the Cathedrals*, 14–25.
102 Dobson, 'Later Middle Ages', 89.
103 Kettle and Johnson, 'Lichfield Cathedral', 156.
104 Edwards, *Secular Cathedrals*, 270–1.
105 PRO STAC 2 28/17 no. 1.

canon if they left the city.[106] These formal responsibilities came to be replaced by personal links and perhaps a close relationship but one that did not always extend to membership of their households. At some cathedrals minor clergy from all four ranks were assigned to residentiaries, though not all could be because they outnumbered the resident canons. The vicars at Salisbury and Exeter escorted their masters to services, thereby advertising their status.[107] Canons' wills sometimes refer to their personal vicars choral or choristers: in 1498 Canon John Austell of Wells bequeathed a silver salt cellar to his vicar, John Fox.[108] Three senior dignitaries at Exeter in the 1450s, the dean, precentor and chancellor, had chaplains who were chantry priests in the cathedral.[109] Minor clergy can be found acting for residentiaries in a variety of capacities; as feoffees, proctors, witness and executors. At most cathedrals there was a handful of highly valued minor clergy who held positions of trust and played an important part in its administration. They were recognised by the canons who frequently chose them as their executors. Robert Burgh, a vicar at Wells, acted as executor to as many as five canons between 1400 and 1422; similar figures can be found at Exeter.[110]

Outside their households canons might have other dependents whose links with them were more distant. They employed a whole range of proctors, often local clergy, to represent them on an occasional basis on cathedral business or when they were instituted to a new benefice. Archdeacons often delegated their responsibilities to officials, usually members of the local parish clergy, and employed registrars and receivers. Canons who were pluralist non-resident rectors of parishes appointed curates to carry out their pastoral duties. John Hody, a Wells residentiary and absentee rector of Witheridge (Devon), had a curate there and Richard Melhuysch, a local landowner who was styled 'gentleman', acted as his proctor.[111] The parish clergy regularly feature in canons' wills receiving small bequests in return for prayers and masses for their souls. Even such small sums would have been a valuable additions to the income of these clergy.

Canons' Hospitality

According to Mayor John Shillingford of Exeter in 1448 the residentiaries of the cathedral provided 'good cheer and right welcome, good welfare, and great feasts'.[112] Two centuries later, another Exeter citizen, John Hooker, praised their

---

106 HCA Baylis i, fo. 37v.
107 See note 104; Reg. Lacy Exeter, i, 158–9.
108 Somerset Medieval Wills 1383–1500, 371.
109 Orme, Minor Clergy, 29, 65; Reg. Lacy Exeter, iv, 23–7.
110 Somerset Medieval Wills 1383–1500, 68, 76, 87, 92, 107.
111 Reg. Lacy Exeter, ii, 220.
112 Letters and Papers of John Shillingford, ed. S. A. Moore, Camden Society, New Series, ii, 1871, 57.

liberality when recalling the leading residentiaries of his youth in the 1530s and 1540s.[113] Hospitality was a basic function of all medieval households. Even the two priests of Munden's chantry in Bridport, Dorset, who had only one servant, dispensed it on a considerable scale, feeding at least two or three and up to five or six guests a week.[114] In the modest noble household of Dame Alice Bryene in 1412–13 it was common for twenty people to attend dinner, about half of whom would be guests.[115] Hospitality was a particular obligation of resident canons and a religious and charitable duty following Old Testament and apostolic traditions.[116] Bishop Lacy of Exeter saw the models of canons' hospitality in Abraham and Lot, Abraham being known for the generosity of his welcome to all strangers, while Lot, in Sodom, put his responsibility as a host before his duty as a father. Lacy also considered hospitality as a charitable duty, providing food and clothing for Christ's poor.[117] The scale of hospitality expected of residentiaries in England was recognised as 'heavy and costly' in a petition made to the Curia in 1463.[118] The daily payments made to residents were intended to meet these costs and enable canons to be liberal. Cathedral statutes set out the general principle of hospitality and the detailed obligations were determined and carefully regulated by custom and practice. In December 1403 it was established just who was entitled to a place at the table of the hebdomary canon at Lincoln; eight office holders among the minor clergy are listed but no others were entitled to the privilege.[119] The heaviest burden at all cathedrals fell during a canon's week as hebdomary when he had to feed large sections of the choir on Sunday. In general, dignitaries were expected not only to be in residence for longer periods of the year but also to undertake greater hospitality according to the custom of the cathedral. Up to 1344 the dean of Chichester was required to treat the whole choir on the four principal feasts of the year and to invite the canons separately for eight days beforehand, though the pope ordered this statute to be revoked.[120] The custom at Wells into the sixteenth century was for dignitaries to entertain the canons and vicars during the week of Pentecost.[121] At Salisbury the choristers dined at canons' tables throughout the Christmas festivities.[122] The obligations of hospitality were considered important enough to be enforced by both bishops and chapters up to the Reformation. Complaints about the failure of residents

113 DRO ECA Exeter Book 51 fos 341r, 345r, 346v.
114 K. Wood-Legh, A Small Household of the XV Century, being the account book of Munden's chantry, Bridport, Manchester, 1956. The figures are taken from a survey of the years 1454–5, 1455–6, 1456–7.
115 The Household of Dame Alice Bryene, ed. V. Redstone, 2nd edition, Bungay, 1984.
116 For a general discussion see Edwards, Secular Cathedrals, 59–61.
117 Reg. Lacy Exeter, iv, 290.
118 CPL xi, 636.
119 LAO D&C A/2/29 fo. 5v.
120 CPL iii, 117.
121 Wells HMC, ii, 222.
122 Salisbury D&C Reg. Burgh fo. 18r.

to keep hospitality are a familiar theme of episcopal visitations and chapter meetings.

The practice of hospitality by canons can be observed on a variety of occasions. On an everyday basis local clergy were entertained. Some travellers, particularly more important ones, stayed in canons' houses. Royal justices and ecclesiastical officials who came to cathedral cities on business regularly received hospitality. In the early sixteenth century resident canons of Exeter were required to be in the city during the assizes to entertain visiting justices.[123] Thomas Bekyngton, canon of Wells, royal servant and later a bishop, has left a detailed picture of what must have been a common practice, a traveller being entertained on his journey. In the summer of 1442 he set out on a diplomatic mission to France, taking the land route via Plymouth. He called first at Wells where he was entertained to dinner by Master John Bernard and afterwards took wine with the precentor before being installed personally to his prebend in the cathedral. Arriving at Exeter a few days later he spent a week in the city dining with six different canons. On his return in 1443 he passed through the city again, spending only one night but this was long enough to receive gifts of horses from two canons.[124] It was usual for these important travellers to be entertained by canons. The papal legate, en route for Scotland in March 1486, broke his journey at York and stayed in the deanery.[125] From time to time distinguished visitors came to the close. Most cathedrals received royal visits. When Edward II came to Lichfield in 1323 he stayed in the bishop's palace and Queen Isabella at the deanery.[126] The lavish entertainment required would have strained the resources of the poorer canons. The royal entourage no doubt spread across both the close and the city. On Friday 5 February 1473 the duke of Clarence and the earls of Warwick, Salisbury and Richmond visited Salisbury Cathedral and were entertained by the precentor where they stayed until the following day.[127] Other exceptional events such as the enthronement of a bishop or election of a dean were marked by celebrations and feasting attended by important visitors. Richard Scrope's enthronement as bishop of Lichfield on the feast of St Peter and St Paul 1387 was particularly splendid, attended by Richard II, Queen Anne, and many nobles including Rober de Vere, duke of Ireland, and the earls of Suffolk and Salisbury, as well as the archbishops of Dublin and York.[128] Not all enthronements were so lavish but even a more modest decanal election brought many guests. Following his election as dean of Lichfield in 1321 Sephen Segrave gave a feast for twenty-one knights and 'a great number of vassals'.[129]

The provision of hospitality was in part a charitable duty; feeding the poor

[123] Oliver, Lives, 472.
[124] Correspondance of Thomas Beckington, ii, 177–9, 240.
[125] L. Attreed, York House Books 1461–90, 2 vols, Stroud, 1991, ii, 470–1.
[126] Bod Lib Ashmole Ms 794 fo. 6v.
[127] Salisbury D&C Reg. Machon fo. 56r.
[128] LJRO D30/2/1/1 fo. 15r.
[129] Savage, Magnum Registrum Album, no. 581.

was one of the seven works of mercy. The poor were remembered at canons' feasts but there is rarely direct evidence except where it was formalised. At York in the mid-fourteenth century, according to custom, the dean fed forty paupers at Easter each year and at Lincoln the occupant of the house known as Atherstone Place was obliged to feed a hundred paupers three times a year.[130] The food at canons' tables was probably as fine as the rest of their houses. Few details survive, though we know that Dean Worsley of St Paul's regularly spent £40 a year on food for his household in the 1480s and occasionally as much as £60.[131] According to a late fifteenth century model household an esquire was expected to spend £24 a year on food and fuel.[132] This would suggest that the dean lived in a style commensurate with his status as a senior cleric. Chance has preserved a letter from Canon George Trevelyan of Exeter (d.1526) showing the interest he took in his table. Writing to his brother he asked him to send by carrier 'six great congers and a dozen puffins'.[133] Both Worsley and Trevelyan confirm the impression that canons lived comfortably in a manner that emphasised their status, wealth and privileges and saw no contradiction between the lifestyle of a gentleman and that of a cleric.

---

130 York D&C H1/3 fo. 51r; Jones, Lincoln Houses, iii, 106.
131 See note 89.
132 C. Dyer, Standards of Living in the Later Middle Ages, Cambridge, 1989, 70, Table 5.
133 The Trevelyan Letters to 1840, ed. M. Siraut, SRS, vol. lxxx, 1990, 4.

7

The Interests and Activities
of Residentiary Canons, I:
Religious Interests

Medieval pilgrims visiting Lincoln Minster around 1500 were vividly reminded of the generations of canons who had served it. As they made their way through the nave and aisles to St Hugh's shrine in the retro choir they passed many of their elaborate tombs and burial places. These contain many insights into how canons saw themselves and wished to be seen. Though virtually none survive intact today, they were faithfully recorded in 1641 by Canon Robert Sanderson, a leading Anglican divine and later bishop of the diocese.[1] He noted fifty-four tombs of canons who died before 1540, most of them from the late fourteenth and fifteenth centuries. The custom at Lincoln was for canons to have more than a simple outline of their lives inscribed on their tomb slabs containing their names, the principal benefices they held and the date of their death, together with a brief invocation for Divine mercy. In addition they included moral and religious verses and images and often a portrait in brass with an idealised rather than realistic likeness. Though these brasses have been lost, surviving examples in other cathedrals show canons were conscious of their status and were depicted robed in elaborate and richly decorated vestments. John Beverley (d.1473) left instructions for his image to show him dressed in his choir robes.[2] Some emphasised their piety and were shown kneeling before a crucifix. Both Hamo Belers and John Haddon had themselves portrayed kneeling in prayer to the Virgin whereas John Crosby asked for his image to be flanked by angels.[3] Alongside their piety canons emphasised their birth and lineage. Coats of arms and heraldic devices were often included on their tomb slabs, even if few went as far as Philip Tilney in elaborating his descent and family connections in an inscription and two verses.[4] John Breton included his rebus, a hog's head cask or

---

[1] Sanderson and Peck, *Lincoln Cathedral: An Exact Copy of All the Ancient Monumental Inscriptions As In 1641*.
[2] LAO D&C A/2/35 fos 136v–137r.
[3] Sanderson and Peck, *Lincoln Cathedral*, 27 (Belers), 23 (Haddon, Crosby); LAO D&C A/2/35 fos 86v–87r.
[4] Sanderson and Peck, *Lincoln Cathedral*, 18–19.

ton with Bre over it.[5] The literate pilgrim may have paused to read some of the inscriptions on the tomb slabs. Like their brothers at York and elsewhere, the canons of Lincoln were conscious of and took pride in their status as residents and usually described themselves not simply as canons but as residentiaries of the cathedral.[6] They seem to have chosen their inscriptions with some care if not a great deal of originality. Virtually all that go beyond the basic biographical outline make some reference to death and decay. Typical of these is Philip Tilney who asked the passing pilgrim to 'consyder here a caryon wormes to fede'.[7] John Marshall made the same point in a more poetic fashion quoting in Latin a well known verse 'As the rose pales without the sun; so man passes away; now living, now abandoned'.[8] This is one of the few inscriptions that quotes a known literary source. The rest seem to be original compositions on familiar themes displaying their author's skills in Latin verse, usually hexameters. John Breton's inscription began '*Sub pedibus stratus et vermibus associatus, Sum desolatus, sis Christe mei miseratus.*'[9] Robert Mason composed two autobiographical verses which were placed each side of his head on his tomb slab. He ended his verses like several others with a request for the prayers of passing pilgrims; John Breton asked them to say the Pater Noster and Ave Maria.[10] The inscriptions were also used to express canons' devotion and seek God's mercy. Thomas Loughborough and Martin Joyner declared their faith in the resurrection and Peter Partrich sought Christ's mercy through his Holy Cross.[11] A sense of outrage still echoes from John Rouceby's inscription which recorded that he had been wickedly killed in an act of premeditated murder and named his murderer.[12] The most interesting monument was that of Dean Sheppey who died in 1412.[13] He appears as an exemplary late medieval senior cleric, a devout and educated man. His brass showed him kneeling with two scrolls coming from his mouth. These express his devotion to the relatively new cult of the five wounds of Christ. Below his skill in Latin was demonstrated with a verse in hexameters in which he is described as a cheerful, courteous white-haired old man (*canus . . . gratus et humanus*) before reminding the reader that he too will die and asking for his prayers.

The Pastoral Interests and Activities of Canons

Cathedral canons were not simply the career minded pluralists advancing through royal and ecclesiastical service that some contemporary critics complained of, or for that matter a list of their benefices and offices might suggest.

5   Ibid., 21.
6   Dobson, 'Residentiary Canons', 146, 169.
7   See note 6.
8   Sanderson and Peck, *Lincoln Cathedral*, 27.
9   Ibid., 21.
10 Ibid., 30 (Mason), 21 (Breton).
11 Ibid., 30–1 (Loughborough), 30 (Joyner), 26 (Partrich).
12 Ibid., 29.
13 Ibid., 14.

As pluralists resident at their cathedrals they were rarely involved in pastoral work at a parish level, a duty that was left to paid chaplains. But even at this level there are some exceptions to indicate that a minority were active. A handful of Exeter residentiaries were appointed penitentiaries in a rural deanery to hear the confessions of the local clergy. The longest serving, William Browning, was appointed twelve times between 1433 and his death in 1454, and continuously from 1447. He was usually appointed to one of the deaneries where he held a parish.[14] Although in general canons efforts were concentrated on the administrative work of the Church this involved them in some pastoral activities. Diocesan administration often had a pastoral dimension such as the visitation of religious houses and matrimonial cases, and particularly in the consistory court over which they frequently presided, and where many had begun their careers as junior officials. The work of Jonathan Hughes has shown the seriousness and pastoral zeal of the York diocesan administrators in the late fourteenth and early fifteenth centuries. Many of those most closely involved were residentiaries at the Minster. Men like John Newton, Thomas Dalby, Thomas Walleworth and later Robert Wolvenden combined residence with running the diocese.[15] Having begun his career in the service of Bishop Arundel of Ely in the 1370s, John Newton followed his master to York as vicar general from 1390 to 1396. He entered residence in 1393 on his resignation as master of Peterhouse at Cambridge, and remained until his death in 1414.[16] Both as individuals and chapters canons had some pastoral responsibilities for their own prebendal churches and those appropriated to the common fund as well as others that came within the cathedral's jurisdiction. In some cities, such as Exeter and Lichfield, this could be quite extensive. Some seventy-five churches and chapels belonged to the dean and chapter of Lichfield or were attached to prebends and the city came within the jurisdiction of the dean.[17] Collectively the chapter supervised the clergy serving the three chapels in the city.[18] Residentiaries exercised their pastoral duties by appointing the parish clergy and carrying out visitations. The survival of his register has allowed us to observe Dean Chandler of Salisbury making regular personal visitations of the cathedral's prebendal parishes in 1405, 1408–09 and 1412.[19] In addition, by virtue of their office, deans had particular responsibilities for the pastoral supervision of the cathedral clergy.[20]

While few resident canons had pastoral contact with the laity through their parishes a larger number reached them through the pulpit. All nine secular cathedrals had some formal arrangements for the preaching of sermons, though

[14] *Reg. Lacy Exeter* ii, 277, 324, 373, 411; vol iii, 23, 66, 101, 139, 165, 193.
[15] Hughes, *Pastors and Visionaries*, 178–92.
[16] Ibid., 178–9, 200–1, 204–5, 217.
[17] Kettle and Johnson, 'Lichfield Cathedral', 146–7, 155, 161–2.
[18] Kettle, 'City and Close', 160–1.
[19] T. C. B. Timmins, *The Register of John Chandler, Dean of Salisbury 1404–17*, WRS, xxxix, Devizes, 1984, 1–49, 72–106, 107–28.
[20] This is discussed in Edwards, *Secular Cathedrals*, 146–8.

this did not have the high priority it later assumed after the Reformation. Sermons were the particular responsibility of the chancellor who was expected to provide preachers or preach himself.[21] The detailed provision of sermons varied according to custom at each cathedral. At Exeter they were given at Advent and Lent but at Lincoln a more extensive course was laid down in the twelfth century requiring weekly sermons each Sunday and on six major feasts.[22] Some of these were associated with the great processions held on these occasions. At Chichester the two archdeacons were expected to preach on Ash Wednesday and Maundy Thursday.[23] These sermons were specifically intended for the laity and were often preached in the nave. There is circumstantial evidence that they were well attended; in 1437 Bishop Alnwick of Lincoln complained in his visitation that the vergers were not keeping order among the laity while the sermon was being preached.[24] Among the miscellaneous accounts at Exeter there are details of the sermons given in the late fourteenth and late fifteenth century. They show that the bulk of the preaching was done by the local Franciscan and Dominican friars. Canons played a much smaller part but the few with a reputation as preachers regularly gave sermons; three are known in the 1390s and 1400s and a further three between 1486 and 1501.[25] When neither friars nor canons preached local clergy were invited in their place. Cathedral libraries contained books of sermons providing models and guidance for those who wished to develop their skills. To encourage this Treasurer Skelton of Lincoln gave a number of books to the cathedral in 1501, including a Bible and concordance and two volumes of sermons.[26] Alongside sermons in English for the laity there was also preaching in Latin intended for the clergy; episcopal visitations and enthronements often included a Latin sermon.

Some residentiaries were undoubtedly skilled and highly regarded preachers. The most popular among the Exeter canons of the late fifteenth century was John Taylor, the chancellor, who preached as many as fifteen times between 1487 and 1491.[27] Almost as regular a preacher, though over a longer period, was Peter Carslegh, who was not yet a canon when he started in 1487. He gained a high reputation and was heard outside the cathedral, in parish churches and on great

---

[21] The general background to preaching in cathedrals can be found in Edwards, *Secular Cathedrals*, 216 and G. R. Owst, *Preaching in Medieval England*, Cambridge, 1926, 155–6.

[22] Lepine, *Canons of Exeter Cathedral*, 203–5; Owen, 'Historical Survey 1091–1450', 118, 142, 172. In 1390 the Lincoln chapter made alternative arrangements for the Carmelite friar Stephen Patrington to preach in the absence of the chancellor (LAO D&C A/2/27 fos 35v–36r).

[23] Edwards, *Secular Cathedrals*, 250.

[24] Owst, *Preaching in Medieval England*, 157.

[25] The late fourteenth-century preachers were John Gorewell, Martin Lercedekne and Robert Rygge (DRO D&C 3773 fos 22r, 28r, 42r). The late fifteenth century preachers were John Taylor, Peter Carslegh and William Sumaister (DRO D&C 3762).

[26] Bowker, 'Historical Survey', 172.

[27] DRO D&C 3762 s. a. 1487–92.

occasions such as the funeral of the countess of Devon in 1527.[28] Most cathedrals seem to have had similar figures; at Lincoln Thomas Duffield's reputation was such that he was chosen by Bishop Alnwick to preach nineteen sermons during his visitations in 1440–41.[29] We know most about the preaching of Richard FitzRalph while he was dean of Lichfield and resident there in the mid 1340s. His sermon diary records that he preached regularly in English to the people in the cathedral and also sometimes travelled to neighbouring towns and villages. On two occasions he spoke in the open in the cemetery of St John's Hospital in Lichfield.[30] By the early sixteenth century a tradition of promoting preaching by the deans of Lichfield seems to have developed. John Yotton (d.1512) endowed a priest to preach the gospel without charge in Lichfield and neighbouring parishes and his successor, Ralph Collingwood (d.1521), was noted for his practice of preaching to the people every Sunday for half an hour.[31] In a practical way Simon Alcock, a fifteenth century residentiary at Lincoln, sought to encourage preaching by writing a manual of instruction of which several copies survive.[32] Two individuals stand out among these noted preachers. Giles Redmere, who resided at Lincoln a century and a half before Simon Alcock, was perhaps unique. Bishop Dalderby had such a high opinion of his ability that in 1313 he granted an indulgence of forty days to all those who heard him preach.[33] In 1463 Humphrey Stafford, earl of Devon, was so impressed with the skills of Nicholas Gosse, the chancellor of Exeter, that in his will he asked him, together with the warden of the Franciscan Friars at Exeter, to preach a sermon in every parish church in the five South-Western counties of Somerset, Dorset, Wiltshire, Devon and Cornwall for the sake of his soul.[34] Unfortunately no evidence survives to indicate whether this massive and unusual undertaking was ever carried out. Virtually all these noted preachers shared one common characteristic: they had studied theology and many had gained doctorates.

Canons' Personal Devotion

In his pioneering study of the residentiary canons of York Professor Dobson described them as 'highly orthodox and conventionally pious', a judgement that applies equally well to their colleagues in the other eight secular cathedrals.[35]

[28] DRO D&C 3762 s. a. 1487–1500; Lepine, 'Courtenays and Exeter Cathedral', 46.
[29] A. H. Thompson, *Visitations of Religious Houses in the Diocese of Lincoln, iii*, LRS, xxi, 1929, Appendix III, 418–19.
[30] A. Gwynn, 'The Sermon-Diary of Richard FitzRalph', *Proceedings of the Royal Irish Academy*, xliv, Section C, 1–57.
[31] BRUC 667 (Yotton), 149 (Collingwood).
[32] BRUO i, 18–19.
[33] LAO Reg III (Reg. Dalderby) fo. 281r.
[34] *Somerset Medieval Wills 1383–1500*, 201.
[35] Dobson, 'Residentiary Canons', 169.

Canons' personal devotion emerges most clearly from their wills and the provisions they made for their souls. Despite their pitfalls and limitations, wills, with careful use, can yield insights into canons' personal devotion among the conventional concerns and expressions.[36] However, they only record an individual's preoccupations as he faced death rather than how he lived his life. John Shillingford, a canon of Salisbury, though not a residentiary, no doubt spoke for them all when he confessed that he had spent too much of his time on worldly affairs.[37] What emerges from wills and other evidence is a faithful reflection of late medieval piety: an awareness of death and judgement; a concern for an individual's soul which led to the founding of masses, obits and chantries and much almsgiving; devotion to saints; pilgrimages and membership of gilds and confraternities; and an interest in the liturgy. As might be expected from an educated clerical elite, canons were more precise and detailed than the laity in their descriptions of God when making their wills. In a study of Hull almost all the citizens refer to God simply as Almighty God, whereas canons are generally more explicit.[38] Many refer to God as their creator and introduce the idea of redemption, referring to Him as their redeemer or saviour, or to His precious blood. With characteristic thoroughness Precentor Sturgeon of St Paul's began his will with a clear theological definition 'In the blessed name of the Holy Trinity, the Father, the Son, the Holy Ghost, three persons in one substance'.[39] Far fewer wills make any reference to Jesus Christ. The fear of ultimate judgement underlay all wills though it often remains implicit in the provisions for the testator's soul. Some rejected worldliness and spoke of themselves and their bodies in disparaging terms. In the early fifteenth century the York residentiaries John Newton, Richard Pittes and William Waltham included penitential statements of their unworthiness at a time when such statements were unusual.[40] Precentor Sturgeon stated starkly that he was 'most unworthy to have that worshipful name and office of priest'.[41] John Cutler, the treasurer of Lincoln from 1501–08, opened his will with a long paragraph 'beseeching his gracious Godhead of his infinite great mercy to pardon and forgive me of all of my trespasses and offenses'.[42]

Canons enthusiastically shared the widespread medieval devotion to saints and their relics. The Virgin's immense popularity is well reflected both in general

---

[36] The interpretation of medieval wills is discussed in C. Burgess, ' "By Quick and by Dead": Wills and Pious Provision in late Medieval Bristol', *EHR*, 837–58, and P. Heath, 'Urban Piety in the Later Middle Ages: the Evidence of Hull Wills', in R. B. Dobson, *The Church, Politics and Patronage in the Fifteenth Century*, Gloucester, 1984. The difficulties encountered with a group of clerical wills are considered in Lepine, *Canons of Exeter Cathedral*, 205–7.

[37] *Reg. Stafford Exeter*, 387.

[38] Heath, op.cit. note 36.

[39] Furnivall, *Fifty Earliest English Wills*, 131–4.

[40] Hughes, *Pastors and Visionaries*, 218.

[41] See note 39.

[42] LAO D&C A/3/3 fos 18r–19r.

invocations and commendations in their wills and in many other ways. Burial in Lady chapels or in front of images of the Virgin was commonly requested. The Exeter canon William Puntingdon established his obit at Our Lady's altar and asked for it to be held on the day after the feast of the Purification of the Blessed Virgin Mary.[43] Robert Mason expressed his devotion by giving a silver gilt figure of Our Lady to be placed on the high altar of Lincoln cathedral in 1493. An inventory of 1536 reveals this to have been a large and splendid madonna and child richly encrusted with jewels and pearls.[44] His fellow canon Nicholas Wymbush was more generous still, bequeathing half the residue of his estate to be spent in her honour.[45] At all cathedrals the cult of the Virgin was developed and enhanced as Lady chapels were built and the liturgical importance of the feasts associated with the Virgin and her mother St Anne increased; indeed several included her as one of their patrons. The apostles SS Peter, Paul and Andrew were frequently mentioned in the invocations of wills. Some ranged widely and eclectically: John Belvoir (d.1391), the sub dean of Lincoln, called on the prayers of five saints SS Thomas, Martin, Nicholas, Katherine and Margaret.[46] In 1443 Treasurer Symondsburgh asked for permission to be buried in front of the image of St Christopher at Salisbury.[47] John Beverley's devotion to the early church fathers was more unusual. In his will of 1473 he invoked SS Augustine, Gregory, Ambrose, Jerome and Bernard.[48] New cults were supported; Dean Sheppey's interest in the Five Wounds has been noted and it remained popular among residentiaries up to the Reformation; John Cutler of Lincoln (d.1508) requested five masses of the Five Wounds to be celebrated on the day before his funeral.[49] At Lichfield Dean Heywood was instrumental in promoting the cults of the Holy Name and St Anne in the 1460s and 1470s.[50]

Quite what drew individuals to particular saints is difficult to say. No doubt the motivation behind them was often personal and remains hidden but some themes can be observed. A cathedral's patron saints were a popular choice, St Hugh at Lincoln, St Chad at Lichfield, and St Osmund at Salisbury where the chancellor John Dogett gave £10 to his shrine in 1501.[51] Several Exeter canons chose the cathedral's three patrons SS Peter and Paul and the Virgin.[52] Some

[43] DRO D&C 2129.
[44] LAO D&C A/3/1 fo. 123r; Wordsworth, 'Inventories of Plate, Vestments etc, Belonging to the Cathedral Church of the Blessed Mary of Lincoln', *Archaeologia*, liii, 1892, 16.
[45] LAO D&C A/2/35 fos 87v–88r.
[46] LAO D&C A/2/28 fo. 41.
[47] Wordsworth, *Salisbury Ceremonies and Processions*, 293.
[48] See note 2.
[49] LAO D&C A/3/3 fos 18r–19r. Another Lincoln canon, Simon Stallworthy (d.1511), expressed his devotion to the cult of the five wounds (PRO PROB 11/17 fo. 163r).
[50] Kettle, 'City and Close', 163.
[51] Wordsworth, *Salisbury Ceremonies and Processions*, 281.
[52] Lepine, *Canons of Exeter Cathedral*, 212.

residentiaries chose their namesakes as patron saints. This, perhaps, explains Dean Andrew Kilkenny's embellishment of St Andrew's chapel in Exeter cathedral where he was buried and established his obit. As well as paying for its decoration and supplying new vestments and altar vessels, in 1299 he enhanced its liturgy by instituting a procession to St Andrew's altar on the vigil of the saint's feast day.[53] The same motive seems to lie behind Chancellor Nicholas Bradbridge's request to be buried in front of the image of St Nicholas in Lincoln Minster.[54] Local saints and cults attracted the interest of canons. The York residentiaries played a central role in developing the cult of archbishop Scrope in spite of official opposition.[55] The South-West was a particularly fruitful source of local cults which attracted the attention of the canons resident at its cathedral. A fourteenth-century dean, Bartholomew of St Lawrence, gave some of the bones of St Brannoc to the cathedral, which he had probably acquired as dean since Brannoc was associated with the north Devon village of Braunton, whose church was appropriated to the deanery.[56] A similar connection brought St Urith to the notice of Arnulph Colyns (d.1490) who was rector of Chittlehampton in Devon where she was buried. He bequeathed 13s 4d to the church there in her honour.[57] Precentor Keyes (d.1477) venerated the local Exeter virgin and martyr St Sidwell.[58] John Taylor, a distinguished preacher and theologian, took a close interest in the cult of St Michael at St Michael's Mount in Cornwall. In 1479 he presented the chapel with a copy of the *Revelatio S. Michaelis in monte tumba* which set out its origins.[59] The possession of relics by individual canons was rarer but not unknown. In the 1420s there were three pieces of the true cross in the Close at Exeter, two of them owned by canons.[60] One of them formed part of the unusually large collection of Martin Lercedekne that also contained some of the Virgin's milk and a reliquary with an unspecified number of relics.[61] The presence of St Chad's bones in the cathedral in Birmingham is due to a canon of Lichfield, Arthur Dudley, who during the Reformation stole them from his cathedral in order to save them from the reformers.[62] In general though, it was cathedrals rather than individual canons that held large collections of relics.

Shortcomings in the evidence make it hard to assess how much residentiaries

---

53 DRO D&C 2864, 394.

54 Cole, *Lincoln Chapter Acts 1520–36*, 159–60.

55 Hughes, *Pastors and Visionaries*, 305–15.

56 Orme, *Exeter Cathedral*, 83.

57 PRO PROB 11/ 8 fo. 273; BRUO i, 472. The cult of St Urith is examined in N. I. Orme ed., *Nicholas Roscarrock's Lives of the Saints: Cornwall and Devon*, DCRS, New Series xxxv, 1992, 137–9.

58 Sidwell's cult is considered in M. J. Swanton, *St Sidwell: An Exeter Legend*, Exeter, 1986.

59 *BRUO* iii, 1850–1.

60 Lepine, *Canons of Exeter Cathedral*, 210.

61 *Reg. Chichele Canterbury*, ii, 476–82.

62 W. N. Landor, *Staffordshire Incumbents and Parochial Records 1530–1680*, Wm Salt Archaeological Society, Third Series, 1915, 140.

shared the medieval enthusiasm for pilgrimages; the names of the countless visitors to the many shrines are not recorded.[63] The occasional references are almost certainly a considerable underestimate. Many had travelled to Rome on ecclesiastical business in the course of their careers and while they were there probably visited the shrines of the city, which was considered the second holiest place after the Holy Land. The scattered examples known shown canons visiting popular shrines in England and overseas. Walter Clopton, an Exeter residentiary, was granted permission to make a pilgrimage to the East Anglian shrines of Walsingham and Bury St Edmunds in 1328.[64] The York canon Robert Langton's destination in 1510 was Santiago di Compostella and Rome.[65] A more personal note was struck by Geoffrey Simeon in 1490. When asking the Lincoln chapter for permission to visit the Holy Places in Rome he explained that this had been his fervent wish since he was a boy.[66] He seems to have set a precedent, for three years later Thomas Hill made a similar request and another was made by Nicholas Bradbridge in 1516.[67] The Exeter canon John Mogrich (d.1524) left instructions for a servant to make a pilgrimage to Walsingham after his death.[68] Much more is known about residentiaries' participation in another expression of popular piety, fraternities and guilds. These were widely supported by canons through membership, bequests and sometimes active involvement. Throughout its history the Corpus Christi Guild at York had a high membership among the Minster clergy whose residentiaries were among its leading figures and two of whom sponsored its incorporation in 1458–59.[69] A similar role was played by the Lincoln residentiaries in the Corpus Christi Guild at Boston.[70] Both of these guilds were large and prestigious with a national importance. The most prominent clerics were often members of the fraternities of leading religious houses such as Christ Church Canterbury, Durham and St Albans. Canons were as likely to take an interest in local fraternities or those in places they had a connection with. Richard Chesterfield, a Lincoln residentiary, made generous bequests of 40s each to St Mary's and the Holy Cross guilds in his birthplace Chesterfield as well as smaller ones to the Holy Trinity and Corpus Christi guilds at Newark while his colleague Robert Aiscough made them to the guilds of St Anne and

---

[63] The standard works on pilgrimages are R. C. Finucane, *Miracles and Pilgrims: Popular Beliefs in Medieval England*, 1977, and J. Sumption, *Pilgrimage: An Image of Medieval Religion*, 1975.

[64] *Reg. Grandisson Exeter* i, 467.

[65] YML H3/1 fo. 50v.

[66] LAO D&C A/3/1 fos 69v, 70r.

[67] Ibid. fo. 82r (Hill); Bowker, *Secular Clergy*, 163. The Salisbury canon John Hurleigh visited the Holy Land with the earl of Worcester in 1459 (BRUO ii, 988).

[68] PRO PROB 11/ 21 fo. 182v.

[69] R. H. Scaife, *The Register of the Guild of Corpus Christi in the City of York; with an appendix of Illustrative Documents, Containing some Account of the Hospital of St Thomas without Mickelgate-Bar in the Suburbs of the City*, SS, lvii, 1872, 14 passim.

[70] P. Thompson, *The History and Antiquities of Boston*, Boston, 1856, 373–5, 749–53.

the Ploughgild in Lincoln.[71] Guilds were the main focus of the piety of another Lincoln canon, Philip Tilney. He was a leading figure in the Guild of Corpus Christi in Boston, served as its alderman, and asked to be buried in the choir of its chapel. In 1445 he helped found a new guild there dedicated to Our Lady. The full extent of his interest in guilds emerges in his will of 1453. Not only did he give the large sum of £20 to the Corpus Christi Guild and payed each of its chaplains to say a trental for him, he also made smaller bequests of a few shillings to six other guilds in Boston, where he originated, and one in Lincoln.[72] As individuals and as a chapter canons were closely involved in the organisation of the fraternities that existed in most secular cathedrals in the late middle ages.[73]

The anchorites common across medieval England living a solitary religious life received encouragement from canons; small bequests can regularly be found in their wills.[74] Geoffrey Scrope, who was resident at Lincoln from 1360, and perhaps earlier, until his death in 1383, was a patron of recluses by family background and personal inclination. The Scropes and possibly Geoffrey himself were supporters and followers of the leading English mystic Richard Rolle of Hampole. He was certainly a patron of the anchoress Margaret Kirkby who helped draw up an account of Rolle's miracles. He also supported anchorites at Doncaster, Kirkby Wisk, Stamford and one at Holy Trinity church in Lincoln. His interest in the solitary life was further expressed in his gifts to five religious houses of the Carthusian order which emphasised a retreat from the world into contemplative and mystical devotion.[75] Scrope was unusual in the depth of his interest but not unique. Other Lincoln residentiaries supported anchorites in the city, among them his contemporary John Belvoir (d.1391) and Philip Tilney (d.1453).[76] At much the same time the Exeter residentiaries were fostering local recluses. A group of six were patrons of an Exeter anchoress, Dame Alice Bernard, who was enclosed at St Leonard's church there from 1397 until at least 1425 and probably 1435.[77] The most important of these canons was John Dodyngton who carried out the bishop's commission to enclose her and may have acted as her confessor.[78] Chichester cathedral was perhaps unique in having an anchorite in the Close at the beginning of the fifteenth century. William Bolle had been one of the cathedral's minor clergy and held a local rectory, Aldrington, before his enclosure in 1402 and is known to have been living in 1418.[79] No canon is known to tried to live the solitary life of the anchorite but one or two gave up the

---

71 LAO D&C A/2/29 fos 13r–14v (Chesterfield); A/2/35 fos 119v–120r.
72 Thompson op.cit. 373–5; CPR 1441–6, 333; LAO D&C A/2/35 fos 21v–22v.
73 These are more fully discussed in Chapter 1.
74 The standard work on anchorites is A. K. Warren, *Anchorites and their Patrons in Medieval England*, 1985.
75 Hughes, *Pastors and Visionaries*, 87; Foster, *Lincoln Wills*, i, 11–19.
76 LAO D&C A/2/28 fo. 41 (Belvoir); A/2/35 fos 21v–22v.
77 Warren, *Anchorites*, 268–74.
78 *Reg. Stafford Exeter*, 99.
79 M. E. C. Walcott, 'The Bishops of Chichester from Stigand to Sherborne', SAC xxix, 33–4.

cathedral cloister for a monastic one. After twenty years service to the bishops of Exeter Thomas Henton left his canonical house in the close and entered Barlinch Priory in Somerset in November 1329, where he was still living three years later. Barlinch was an Augustinian house with a rule similar to the cathedral's.[80] The contrast was much greater for Nicholas Hereford, who after a decade in the Close at Hereford from 1406/7–17, left for the greater austerity of the Charterhouse in Coventry where he ended his life. His religious vocation had led him from Lollardy, for which he was tried, excommunicated and imprisoned, to the quiet comfort of residence at Hereford, and finally to the rigors of the Carthusian life.[81]

Although much of the cathedral liturgy was primarily the responsibility of the bishop and minor clergy some canons took a particular interest and all chapters exercised some degree of supervision. Major liturgical innovations were usually the work of bishops and it was the minor clergy who bore the brunt of performing them. It is uncertain how many of the eight daily offices residentiaries attended beyond the minimum set out in the statutes, though it is unlikely that they were present at more than the daily mass and one of the other offices. However, we know that the Exeter residentiaries attended obits and funerals in the cathedral regularly and some may have attended several of the daily offices.[82] Some of their devotions were performed in the private chapels of their houses in the close. The predominance of liturgical texts among canons' books also suggests a conscientious approach to worship. Chapters could expect to be consulted about liturgical developments and asked for their consent. Their supervisory role was taken seriously and conscientiously discharged. This forms an important and recurring theme in chapter act books which record a good deal of the mundane day to day disciplining of the minor clergy's behaviour in the choir to maintain liturgical standards. After the Dean Denton's visitation of Lichfield cathedral in 1522 the chapter carried out a thorough reform of the minor clergy the following year. Proper clerical dress was imposed on the vicars, the choristers were admonished to say matins and the hours of the Blessed Virgin Mary 'clearly and devoutly', and the rites of the Sarum missal introduced for parts of the liturgy.[83] Nearly a decade later, in 1531, the chapter sought to enhance the liturgy by requiring the choristers to attend midnight matins on solemn feasts and the chantry priests to be present at mass and vespers on feast days.[84] Clearly there was no lack of vigour in the cathedral's life at Lichfield on the eve of the Reformation. The Hereford chapter was also active in the 1520s, instituting two new antiphons to be sung by the choir in the nave.[85] In 1530 it instituted a procession to be held on each

[80] *Reg. Grandisson Exeter* i, 536–7, ii, 667.
[81] BRUO ii, 913–15; HCA R149–50, R463–7.
[82] Lepine, *Canons of Exeter Cathedral*, 176.
[83] LJRO D30/2/1/3 fos 134v, 138r–139r.
[84] LJRO D30/2/1/4 fo. 75r.
[85] HCA Baylis i, fo. 37r.

feast of the Virgin.[86] As individuals the most effective way canons augmented divine worship in their cathedrals was through the foundation of obits and chantries which greatly increased the number of masses being celebrated. This was often a conscious aim, and, as we have seen in Andrew Kilkenny's case, might be linked to the cult of a particular saint. Sometimes a liturgical dimension was incorporated more explicitly in an obit. John Hewish, a Wells residentiary who died in 1363, set aside 10s from his obit to pay for an annual procession to the image of the Virgin at the entrance to the choir on the eve of her Nativity.[87] The Exeter canon John Orum (d.1436) gave his cathedral the substantial sum of £40 for the choristers to sing an antiphon in the north porch where he was buried.[88] Precentor Upton of Salisbury acquired considerable liturgical expertise. The elaborate burial of Sir Walter Hungerford in the cathedral in 1449 was organised by him after careful discussion in chapter.[89] On the next great ceremonial occasion, the enthronement of Bishop Beauchamp in 1451, the organisation was again left in his hands.[90] Upton was well qualified for this work having written a book on heraldry and knighthood.[91] Not surprisingly deans were amongst the most active individuals of the chapter in developing the liturgy. At Salisbury Dean Chandler promised to provide 4s a year for the choristers to carry two candles to be lit during the elevation of the host on major feasts.[92] It was Dean Denton who provided the funds, a total of £40, for new copes, incense and candles for the procession on the feast of the Purification of the Virgin at Lichfield in 1523.[93] His predecessor Dean Heywood was also a notable benefactor of the cathedral liturgy.[94]

During their last years and particularly as they approached death residentiaries' thoughts and activities became preoccupied with making provisions for their souls. In this they shared the widespread belief of the late middle ages in the doctrine of purgatory and the pre-eminence of the mass as a means of intercession and source of spiritual benefits. The notion of purgatory as an intermediate stage between heaven and hell, where those not condemned to the latter or ready for the former were punished for their sins and purified for heaven, developed during the twelfth and thirteenth centuries. It contained the souls of those pardoned of guilt but not of pain, those who had repented of their sins but not expiated them. The Church proclaimed that the pain of souls in purgatory could be relieved by good works such as prayers and almsgiving. As the mass was considered the most effective form of intercession there was a multiplication of masses on a huge scale,

[86] Ibid. fo. 66r.
[87] HMC Wells ii, 626.
[88] Reg. Lacy Exeter iv, 23–7.
[89] Salisbury D&C Reg. Burgh fo. 23.
[90] Ibid. fo. 35r.
[91] BRUO iii, 1933–4.
[92] Wordsworth, Ceremonies and Processions, 278.
[93] LJRO D30/2/1/4 fos 138r–139r.
[94] See Chapter 9.

which from the fourteenth century was channelled into chantries, obits, trentals (thirty masses said in quick succession), and prayers in religious houses. In spite of doctrines to the contrary it was popularly believed that the greater the number of masses, the greater the spiritual benefits resulting in less, or even no time spent in purgatory. Canons, despite their education, shared this mechanical approach. Fears of the uncertainty of death and distrust of executors led many residentiaries to establish obits and chantries before they died. There were spiritual benefits to be derived from this as the founder could be prayed for while he was alive as well as after his death. The first provision usually made was for a Christian burial. Most cathedrals seem to have had their own customs for the scale of canon's funeral, though few details survive. As a result of a dispute in 1328 between the sacrist and canons of Lichfield over the distribution of candles and torches and the tolling of the bell we know something of the customs practiced there.[95] Other details can be inferred from wills; the number and size of the candles to burn round the body; payments to the clergy attending the funeral or saying prayers, some of whom would be clothed in black and carrying torches; the ringing of bells; distributions to the poor; and the provision of a feast. Altogether a typical canon's funeral was a grand and solemn occasion that reminded the community of his status and wealth as much as his house and household had done while he was alive. Dean Kilkenny of Exeter's in 1302 cost £34 3s which included 60lbs of wax for candles and £12 15s 11d spent on bread for the poor.[96] The funerals of some wealthy fifteenth century York canons cost £70 or £80.[97] Roger Nassington's funeral banquet at Lichfield in 1364 was lavish; 114s 9d was spent on fish and some forty guests were entertained.[98] A minority reacted against this extravagance disparaging their unworthy bodies and asking for a modest funeral without worldly pomp, though this should be understood in relative terms.[99]

Anxiety and urgency underlay some of the arrangements made by residentiaries for masses to be said after their deaths. Not content with the longer term and more regular benefits from an obit or chantry, they asked for hundreds and sometimes as many as a thousand masses to be said as soon as possible after their deaths; John Beverley of Lincoln wanted sixty-five priests to say twenty masses each for his soul.[100] Only the large numbers of chantry priests in cathedrals enabled these requests to be carried out. Even so it would have taken considerable organisation to effect the Exeter canon John Flower's instruction to have a hundred masses said within three days of his death in 1463.[101] Another Exeter canon, Martin Lercedekne, showed particular attention to liturgical and theological detail in the arrangements he made in 1433 for 600 masses, a hundred

95 Savage, *Magnum Registrum Album*, no. 708.
96 DRO D&C 2846.
97 *Test Ebor* iii, 46–7, 143–4.
98 Cox, *Lichfield Muniments*, 225–30
99 Several York canons made requests of this sort, Hughes, *Pastors and Visionaries*, 218.
100 See note 2.
101 DRO Chanter Ms 12 part 1 (Reg. Neville Exeter) fo. 138.

each of the Trinity, Cross, Holy Spirit, St Mary, All Saints and the requiem.[102]
A similar motive lay behind the establishment of temporary chantries, priests
employed to celebrate for a canon's soul for a specified number of years, perhaps
two or three. The scale of these arrangements could be quite considerable. At
Lincoln in the 1470s three residentiaries employed six chaplains between them
for a total of ten years.[103] Prayers as well as masses were requested both from
individuals and religious houses, usually in return for a small gift. Indulgences
were offered to those who prayed for the souls of canons. Generally these have
been badly recorded and so are difficult to quantify but at Lincoln they were
granted in abundance in the early fourteenth century and were conscientiously
entered in the episcopal registers. Between 1310 and 1330 the executors of a
dozen residentiaries were granted indulgences of forty days for those praying for
their souls by Bishop Dalderby and Bishop Burghersh.[104] Isolated examples are
known from elsewhere, such as Exeter. More unusual commemorations were
established from time to time. Martin Dyer's wish was for a special peal of bells
at matins and vespers on his obit day.[105]

Obits and perpetual chantries were designed to provide longer term spiritual
benefits. Of the two obits were more common because they were easier and
cheaper to establish. They were usually founded with a sum of money, either a
capital sum or an income such as rent, and were intended either for a fixed term
of years or in perpetuity depending on the size of the endowment. By the fifteenth
century the average cost of an obit at Exeter cathedral was £1 a year and many
resident canons founded twenty year obits with the residence payments they were
entitled to in the year after their death. The overwhelming majority of residentiaries established obits or chantries in their cathedrals even if they were buried
elsewhere. Lists of them have been preserved in most cathedral archives. Some
founded several in churches they had connections with; Edmund Hanson
(d.1511) was buried in Lincoln cathedral but established obits at Cambridge and
Tattershall.[106] They were used as an opportunity to repay the kindness of kin and
benefactors who were granted a share of the spiritual benefits of the prayers and
masses by the founder, and thus give an insight into the operation of patronage
in medieval society. The Salisbury residentiary William Werkman listed five
benefactors including a former residentiary John Chitterne.[107] The income of an
obit was carefully allocated and often included almsgiving as well as payments
to the clergy officiating and participating. The archdeacon of Totnes, Thomas

102 See note 61.
103 Alexander Prowet employed two chaplains for five years, Robert Aiscough three for
     three years and Robert Wymbush one for two years (LAO D&C A/2/35 fos
     118v–119r, 119v–120v; A/2/36 fos 97v–98r).
104 LAO Reg. III (Reg. Dalderby) fos 181r, 213v, 265r, 278r, 347r, 356r, 366r, 371r, 376r,
     392v; Reg V (Reg. Burghersh) fos 287r, 435r.
105 DRO Chanter Ms 12 part 1 (Reg. Neville Exeter) fo. 23v.
106 LAO D&C A/3/4 fos 39v–40r.
107 PRO PROB 11/ 3 fo. 52.

Charlton (d.1330), set aside 12d for the Dominican and Franciscan friars of Exeter and 4d for the poor.[108]

Perpetual chantries were relatively expensive to found because of the greater endowment needed and the cost of a royal licence. The executors of Dean Kilkenny spent nearly £50 at the beginning of the fourteenth century establishing his in Exeter cathedral. A third of this was used to purchase an advowson as an endowment, the royal licence to transfer it to the cathedral cost almost as much and the remainder was spent on repairing the chancel and employing a chaplain there.[109] This was a comparatively modest outlay; William Bosco gave the vicars choral of Lichfield 140 marks to establish his in 1325 and a century later John Frank gave the dean and chapter of Salisbury his manor of Edmosham in Dorset.[110] In a relatively poor cathedral without many valuable prebends few chantries were established by canons. Between 1280 and 1540 only eleven canons founded chantries in Exeter cathedral, though there were six episcopal foundations over the same period.[111] By contrast there were considerably more in the richer cathedrals of York and Lincoln which had some very wealthy prebends. At the latter over a similar period, 1300–1540, there were twenty-one foundations by residentiaries.[112] There were even more at York, over sixty the majority of which were the work of canons.[113] Like obits, chantries were carefully planned and their foundation documents set out in detail who the beneficiaries were, how the income should be distributed and often many of the liturgical details. William Bosco, the chancellor of Lichfield, intended his to honour the cathedral's patron St Chad whose mass was to be said every day at the altar dedicated to him in the nave. During the mass he would be prayed for by name in the second collect. He would also have the office of the dead said daily for the benefit of his soul and a requiem mass would be celebrated annually after which 7s were to be distributed to the poor in bread, pease or beans.[114] John Frank was more precise still in his will of 1433. The masses to be said each day of the week were set out, beginning on Sunday with the mass of the Trinity followed by masses of the angels, apostles, martyrs, confessors, virgins and of Our Lady on Saturday. In addition he wrote the prayers to be used during it to ensure that his name was included.[115] Vanity and piety were combined in many chantries, the grandest of which attempted to provide a form of immortality on earth. By 1500 secular cathedrals had become great engines of prayer for the souls of the generations of their clergy.

---

108 DRO D&C 2223.
109 See note 96.
110 Savage, *Magnum Registrum Album*, no. 694 (Bosco); *Reg. Chichele Canterbury* ii, 591–5 (Frank).
111 Orme, *Minor Clergy*, 133–7.
112 Bradshaw and Wordsworth, *Lincoln Statutes*, iii, 589–99.
113 Dobson, 'Later Middle Ages', 95.
114 Savage, *Magnum Registrum Album*, no. 694.
115 *Reg. Chichele Canterbury* ii, 591–5.

Almsgiving was practised generously by resident canons and was as much intended for the welfare of their souls as masses and obits.[116] There was no distinction between religion and charity in the medieval mind. Charity was an essential part of the Christian life and had been practised by Christ. Popular devotion stressed the importance of the seven works of mercy: to feed the hungry; give drink to the thirsty; clothe the naked; visit the prisoner; shelter the stranger; visit the sick; and bury the dead. All charitable giving was religious in motive, intended to benefit an individual's soul and those of the faithful departed, for it was both expected and desired that recipients of alms would pray for the donors. Wills tell us a great deal about the charitable interests and intentions of canons at and after their deaths. It is much harder to find direct evidence of almsgiving while they were alive, though it undoubtedly went on, if perhaps on a relatively modest scale. The hospitality kept by residentiaries had a charitable dimension and was partly intended to feed the poor. The Exeter residentiaries of the 1530s had a reputation for liberality to the poor.[117] Collectively chapters practised almsgiving more formally; on Maundy Thursday 1339 the dean and chapter of Exeter fed sixty paupers with bread and drink and gave them 1d each.[118] Post-mortem charity was an obligation of residentiaries who at most cathedrals were granted their income from residence for a year after their deaths to enable them to meet it. The principal forms of charity were gifts to churches and religious houses, educational bequests (which will be discussed in the next chapter), alms for the poor, and public works, such as the upkeep of bridges and roads. Canons' families and wider kin frequently appear in their wills but generally occupy a less prominent part in them than in those of the laity. The celibate clergy had no wives or legitimate children who, according to medieval custom, were entitled to a third each of his estate. Bequests to kin tended to be modest, small sums of money, pieces of plate, or household items.[119] Greater generosity was shown to kin bound for a career in the Church. Provision for their education is a common theme of their wills. Most of canons' charity was focused on the people and places they had some connection with or responsibility for, particularly their birthplaces and places where they were beneficed, as well as kinsfolk. A few weeks before his death in 1460 Thomas Salisbury, the archdeacon of Bedford, cast his mind back to the places he had been associated with during his life. Many were remembered in his will from his family and connections at his birthplace, Stow on the Wold, to Shrewsbury where he had been dean of the collegiate church of St Chad, and

---

116 For a general discussion of medieval charity see Swanson, *Church and Society*, Chapter 6 and M. Rubin, *Charity and Community in Medieval Cambridge*, Cambridge, 1987, Chapter 3.
117 DRO ECA Exeter Book 51 fos 342r, 345r.
118 DRO D&C 2792.
119 This was the pattern at Exeter between 1300 and 1455 (Lepine, *Canons of Exeter Cathedral*, 223).

his parish churches of Peasemore near Newbury, Kettering and Yelvertoft, as well as the Close in Lincoln.[120]

Many were as meticulous as Salisbury in remembering the places they were connected with. Even so, few provided for all their benefices, instead making bequests to those they felt closest to or the churches they still held at their deaths. The other cathedrals and collegiate churches in which they held prebends were often remembered but in contrasting ways according to the closeness of their connection. Some were generous and sought prayers and founded an obit, but others made a more perfunctory gesture with a small gift indicating only distant links with the church or made no bequest at all. The prebendal churches and estates of residentiaries in their own cathedrals in particular received bequests, and a significant minority chose to be buried there rather than in the cathedral, like William Smith (d. 1528), archdeacon of Lincoln and prebendary of Sutton cum Buckingham, who wished to be interred in the chancel of Buckingham church.[121] The types of gifts to parish churches varied widely, though they were generally small: vestments and liturgical books occur most frequently, followed by donations to the fabric, altar plate and vessels. William Smith was unusual in both the generosity and nature of his bequest to Buckingham church, a contribution of £4 towards the cost of a pair of organs.[122] Scarcely a will survives without some bequests to religious house. As with parish churches these tended to be small gifts of a few shillings in return for prayers for the testator's soul. Even after a fifty-year career at Exeter, Nicholas Braybrooke left nothing to the religious houses of the diocese, preferring instead to support the friars at Guildford and the important monasteries at Chertsey and Merton all of which were in his native diocese of Winchester.[123] The friars, principally Dominicans and Franciscans, received most bequests. Virtually all residentiaries gave something to each of the houses in their cathedral cities. Fewer gifts were made to other orders, a reflection of the slackening of interest in the well established orders, such as the Benedictines and Cistercians, in medieval piety. The bequests that were made were often the result of a personal connection or a particular interest in monasticism. Archdeacon Smith's donations to the nuns at Delapre Abbey near Northampton were prompted by the presence of two cousins and a niece there.[124] John Belvoir (d.1391), the subdean of Lincoln, chose to support thirteen houses, including most of those in his native archdeaconry of Leicester.[125]

Hospitals did not receive as many alms as churches or religious houses, partly because donors preferred to make provisions for the poor and sick as individuals. Those in a residentiary's diocese or cathedral city were most likely to be recipients of a few shillings. By contrast their inmates and the poor in general were much

---

[120] LAO D&C A/2/35 fos 85v–87r.
[121] Cole, *Lincoln Chapter Acts 1520–36*, 91–4.
[122] Ibid.
[123] Reg. Arundel Canterbury i, fo. 165r.
[124] See note 121.
[125] LAO D&C A/2/28 fo. 41r.

more generously treated. In many cases this formed the largest proportion of canons' almsgiving, though it is impossible to calculate how much was given because bequests were often generalised, lacking figures or totals, and the instructions given in wills may not have been carried out. The intentions set out in wills could be lavish; the Wells residentiary Richard Bruton (d.1417) carefully allocated over £50 to the poor of the places he was connected with, much of it explicitly for the sake of the souls of his kin and benefactors.[126] The usual sums left by canons to individuals ranged from ½d to 3d but sometimes gifts might be in kind, bread, clothing or sheets and blankets, or for particular purposes such as the payment of taxes. Specific types of recipients might be singled out: sick paupers, mothers in childbirth, prisoners, and deserving girls who were given marriage portions, reflecting the seven works of mercy. Almsgiving to the poor after a canon's death usually began at his funeral which invariably made provision for them. Their funerals were often the occasion for substantial distributions of money, food and clothing; in 1460 the poor of Lincoln shared 100s given by Nicholas Wymbush and an equal sum from Thomas Salisbury who also paid for twelve of them to be dressed in black and carry torches on the day of his burial.[127] These payments might continue in subsequent weeks. William Skelton of Lincoln wanted his executors to distribute £10 to the poor a week after his death, and to give 2d each week to prisoners, the poor or the sick for a year afterwards.[128] If the residue of an estate was given to the poor payments were spread over several years. On a smaller scale but over a longer period paupers received modest sums from the income of some canons' obits. In their charity to the poor residentiaries showed a strong sense of responsibility for their prebendal churches and estates, parish churches and cathedral cities. Paupers from all three were regularly and carefully singled out as recipients. Precentor Hickeling of Exeter (d.1416) set aside part of the residue of his estate for the poor parishioners and tenants of the dean and chapter.[129] His contemporary at Wells and Exeter, Robert Rygge, was more explicit in directing part of the residue of his estate to be used to make up for his negligence in the place where he had been beneficed and from which he had drawn an income.[130] The community as a whole benefited from gifts for the repair of roads and bridges, a common theme in medieval wills and those of canons. No doubt this was partly a consequence of their familiarity with their short comings as they travelled extensively on ecclesiastical business. Richard Bruton must have known the road from Wells to the episcopal palace at Wookey well, having travelled it many times as the bishop's vicar general and president of the consistory court, and bequeathed 20s for its repair in 1417.[131]

Despite being among the wealthiest clergy of their day, few residentiaries had

126 *Somerset Medieval Wills 1383–1500*, 87–98.
127 LAO D&C A/2/35 fos 87v–88r (Wymbush), 85v–87r (Salisbury).
128 LAO D&C A/3/2 fos 12v–15r.
129 *Reg. Stafford Exeter*, 410–11.
130 PRO PROB 11/2A fo. 161v.
131 See note 126.

the resources to establish their own foundations. Even the great ecclesiastics resident at York Minster, who were among the richest residentiaries in the kingdom, rarely founded religious houses, confining their energies to creating chantries. Generally, new foundations by the clergy were the work of the episcopate. However, there were a handful of exceptions, most of them small hospitals for the poor and sick, founded by canons. The most remarkable of these was the transformation of the parish church at Manchester into a collegiate body, the forerunner of the present cathedral, by Thomas de la Warr in 1421. He was not only rector of the church by had been lord of Manchester since inheriting the barony of de la Warr from his brother in 1398.[132] The wealth this brought him provided the opportunity to found the collegiate church and endow it generously. The new foundation was established with a master, eight chaplains, four clerks and six choristers and was intended as a chantry to pray for the souls of Henry V, Bishop Burghill of Lichfield and the de la Warr family.[133] Thomas de la Warr may have modelled it on the corporate life at Lincoln where he was resident for over a decade from 1385/6–96/7.[134] His contemporary in the Close at Lincoln, Thomas Aston, refounded the hospital at Spital-on-the Street, some ten miles north of the city, in the 1390s. The existing chantry there under the patronage of the dean and chapter was turned into a hospital for seven paupers. These were to be chosen with some care to ensure they were deserving cases and might include any old or sick clergy provided there was a vacancy. As with all other foundations the beneficiaries were expected to pray for the souls of the founder, his kin and benefactors, including John of Gaunt and his consort Katherine Swynford and the dean and chapter of Lincoln. The inmates of Aston's hospital were asked to say twenty Paternosters with the Ave, recite the creed three times and after vespers repeat the psalm *De Profundis*.[135] John Stevens' almshouse was unusual in being even more closely linked to the cathedral where he was resident, Exeter. Known as 'Our Lady House', it was founded around 1450 for thirteen poor men, to represent Christ and the twelve apostles. Servants of the chapter and residentiaries had priority of admission, as did those who could help 'priests in the administration of the sacrament'.[136] Thomas Milley, like Aston, refounded an existing almshouse at Lichfield; it provided for fifteen women.[137] The canons of Lincoln, Lichfield and Exeter supported these founda-tions at their inception and subsequently; they feature in their wills.[138]

Executor's accounts enable us to gain some impression of how many of these

---

[132] BRUO ii, 1111.

[133] CPL vii, 475.

[134] Edwards, *Secular Cathedrals*, 345–7.

[135] E. Venables, 'An Historical Notice of the Hospital of "Spital-on-the-Street" Lincolnshire', AASRP, xx, 1889–90, 264–98.

[136] DRO D&C 4593, 3625 fos 171v–172v.

[137] VCH *Staffordshire*, iii, 275–8.

[138] Two Exeter canons, John Morton and John Pyttes left small sums to Stevens Almshouse (DRO Chanter Ms 12 part 1 fo. 139r, Chanter Ms 12 part 2 fo. 51v).

intentions were carried out. Unfortunately they are scarce, but those of Dean Kilkenny of Exeter yield a fascinating and detailed picture of almsgiving by an important and wealthy cleric at the beginning of the fourteenth century, as well as revealing how extensive and executor's discretion and activities might be. The dean's estate was valued at £916 18s ¾d, the equivalent of a wealthy York residentiary, of which £200 was spent on almsgiving, amounting to a quarter of the estate as £105 was written off in bad debts. It was spent over the nine years, 1302–c.1311, that the accounts cover. Although the dean's will does not survive, the accounts make it clear that most of this was spent at the discretion of his principal executor and kinsman William Kilkenny. Only £20 was given in the form of legacies, mainly to local religious houses, notably the Franciscans in Exeter who received £13. A total of £12 15s 11d was given to the poor at the dean's funeral. Some £50 was given in small sums by William Kilkenny in what seems to be a rather ad hoc manner to a variety of individuals, mainly the wives and families of tenants. Only one payment, a modest 47s to prisoners, is actually described as a work of mercy. The largest distribution, of £103, reflects the dean's sense of responsibility to the places from which he drew his income. It was made to poor tenants and parishioners on seven decanal estates over a three year period from 1304 to 1306 and consisted of cash payments, remission of debts and manorial dues, clothing, marriage portions, and for a few, manumission. A further £32 of debts owed by poor tenants was cancelled. Other gifts, such as religious ornaments to churches, make up the total.[139] Christian charity on this scale was unusual because of Kilkenny's exceptional wealth, but the principle and its practice, if more modestly was accepted by all residentiaries.

The general impression of religious orthodoxy and conservatism of residentiaries is reinforced by an examination of the nine chapters in the late 1520s and 1530s. There were few reforming voices from within the residentiary body. The full extent of their conservatism emerges as the Henrician Reformation got underway in the early 1530s in their responses to the royal supremacy and the dissolution of the monasteries. With few exceptions there was no enthusiasm and little sympathy. While most flowed with the tide and accepted change a small minority actively opposed it, at the cost of further preferment and in some cases their careers and even their lives. Henry Litherland, the treasurer of Lincoln, preached against the supremacy in 1534 and four years later was executed for his part in the Pilgrimage of Grace.[140] His colleague at Lincoln, James Mallet, a former chaplain of Katherine of Aragon, survived for a little longer but was executed for treason in 1542.[141] A similar fate had befallen Edward Powell of Salisbury in 1540.[142] Where the issue of reform was raised in a chapter it was usually on the appointment of an outsider, otherwise chapter act books are

139 See note 96.
140 *BRUO 1500–1540* 371.
141 *BRUC* 386–7.
142 *BRUO* iii, 1510–11.

almost silent on the issue. The arrival of a reforming dean, Simon Heynes, among the conservative chapter of Exeter in 1537 provoked a long and acrimonious feud which only died down on his departure.[143] The Salisbury chapter was split on the issue of reform, with the chancellor, Thomas Parker, an ally of Cromwell and supported by a reforming bishop, Nicholas Shaxton, leading the protests to the king about the respect still given to the pope in the cathedral. His conservative opponents seem to have lead a rearguard action of passive resistance to him. An anonymous set of 'Articles for the Reform for the Church of Salisbury' of 1537 complained of the failure to keep proper chapter meetings or records of decisions made and the poor state of the accounts. It went on to denounce the observation of certain saints days and use of relics against the king's wishes.[144] More effective in hindering reform was the deprivation of Bishop Shaxton in 1539 and his replacement by the more conservative Bishop Capon.[145] At Salisbury, as elsewhere, the Henrician Reformation left the secular cathedrals comparatively unscathed. Radical change was postponed until the Edwardian Reformation and the dissolution of the chantries in 1548.

The Moral Failings of Canons

Flagrant breaches of clerical discipline by residentiaries were rare. Their failure to live up to their religious vocations lay more in their readiness to accept a comfortable life in the close. The most serious charges made against John Paxton by Bishop Rede of Chichester during his visitation of the cathedral in 1403 were that he had pilfered some of its timber, misappropriated 20s from the fabric fund and used St Faith's chapel as a short cut when going to and from his house to the choir for services.[146] Paxton's lapses were typical; there are remarkably few records of more serious failings or criminal activity, though some individuals stand out. The perennial problem of clerical incontinence did affect canons, but by comparison with the minor clergy, whose punishment for fornication was regular and frequent, they seem remarkably chaste. This is no doubt to some extent a distortion resulting from their status which protected them from disciplinary proceedings. Even so residentiaries were from time to time punished. The unfortunate William Chokke of Wells admitted the charge of adultery against him in 1491 and offered to pay a £10 fine should he repeat the offence. The chapter were not convinced by his protestations and banished him from the Close and city for two years with the loss of his residence payments.[147] This

143 Orme, *Exeter Cathedral*, 94–9.
144 Salisbury D&C Reg. Blacker fo. 151.
145 See Edwards, 'Salisbury Cathedral', 185–6, for a fuller account of this.
146 *Reg. Reade Chichester*, 116–17.
147 HMC *Wells* ii, 122.

suggests they expected high standards of behaviour from canons. Another Wells canon, John Edmonds, was treated more leniently for the same offence in 1510 when he was fined 33s 4d to pay for some new vestments.[148] Thomas Blythe of Lichfield was found guilty of incontinence twice, first in 1525 and again in 1528.[149] In the calm of the close some sought to clear their consciences by seeking absolution for the misdemeanours of their youth. In 1398 Richard Tyttesbury of Exeter received papal absolution for his behaviour as a rowdy and ambitious student at Oxford where he had become involved in a brawl, revealed confessions and said mass in unconsecrated places.[150] Ambition led the most headstrong into trouble in the course of their early careers; William Gulden's use of violence to gain a canonry has already been seen.[151] Such lapses resulted in a small proportion being excommunicated and more rarely imprisoned. Most of these events had occurred before they entered residence and were frequently connected with disputes over benefices and failure to pay papal dues.[152] Criminal activity was more unusual still, though canons were occasionally charged with debt, trespass and nuisance. An exceptional and protracted case of debt resulted in the imprisonment of the Exeter residentiary William Pencrich at the suit of the city's mayor.[153] Brawling in the close or city was more likely to involve canons' servants than the canons themselves, though the jury in a case in the Close of Exeter in 1426 reported that Canon Redman had attacked a citizen, to which he replied that he was acting in self-defence.[154]

Heresy was virtually unknown among canons, indeed they were normally in the forefront of efforts to stamp it out. The most serious case was that of Nicholas Hereford, who as we have seen resided at Hereford in the early fifteenth century. He took up Wycliffite ideas while studying theology at Oxford. Having been condemned at the 'Earthquake Council' at Black Friars in 1382 and excommunicated, he fled abroad seeking papal support. Instead, he was again condemned and this time imprisoned for life. A chance riot in June 1385 enabled him to escape but on his return to England he was imprisoned for a second time in 1387. Following his recantation and absolution in 1391 he was restored to favour which included presentation to the treasurership of Hereford. Back in his native diocese he was active with the bishop in Lollard trials where he seems to have remained until his withdrawal to the Charterhouse in Coventry in 1417.[155] Robert Rygge, who combined residence at Wells and Exeter, was another canon known to have

---

148 Ibid. 219–20.
149 LJRO D30/2/1/4 fos 19r, 47v.
150 CPL v, 88–9.
151 See Chapter 2.
152 See Chapter 2 for some examples of this.
153 PRO C1/17/322.
154 DRO MCR 4–5 Hen V. A fuller account of the episode from Redman's point of view can be found in Reg. Lacy Exeter i, 158–9.
155 BRUO ii, 913–15.

been associated with Wycliffite ideas, though in his case it was little more than a brief flirtation rather than the commitment shown by Nicholas Hereford. When chancellor of Oxford university in 1382 he was accused of having some sympathy with heretical views or at least being prepared to turn a blind eye to them. Unlike Hereford, he quickly submitted himself to the authority of Archbishop Courtenay and subsequently took vigorous action against the Oxford Lollards.[156] Much more typical were the roles of Geoffrey Scrope and Thomas Cotte, two Lincoln residentiaries of the early 1380s, in combatting heresy. They were entrusted by Bishop Buckingham with the examination of the views of the leading Lollard William Swinderby.[157] Many residentiaries at other cathedrals were also active against heresy either in the course of the duties as diocesan officials or by special commission from the bishop.

Two contrasting residents at Exeter stand out as examples of the turbulent priests occasionally found in chapters. William Pyl was being disciplined by one authority or another almost continually from the time he obtained his canonry in 1371 until his death in 1392. The acquisition of his prebend took eight years and led him to be outlawed and imprisoned. There was also trouble over his presentation to the rectory of Combe in Teignhead (Devon). Disputed rights of presentation led to an order for the sequestration of his goods in 1375 and the case dragged on for another three years.[158] Once in possession he neglected his parish and was punished with a further sequestration in 1391.[159] The dean and chapter had four brushes with him: twice in 1383 over debt and failing to keep proper residence; in 1389 for not keeping sufficient hospitality; and in 1392 in a quarrel with a vicar choral.[160] The citizens of Exeter found him equally difficult to deal with. In the fourteen years 1378–92 he was involved in nineteen cases in the mayor's court for debt, trespass and damage, and in three of them was fined for using violence.[161] John Cheyne was less regularly troublesome but became involved in much more serious crimes. In 1401 he was alleged to have been active in the earl of Huntingdon's abortive uprising against Henry IV. It was alleged that he had plotted with the earl to exile the king, that he held £500 worth of Huntingdon's plate and jewels, and that he had treasonably assembled forty archers and kept them at Membland.[162] Nothing is known of the truth of these allegations, though Membland is only a few miles from Cheyne's rectory at Ugborough. The same year he was accused of murder, perhaps in the course of

---

[156] McFarlane, *Wycliffe and English Non-Conformity*, Chapter 4. Two Lincoln canons had similar brushes with Lollardy, Peter Partrich (*BRUO* ii, 1430) and John Hontman (ibid. 987–8).

[157] McFarlane, *Wycliffe and English Non-Conformity*, 108.

[158] *Reg. Brantingham Exeter* i, 200–1, 203.

[159] Ibid. ii, 730–1, 734.

[160] DRO D&C 3550 fos 8v, 9v, 52v, 77v.

[161] DRO MCR 11–12 Rd II, 13–14 Rd II, 14–15 Rd II.

[162] *CPR 1399–1401*, 552; *Calendar of Miscellaneous Inquisitions 1399–1401*, no. 65.

the failed uprising, and in 1405 his goods were declared forfeit.[163] Pyl and Cheyne and a handful of others were exceptional.[164] The majority of residentiaries no doubt had their share of temptations and vexations, but on the whole exercised more self control.

---

[163] *CFR 1399–1405*, 131.

[164] Two other canons were accused of treason: John Whelpdale of Lichfield for his loyalty to the Lancastrian cause in 1471 (*CCR 1468–76* no. 703) and John Harrington of York was caught up in the earl of Lincoln's uprising in 1487 (*BRUO* ii, 874).

8

The Interests and Activities of Residentiary Canons, II: Intellectual and Cultural Interests and Achievements

There can have been few canons who in the course of their working lives in royal and ecclesiastical service did not compile or consult formularies or notebooks containing model documents, legal precedents, cases and learned opinion on most aspects of administration. These *quaterni*, as they are often rather blandly referred to, survive in considerable numbers and give an insight into the intellectual horizons and concerns of their owners. Though predominantly practical, they are not solely utilitarian and often contain miscellaneous jottings on a wide range of subjects. The formulary belonging to the Exeter canon William Browning (d.1455) survives in the British Library and enables us gain some impression of his outlook. The bulk of it is made up documents and cases from the diocesan administration he spent much of his time engaged in and in this respect faithfully reflects his preoccupations. But it also contains a perhaps unique thumbnail sketch of him alongside which are a series of verses in bad Latin.[1] Though his Latin was poor he was familiar with some classical literature; there are quotations from Ovid and Virgil.[2] These are followed by part of the speech, in elegiac couplets, made by Pope John XXIII on his deposition at the Council of Constance in 1415, which Browning probably came across on one of the visits he is known to have made to the Curia around this time.[3] The concluding verses are a series of moral precepts offering useful guidance to a practicing canon lawyer, warning of the need to be honest and listing vices to be avoided. The same collection of manuscripts contains the formulary of another

---

[1] BL Harleian Ms 3300. The sketch is fo. 296r.

[2] Ovid's *Non honor est sed onus assumere nomine honoris* which is quoted among a series of verses about death (H. Walther, *Carmina Medii Aevi Posterioris Latina*, 9 volumes, Gottingen, 1959–86, part II/3 (*Proverbia Sententiaeque Latinitatis Medii Aevi*) no. 19544). The quotation from Virgil's the well known *Omnia vincit amor sed munus vincit amorem*.

[3] *Magnum Oecumenicum Constantiense Concilium*, ed. H. von der hardt, Francofurti-Lipsiae, 1692–1742, iv, 299. For Browning's career see *BRUO* i, 282–3.

Exeter canon, Chancellor Nicholas Gosse (d.1486).[4] It reflects his theological training and interests and mainly consists of a copy of Bishop Quinel of Exeter's *Synodalia* drawn up in the late thirteenth century. This was clearly a working copy and is heavily annotated in the margins. Like Browning's, it reveals some of its owner's wider interests. There is a description of a comet by Henry Sutton and a drawing of it dated 1472; perhaps he saw it? Gosse was particularly interested in prophecy and collected a series of them, mainly taken from the prophecies of Merlin recorded by Geoffrey of Monmouth in his *History of the Kings of Britain*, and including one by the fourteenth-century French friar Jean de Roquetaillade.[5]

In many ways Browning and Gosse were typical of the intellectual strengths and limitations of residentiary chapters. Both were highly educated men who had studied for many years at university.[6] Some were among the leading academic figures of their day, holders of high office in the colleges and universities of Oxford and Cambridge whose learning was recognised by contemporaries; the Exeter residentiaries on the eve of the Reformation had a reputation as scholars and patrons of education.[7] However, few of the greatest scholars of the late medieval period, those with a national or international reputation, spent much time in cathedral closes. Men like Walter Burley, Thomas Bradwardine, John Wycliffe and the humanist scholars William Grocyn and Thomas Linacre were active elsewhere, at the universities or in episcopal households. Even John Colet, the distinguished scholar and reforming dean of St Paul's, preferred to live at the Charterhouse at Sheen rather than his cathedral close.[8] There were a few exceptions to this pattern when closes benefited from the presence of some outstanding individuals. The theologian Richard Fitzralph spent a brief period resident at Lichfield in 1345–46 at much the same time that another distinguished theologian, Thomas Buckingham, was living at Exeter in 1348.[9] Robert Fleming, a leading humanist scholar and the first fifteenth-century Englishman to learn Greek, had a greater impact as dean of Lincoln.[10] He became resident in 1462/3 on his return from the Curia, where he had spent five years in royal and papal service, and stayed until at least 1465/6 and perhaps 1473. After a further period in Rome from 1473 to 1478 he returned to the Close in 1478/9

4 BL Harleian Ms 220. The prophecies are fos 74v–76v.
5 M. Reeves, *The Influence of Prophecy in the Later Middle Ages*, Oxford, 1969, 225–8. A reference to Jerome Herford may be a mistaken reference to Henry Herford a Dominican friar interested in the prophecies of Joachim of Fiore (ibid. 169–70). The prophecies of Merlin appear in Geoffrey of Monmouth's *History of the Kings of Britain*, Part 5.
6 *BRUO* i, 282–3 (Browning), ii, 795 (Gosse).
7 DRO ECA Exeter Book 51 fos 341, 342r, 345r, 346.
8 *BRUO* i, 462–4.
9 A. Gwynn, 'The Sermon Diary of Richard FitzRalph', *Proceedings of the Royal Irish Academy*, xliv Section C; DRO D&C 3766 fo. 2r.
10 His career is set out in *BRUO* ii, 699–700.

and remained until his death in 1483.[11] Another leading humanist, Thomas Chandler, was dean of Hereford and resident there from 1482/3 until he died in 1490.[12] Their contemporary fellow humanist John Gunthorpe occupied a similar position at Wells in the years up to his death in 1498.[13]

Book Ownership

The books canons owned give us some idea of their interests and intellectual horizons. The precise scale of their book ownership is difficult to judge from the fragmentary evidence which survives, but it is clear that it was widespread, as might be expected from such a highly educated elite. Many had at least a shelf of books and some a substantial library. Most inventories of their possessions, a more reliable guide than wills and chance references, list several. Thomas Cotte's inventory, dated 1384, listed twenty-four volumes in his library at Lincoln, and several of them contained two or three works.[14] Martin Collins' at York was exceptional with over 150 volumes, as many as an episcopal or cathedral library.[15] The books canons owned give a generally accurate impression of their interests and reflect their known preoccupations.[16] Canons emerge as practical and conscientious men possessing the books necessary for their position in the Church, with the emphasis on liturgical, legal and theological works in roughly that order of priority, yet also aware of some of the more recent developments in these fields and with broader interests in such subjects as history and literature. Liturgical works dominate. Almost all had their own personal breviary and most also had missals and psalters, though the more specialised musical books such as antiphonals and tropers were less common. With lawyers forming the majority of graduate canons and many of them actively involved in diocesan administration it is not surprising that legal texts formed an important part of their libraries. The basic texts of civil and canon law appear regularly and alongside them the principal commentaries, for these were working libraries. The Hereford residentiary Richard Rudhale (d.1476) built up much of his collection of nine books in Italy while studying at Padua in the early 1440s where he bought and had copied four commentaries on canon law. One of these shows his awareness of more recent scholarship and contains commentaries on the Decretals by Italian

---

[11] LAO D&C Bj/2/16 s. a. 1462/3–65/6, Bj/3/1, Bj/3/2 s. a. 1480/1–82/3.

[12] HCA R518–25, R170–3.

[13] No residence figures survive for this period but Gunthorpe is recorded as present at Wells in 1493 and 1496 and called a residentiary in 1498 (HMC Wells ii, 133–4, 146, 150).

[14] LAO D&C Dvi/14/1.

[15] Test Ebor iv, 279–307.

[16] The book ownership of the Exeter canons of 1300–1455 is analysed in Lepine, Canons of Exeter Cathedral, 243–54. The following discussion is based on this and the evidence of the surviving wills of residentiaries at other cathedrals.

Masters of c.1400.[17] These remained in regular use at Hereford where he acted
as vicar general to successive bishops in the 1450s and 1470s.[18]

Theological books were generally less common, with works by Augustine and
Aquinas widely owned together with academic commentaries by authors such as
Robert Holcote and William of Nottingham. Popular compilations of theology
can also be found in these libraries. Chancellor Cotte of Lincoln, a doctor of
theology, included works by Augustine, Aquinas and Anselm, Boethius' *Conso-
lation of Philosophy*, and several commentaries on the gospels in his collection.[19]
The works of the mystic Richard Rolle, mainly his commentaries, were popular
among residentiaries. Henry Webber, who ran both the cathedral and the diocese
from the deanery at Exeter for most of the 1460s and 1470s, was particularly
concerned with combating heresy.[20] He owned copies of William Woodford's
Tract Against Wycliffe and Richard Ullerston's *Defensorium Dotacionis Ecclesie*, a
defence of Church property, one of the issues raised by Wycliffe, as well as
Wycliffe's own *De Mandatis*.[21] Bibles are surprisingly rarely listed. Canons'
conscientiousness is reflected in their widespread possession of practical handbooks for priests, particularly the *Pupilla Oculi* by John Burgo, which quickly
circulated among them after its production in the early 1380s. Books of sermons
and the lives of saints, especially the *Legenda Aurea* of James of Voragaine, were
as common. History was the most popular subject of the non-religious books.
There was often space for a volume of chronicles in their libraries. Thomas
Austell's included one containing works by Geoffrey of Monmouth and Henry
of Huntingdon among others.[22] Other subjects are found less frequently but
there are examples of grammar books, medical treatises, and classical literature.
Science is hardly represented beyond Bartholomew the Englishman's encyclo-
pedia *De Proprietatibus Rerum* which was relatively widespread. One of the more
curious interests was Simon Stalworth's in the Turks. He owned two books about
them one of which was a tract about their customs. In all other respects he seems
to have had a conventional career in royal service and a long period in residence
at Lincoln.[23]

Though book ownership broadly reflects canons' academic training, their
interests ranged more widely. William Duffield (d.1453) had a significant collection of medical books but did not qualify in medicine.[24] Canon and civil lawyers
often had one or two theological works in their libraries and non-graduates
owned books. The breadth of interests is well illustrated by the library of some

[17] Thomson, *Hereford Cathedral Library*, xxiii.
[18] *BRUO* iii, 1603.
[19] See note 14.
[20] *BRUO* iii, 2005 sets out his career.
[21] Bod. Lib. Ms Bodley 333; DRO D&C 3516; *BRUO* iii, 2005.
[22] *BRUO* i, 78.
[23] *BRUO* iii, 1733; he was resident from 1489/90 to 1508/9 (LAO D&C Bj/3/2 s. a.
    1489/90–95/6, Bj/3/3 s. a. 1501/2–8/9).
[24] *BRUO* i, 601–2.

thirty books belonging to Owen Lloyd, a Welshman and Exeter residentiary, most of which can still be seen in the cathedral library at Hereford. He trained in civil law, becoming a doctor by 1458, and spent many years in diocesan administration, first at Lichfield and then for nearly a decade at Exeter until his death in 1478.[25] Most of his books were practical legal texts and commentaries but his library also contained some theology, a compendium of Richard Rolle's devotional works and some of his commentaries, the *Pupilla Oculi*, collections of sermons and some classical literature, an anthology of Ovid, Aristotle's *Rhetoric* and work by Terence, which together suggest an interest in preaching. An interest in his native land no doubt accounts for his copy of Gerald of Wales' *Itinerary through Wales*.[26] Much the same impression is given by an examination of a complete library, also from Exeter, which belonged to Dean Kilkenny. Like Lloyd he had a legal and administrative career in the Church, serving as Dean of Arches in 1282.[27] In his large library of sixty-nine volumes law predominated, a total of thirty-one books of the major texts and commentaries. Liturgical works form the second largest group. The dean took his liturgical responsibilities seriously as his possession of several breviaries, missals, and psalters, as well as two tropers, a gradual and an antiphonal suggests. Theology had a smaller place in the library, forming about a tenth of it. The only major authors were Grosseteste and Boethius, the rest being difficult to identify and probably popular compilations. There were three lives of saints, including a *Life of St Richard*, and two books of sermons. His non-religious books consisted of three histories, a copy of the statutes of the realm, a Latin dictionary and a work of classical literature by Seneca.[28]

These were very much working libraries. Fortunately for us some canons annotated their books heavily confirming that they read and thought about them. The Lincoln chancellor Peter Partrich (d.1451) clearly studied his collection of theology extensively. Eleven of his books still remain at Lincoln in the cathedral library and all of them show his annotations. His work went beyond annotation; for several he drew up tables and made indexes and one, Augustine's *City of God*, was partly transcribed by him.[29] He is also known to have transcribed copies of two of Bishop Grosseteste's scientific treatises, a rare venture by a canon into this field.[30] How much of this was done while Partrich was at Lincoln is difficult to say. A leading theologian, he spent much of the period 1408 to 1428 in Oxford but also attended the Council of Constance in 1417 and the Council of Basel in 1432.[31] Thereafter he seems to have spent most of his time at

[25] *BRUO* ii, 1153–4 sets out his career.
[26] Thomson, *Hereford Cathedral Library*, xxiii–iv; Orme, 'Education and Learning', 279.
[27] *The Early Rolls of Merton College Oxford*, ed. J. R. Highfield, OHS, New Series, xviii, 39; CPR 1281–92, 513; Churchill, *Canterbury Administration*, ii, 239.
[28] DRO D&C 2846.
[29] Thomson, *Lincoln Cathedral Library*, xviii.
[30] *BRUO* iii, 1430–1.
[31] Ibid.

Lincoln.[32] Some of his annotations were probably done in the course of his studies at Oxford but it is also probable that they were continued at Lincoln. Other canons are known to have continued their studies in residence. The annotations in Richard Rudhale's legal texts mention his fellow residentiaries at Hereford.[33] Residents at Exeter and Lichfield are known to have copied books; Richard Grenville the *Pupilla Oculi* and John Stevens Richard Rolle's *Commentary on Job* at the former and Roger Walle a volume of history and cathedral statutes at the latter.[34] Canons also commissioned copies. A magnificent edition of the works of Hugo of St Cher in eighteen volumes was presented to Exeter College Oxford in 1469 by Roger Keyes, precentor of Exeter. It was written between 1452 and 1465 to his commission by William Salomon, a Spanish notary.[35] The care canons took with their books indicates how highly they were valued. It was unusual for them to be sold after their deaths. Instead they were given to deserving individuals or institutions, fellow clergy and college libraries being the preferred recipients. This was partly a means of securing prayers for their souls but there was an important underlying aim, the encouragement of learning in the Church. As a result the multiple ownership of books was common. In a remarkable example a breviary can be traced through four generations of Exeter canons in the fifteenth century.[36]

Although the greatest scholars rarely spent much time in cathedrals closes there were some outstanding men among the residentiaries living an active scholarly life. Three individuals, John Newton, John Orum and Thomas Cyrcetur illustrate their qualities and the range of their activities. By any standards John Newton was a remarkable cleric.[37] A distinguished scholar, he rose through the patronage of Bishop Arundel at Ely, entering his service in 1376, and had become a doctor of civil law by 1378. Soon afterwards, in 1382, he became master of Peterhouse College at Cambridge, an office he held for fifteen years. On Arundel's translation to the see of York he returned to his native diocese to become his vicar general in 1390. The reward for this service was his appointment as treasurer of the Minster in 1391 and from 1393 to 1405 and probably until his death in 1414 he was resident there. While in residence he served as Archbishop Scrope's vicar general in 1398 and 1399. Such a bald statement of his career hides

---

[32] He is known to have been resident from 1440/1–49/50 (LAO D&C Bj/2/12–15) and was probably resident for most of the 1430s though no figures survive.

[33] See note 17.

[34] *Reg. Stafford Exeter* 394 (Grenville); DRO Chanter Ms 12 part 1 (Reg. Neville Exeter) fos 125–6 (Stevens); BRUO iii, 1966 (Walle).

[35] A. G. Watson, *Dated and Datable Manuscripts in Oxford Libraries*, 2 vols, Oxford, 1984, i, 131–2.

[36] In 1418 Laurence Haukyn bequeathed his breviary to John Scute who in turn passed it on to John Stevens in 1425. On Stevens' death in 1461 it passed to Henry Webber who bequeathed it to another priest on his death in 1477 (*Reg. Stafford Exeter* 421–2; *Reg. Lacy Exeter* iv, 5–7; DRO D&C 2365).

[37] BRUC 421–2. His career is more fully analysed in Hughes, *Pastors and Visionaries*, 178–9, 200–1.

his scholarly and religious interests and activities at York. With the support of Archbishop Arundel and his circle he helped to make the Minster a centre of scholarship and played an important in spreading awareness of the work and spirituality of Richard Rolle. To this end he compiled a table of chapter headings for Rolle's *Incendium Amoris*, summarising it and adding some of his own observations on the relationship between the active and the contemplative life. Newton and his colleagues in Archbishop Arundel's circle sought to live a mixed life combining the two. He also corrected some manuscripts of Rolle's works using an autographed version.[38] The most eloquent testament to Newton's spirituality and scholarship is his library, of which some eighty-seven books can be identified. Thirty-five of these form a substantial, though not unusual, law collection. Of more interest are his theology books in which Augustine, Aquinas, Gregory and Bernard are well represented. It also included biblical commentaries, books of sermons and work by Anselm and Boethius. One volume contained mystical tracts by John Hovedon, Walter Hilton and Richard Rolle. More remarkable still is his interest in classical literature which forms a substantial part of his library. Among the authors represented in it are Seneca, Macrobius, Frontinus, Cassiodorus and Valerius Maximus. An interest in Ancient Rome also emerges from his historical works that included Giles of Rome's *History of the Destruction of Troy* as well as histories of England by Bede and William of Malmesbury. Newton was also acquainted with the work of Petrach and some of the Italian humanist jurists of the fourteenth century. The bulk of these books remained at the Minster for the use of its clergy. With his bequest Newton effectively refounded the cathedral's library.[39]

Unlike Newton, John Orum (d.1436) studied theology and did not become involved in diocesan administration. He rose from humble beginnings as a vicar choral at Wells whose chapter granted him a dispensation to be absent to study at Oxford in 1388.[40] By 1406 he had gained a doctorate in theology and been appointed archdeacon of Barnstaple. A prebend in Wells followed in 1407/8. For the rest of his career he divided his time between Exeter and Wells, keeping residence in both cathedrals between 1414 and 1421/2, and finally settling at the former during the last fourteen years of his life.[41] Aquinas, Anselm, and Duns Scotus featured among his theological books.[42] Orum's learning enabled him to lecture at Wells and preach at Exeter and elsewhere including the parish church at Woodbury in Devon.[43] A draft of his lectures on the Apocalypse delivered to the clergy at Wells survives. They covered such topics as the unity of the Church, the challenge of heretics and the use of music in church, and used quotations

---

[38] Hughes, *Pastors and Visionaries*, 204–5, 217–23.
[39] BRUC 421–2; Hughes, *Pastors and Visionaries*, 200–1.
[40] BRUO ii, 1405–6.
[41] DRO D&C 3758 fos 122r–163v, 3759 fo. 1v–31v; Colchester, Wells Communars' Accounts, 298.
[42] BRUO ii, 1405–6; Bod Lib Ms Bodley 286.
[43] DRO D&C Vicars Choral 3357.

from the fathers, notably Bernard of Clairvaux.[44] Music in church was one of Orum's particular interests; as we have seen he established an antiphon in Exeter cathedral.[45] His theological interests extended to mysticism; he had a copy of the *Revelations of St Bridget* soon after her canonisation. Thomas Cyrcetur (d.1453) was a slightly older contemporary of Orum's and had entered residence at Wells by 1428 soon after his colleague had retired to Exeter.[46] Like Orum he was a theologian and combined residence at two cathedrals, Salisbury and Wells in the 1430s, an unusual practice. Cyrcetur's gift was for preaching. His books, which he bequeathed to the library at Salisbury, where he had decided to settle from about 1440/1, reveal a great deal about his intellectual outlook and approach to preaching. A recent study of them and his sermons has concluded that his theology was conservative but strongly pastoral. The theology in his library was largely made up of the standard textbooks of the fourteenth century. He was familiar with and used some of the works of Gregory and Anselm. The rest of his books were largely concerned with preaching; an impressive collection of sermons and sermon aids and a copy of the Bible. Like so many of his fellow residentiaries he owned a copy of the *Pupilla Oculi* which became heavily annotated through regular use. Much of Cyrcetur's approach was biblical; the wide range of quotations used in his sermons and notes demonstrate the thoroughness of his knowledge. Preaching was the main focus of his activities; in his own words 'Among all the works of mercy, preaching is most pleasing to God.' In the course of preparing his sermons he compiled indexes of themes and notes on extending and developing ideas. His approach was to teach the basics of the faith as set out in the synodal statutes of the thirteenth century; the fourteen articles of faith, the Ten Commandments, the seven works of mercy, seven deadly sins, seven cardinal virtues and the seven sacraments. From his notes we know some of the themes he returned to and elaborated; the good pastor, the dangers of heresy, confession and penance, and suffering and death. Some of these sermons were preached early in his career as a parish priest at Wellow before he came to Wells and Salisbury, but it is likely he continued at both cathedrals, where regular courses of sermons were given to the laity. Cyrecetur emerges as a conscientious and thoughtful pastor with a strongly developed sense of his role as priest and teacher which he fulfilled in both parish and cathedral close.

The scholarly interests of residentiaries were fostered by cathedral libraries. During the fifteenth century these flourished and were extensively enlarged. Before this a cathedral's books, which were the responsibility of the chancellor, were kept in a rather ad hoc manner at various places around it. Service books were usually chained in the choir, others, such as law texts and books of sermons were placed in the aisles so that the clergy could consult them. The most valuable

---

44 J. I. Catto, 'Wycliff and Wycliffism at Oxford 1356–1439', in Catto, *History of the University of Oxford vol. II*, 258–9.

45 See Chapter 6.

46 The rest of this paragraph is based on R. M. Ball, 'Thomas Cyrcetur, a Fifteenth-Century Theologian and Preacher', *JEH*, xxxvii, 1986, 205–39.

might be kept in chests, as at Hereford where two fourteenth century examples can still be seen. Exeter was the first cathedral to build a new library in 1412, partly to accommodate the growing number of books and partly in response to a bequest conditional on its completion.[47] York, Lincoln and Wells followed soon after. John Newton's munificent gift of books to York Minster in 1414 prompted the building of a library which was completed by 1421–22 with the help of his executor and fellow residentiary Thomas Haxey who supplied the lead for the roof.[48] At the same time, in 1420–22, the new library at Lincoln was being constructed.[49] Episcopal initiative was responsible for the new library above the cloisters at Wells. In his will, drawn up in 1424, Bishop Bubwith gave 1000 marks to complete the north tower and build a library which was to have priority. The residentiaries had already agreed to support it and allocated 300 marks from future entry fines for residence.[50] Around the middle of the fifteenth century work was underway at Salisbury and St Paul's. In January 1445 the Salisbury chapter decided to build a new library and school 'to the honour of God, Our Lady, All Saints and holy mother Church for the increase of faith, knowledge and virtue'.[51] Much less is known about the work at St Paul's but a bequest of books in 1452 refers to a new library.[52] A similar stray reference suggests that rebuilding at Hereford began later and had finished by 1478–9.[53] As at Salisbury and Wells it was built above the cloisters. Construction was in progress at Lichfield in 1490 and completed in 1500 largely at the expense of Dean Heywood and Dean Yotton.[54]

The size of these libraries was relatively modest by the standards of some of the personal libraries of residentiaries. Exeter was one of the larger ones with over 230 books in 1327 and more than 360 by 1506.[55] The York library began modestly with forty books, mostly John Newton's bequest, and by 1536 had grown to 193.[56] Both Hereford and Lincoln had smaller collections of about a hundred. The library at the latter was designed for about a hundred books.[57] The Hereford library was a little bigger, between 112 and 138 volumes and remarkably stable from the twelfth to the fifteenth centuries. Its contents were modernised rather than expanded as new books replaced old ones. The contents of cathedral libraries are less easy to determine.[58] Inventories of 1327 and 1506 give an unusually complete picture of the contents of the library at Exeter. Liturgical,

[47] A. Erskine, V. Hope and J. Lloyd, *Exeter Cathedral*, Exeter, 1988, 46.
[48] C. B. L. Barr, 'The Minster Library', in Aylmer and Cant, *York Minster*, 494–6.
[49] LAO D&C A/2/30 fo. 104r; A/2/32 fo. 14r.
[50] *Somerset Medieval Wills 1501–30*, 326–9.
[51] Salisbury D&C Reg. Hutchins fos 40r, 47r.
[52] Brooke, 'The Earliest Times to 1485', 93.
[53] Thomson, *Hereford Cathedral Library*, xvi–xvii.
[54] Kettle and Johnson, *Lichfield Cathedral*, 166.
[55] Oliver, *Lives*, 301–10, 320–76.
[56] Barr, 'Minster Library', 496.
[57] Thomson, *Lincoln Cathedral Library*, xvii.
[58] See note 53.

theological and legal books predominate, in that order of priority. In 1506 there were about 150 theology books but only half as many on law, perhaps because canons often had their own copies of the principal legal texts. Historical works were well represented but there were few other non-religious books. Scientific and medical works together with classical literature were rare.[59] From what is known of other similar libraries Exeter was fairly typical; civil and canon law and theology predominated at Hereford.[60] Cathedral libraries were used by all their clergy though it is impossible to say to what extent because there are only chance references to books being borrowed, such as the note made of the return of eight books to the library at Lincoln by the executors of Walter Maidstone in 1336.[61] Residentiaries supported their libraries with donations, though generally on a small scale. Cathedral libraries were rarely the recipients of large gifts which were more likely to go to colleges libraries at Oxford or Cambridge.

Educational Patronage

The clergy were among the most generous and most important benefactors of education in medieval England and residentiary canons made a significant contribution to their benefactions. This is hardly surprising given their years of study and academic qualifications, and the careers that a university education had opened up for many of them in royal and ecclesiastical service. They were conscious of their status as the educated elite of the Church and felt a duty to promote the next generation by providing opportunities for learning. Educational bequests commonly appear in their wills. This patronage comprised many forms and institutions according to the inclinations and means of canons; universities, colleges, schools, libraries and individuals were supported. Books, plate, cash, land, buildings and obit foundations were all used to encourage learning. The wealth of residentiaries enabled them to be generous but the creation of new foundations required more resources than most possessed. Generally only those who rose to the episcopate were able to increase educational opportunities on this scale. A handful of former residentiaries established new foundations, notably Walter Stapeldon, a canon and bishop of Exeter, who founded Exeter College at Oxford in 1316.[62] No wealthy resident dignitaries could match Stapeldon's achievement in founding a university college but some founded schools, a smaller and less expensive undertaking. The Wells residentiary John Cole created a grammar school at Faversham in Kent in 1526 and before his death in 1550 the subdean of Lincoln, John Talbot, an illegitimate member of a baronial family, established one at Whitchurch in Shropshire.[63]

Most canons concentrated on supporting an existing institution. The main

[59] See note 55.
[60] See note 53.
[61] See note 57.
[62] Buck, *Politics, Finance and the Church*, chapter 5.
[63] *BRUO* i, 461 (Cole); ib iii, 1844–5 (Talbot).

focus of their benefactions was Oxford and Cambridge colleges which had been so important in the early stages of their careers, though from the fifteenth century some bequests were made to a university rather than a college. While the majority gave to their former colleges a number gave to more than one. Edward Derby, the archdeacon of Stow from 1507 to 1543, generously founded three fellowships at Lincoln College Oxford, his old college, with a gift of £120, but also established one at Brasenose College in 1538.[64] Canons were particularly generous with their books which more often went to a college than the cathedral library and where a significant number remain. The York residentiaries, Richard Andrew and Hugh Trotter, gave the bulk of their libraries to their respective colleges, All Souls at Oxford and Queen's at Cambridge.[65] When money was given it was usually a small sum unless it was intended for a particular purpose such as a building project or to endow fellowships. Archdeacon Southam made a substantial contribution to Lincoln College Oxford, built by Bishop Fleming in whose service he was engaged.[66] Sometimes plate was given, such as the two silver flagons Precentor Porter of Hereford left to New College Oxford in 1524.[67] Both Philip Turville of Lichfield and William Salton of Salisbury encouraged poor scholars by founding loan chests of 100 marks at Oxford in the mid fourteenth century.[68] A generous benefaction was made by John Wyliet, chancellor of Exeter in 1351–83, who gave the bulk of his wealth to his own college, Merton, to found or perhaps re-found an unspecified number of scholarships for poor scholars. They were to be undergraduates, study the arts course for five years, and to be chosen by the college from Wyliet's kin or from the counties near London where the land that supported the scholarships was situated. Two of the scholars were to be chosen by his successors as chancellor of Exeter.[69] Evidence survives showing a fifteenth-century chancellor nominating two of the cathedral's choristers who showed an aptitude for learning to be Wyliet scholars.[70] Richard Dudley, who as precentor was resident at Salisbury from 1517 to his death in 1536, was equally generous to his old college, Oriel at Oxford. In 1521 he gave it the manor and advowson of Swainswick in Somerset to establish two fellowships and six exhibitions.[71] It was much rarer for schools rather than individual pupils to be supported, though as we have seen a handful founded one. Dean Brayleigh paid for a new school-room and house for the schoolmaster of the grammar school at Exeter in 1343–44, and John Austell, a canon of Wells, gave two books to the grammar school there.[72] Parish churches were often recipients of books, many of them

---

[64] BRUO i, 543.
[65] BRUO i 34–5 (Andrew); BRUC 595–6 (Trotter).
[66] BRUO iii, 1732–3.
[67] Ibid. 1503.
[68] Ibid. 1918 (Turville), 1668 (Salton).
[69] *Registrum Annalium Collegii Mertonensis 1483–1521*, ed. H. E. Salter, OHS Old Series, lxxvi, 1923, 513–17.
[70] DRO D&C 3625 fos 182v–183v.
[71] BRUO i, 598–9.
[72] Orme, *Education in the West of England*, 47–8, 85.

liturgical. This was part of a deliberate attempt to raise the standard of clerical ministry by improving the education of the parish clergy. After liturgical works the most common books given to churches were the popular manuals for parish priests, the *Pupilla Oculi* and the *Pars Oculi*. Thomas Aston's donation of the *Pars Oculi* to the vicar of Skellingthorpe, a few miles from the Close at Lincoln, in 1401 was accompanied by the instruction that it was to remain in the church for the use of his successors.[73]

Alongside their support for institutions canons frequently made provisions for individuals, most often to those named and known to them, but also to scholars in general. Robert Wymbush (d.1478), a subdean of Lincoln, paid for the son of a kinsman to go to grammar school for a year and his fellow residentiary Robert Aiscough offered his namesake a set of law texts if he went to university.[74] The Wells residentiary John Upton (d.1396) gave his cousin Walter London the legal books he had already lent him while he was at Oxford.[75] London graduated with an MA by 1403 and went on to become a pluralist on a modest scale in the diocese of Worcester.[76] Upton's patronage makes it clear that canons actively supported individuals during their lives as well as after their deaths. Another Wells residentiary Peter Carslegh (d.1535) is known to have maintained a scholar at Oxford in 1496–97.[77] As we have seen residentiaries' households had an educational function and contained scholars, though it is not clear how much teaching was done in them.[78] This sort of educational patronage played a major part in keeping the higher clergy a mainly self-perpetuating oligarchy with membership of a canon's household and a university education a familiar route into it. While their families and wider kin benefited substantially from this, it was not solely directed towards them. Canons sought out promising individuals, especially from places they had some connection with or responsibility for such as their churches and prebendal estates. Thomas Salisbury, another Lincoln residentiary, allocated £10 from his estate to send the poor of the places where he was beneficed to grammar school, while his colleague John Tilney preferred to send his servant to study at Cambridge for a year.[79] The intention behind some of these provisions was to encourage the next generation of priests. Robert Aiscough's bequest included a copy of the *Pupilla Oculi* if his kinsman became a priest.[80] Nicholas Wymbush, an older kinsman and fellow canon of Robert, was more concerned to help graduates who had not yet found benefices. He gave instructions for ten chaplains at Oxford and Cambridge universities to be given 100s each to pray for him.[81] The patronage of these fifteenth century Lincoln

---

[73] LAO D&C A/2/29 fos 17v–18v.
[74] LAO D&C A/2/36 fos 90r–91r (Wymbush); A/2/35 fos 119v–120r (Aiscough).
[75] *Somerset Medieval Wills 1501–30*, 291–4.
[76] *BRUO* ii, 1158–9.
[77] *BRUO* i, 363–4.
[78] See Chapter 6.
[79] LAO D&C A/2/35 fos 85v–87r (Salisbury), fo. 135r (Tilney).
[80] LAO D&C A/2/35 fos 119v–120r.
[81] LAO D&C A/2/35 fos 87v–88r.

canons echoes that of their counterparts at York and both are typical of residentiaries elsewhere.[82] Such bequests relied considerably on the discretion of executors. Martin Collins simply asked his to choose those they thought most deserving.[83] A strong local commitment underlay much of this support and might be expressed in the guidance given to executors. Dean Froucester of Hereford, like John Wyliet, Thomas Salisbury and many others, directed his patronage to places he was connected with. In his will of 1529 he gave money to help two scholars from his native diocese of Worcester and two Hereford choristers.[84] The Exeter canon, William Browning, was even more specific, asking for twenty-four literate boys from his parishes of Ugborough, where he had grown up, and Berrynabor, to be dressed in black and carry a candle at his funeral. If necessary boys from Exeter were to make up the numbers.[85]

Educational patronage, while it expressed a real concern for the encouragement of learning as well as the advancement of relatives and proteges, also had a strong religious motive. It was regarded as a pious duty, a work of mercy and frequently combined with other provisions for canons' souls; it was commonplace to link support for education with a request for prayers. Chaucer's Clerk of Oxford who had 'but litel gold in cofre: . . . bisily gan for the soules preye of hem that yaf hym wherwith to scoleye'.[86] A bequest for prayers could also be a scholarship. The establishment of obits at university colleges was a popular way of combining the welfare scholars with that of a testator's soul. Indeed, part of the function of many educational institutions was to pray for the souls of its founders and benefactors. Robert Wydow, a Wells residentiary who died in 1505, was unusually explicit in his will. He instructed his executors to find a priest studying theology at either Oxford or Cambridge and pay him 100s for three years 'to pray for me and for all theym that I have been occasion of synne unto'.[87] The Chichester residentiary John Plente (d.1483) founded a chantry at King's College Cambridge, where he had been bursar, with an endowment of £100.[88] This patronage of education was not confined to graduates. The Exeter canon Robert Vaggescombe, a keen sportsman who kept a pack of hounds and spent much of his time in the company and service of the earls of Devon and other local gentry, was nevertheless a generous benefactor of education, though not a graduate himself. He bequeathed £90 for the combined purposes of his soul and education; £10 to a chaplain on condition that he studied at Oxford; £60 to be shared among twelve priests, if possible to be poor priests studying at Oxford; and £20 to poor scholars in general.[89]

[82] Dobson, 'Residentiary Canons', 159–60.
[83] *Test Ebor* iv, 279–307.
[84] BRUO ii, 732.
[85] *Reg. Lacy Exeter* iv, 59–61.
[86] *The Works of Geoffrey Chaucer*, ed., F. N. Robinson, 1957, The Canterbury Tales, General Prologue, lines 296–302.
[87] *Somerset Medieval Wills 1501–30*, 88–9.
[88] PRO PROB 11/ 7 fos 55v–56r.
[89] Reg. Courtenay Canterbury fo. 200.

As well as their private interest and patronage, many canons had a public duty to become involved with education through the offices and dignities they held or through their collective membership of the chapter.[90] Two groups of the minor clergy, the choristers and secondaries, were educated while at the cathedral. The choristers were nominally the responsibility of the precentor, though their day to day supervision was delegated to the succentor or a choir master, and their musical education was provided in the cathedral's song school. The chancellor had two particular educational responsibilities. At all but one of the nine secular cathedrals he nominated the city's grammar master, the exception being Exeter where it was the archdeacon of Exeter's duty. At Lincoln this extended to all the schools in the county. Chapters confirmed the appointment of the chancellor's candidate and exercised a general supervisory role over the city's grammar school up to the Reformation. The chancellor was also required to give lectures in theology or canon law for the clergy, though at Hereford this duty belonged to the prebendary of Episcopi who was also the penitentiary. The performance of this duty depended on the conscientiousness of individual chancellors and the importance placed on it by the chapter. When absentee chancellors failed to delegate their responsibility the lectures no doubt lapsed and this probably happened at most cathedrals from time to time. However, there is a good deal of evidence to suggest that the lectures were considered important and were delivered by well qualified men for much of the later middle ages. Chancellors were invariably theologians or canon lawyers. High standards were maintained at York in the first half of the fourteenth century.[91] In the 1350s the Salisbury chapter took steps to ensure they were given and the non-resident chancellor, Simon Sudbury, appointed a deputy.[92] A century later, in 1454, the chapter, which had recently built a new library and theology school, increased their frequency to one a fortnight.[93] All but two of the fifteenth century chancellors of Lincoln were resident and the exceptions only held the office for three years between them. They were particularly well qualified to lecture, holding higher degrees in theology and two, Thomas Duffield and Peter Partrich, were noted preachers.[94] Collectively the chapter was responsible for the cathedral library, as we have seen. There is some evidence to suggest that this occasionally extended to book production. A number of manuscripts of Richard Rolle's works may have been written at Lichfield in the late fourteenth century for Bishop Scrope.[95] Some chapters had particular responsibilities for educational institutions. The Exeter chapter was the trustee of Exeter College Oxford, holding the church of Gwinear

[90] The educational functions of a cathedral are set out in Orme, 'Education and Learning' and the educational responsibilities of the chancellor are examined in Edwards, *Secular Cathedrals*, 194–205.
[91] Dobson, 'Later Middle Ages', 72.
[92] Edwards, *Secular Cathedrals*, 201–2.
[93] Salisbury D&C Reg. Burgh fos 56r–v.
[94] BRUO i, 600–1 (Duffield), iii, 1430 (Partrich).
[95] Hughes, *Pastors and Visionaries*, 203, 205, 214–15.

on its behalf and appointing its chaplain.[96] Lincoln College Oxford's relationship to Lincoln cathedral was somewhat similar; the chapter were patrons of the Bible clerk there.[97] He was an undergraduate at the college to be chosen from the poor clerks among the cathedral's choristers, like two of the Wyliet scholars at Merton. The Salisbury chapter was closely involved with De Vaux College, a unique institution within its close. It was founded in the thirteenth century by Bishop Bridport to support twenty scholars studying theology and the liberal arts at a time when Salisbury was briefly a centre of advanced learning. During the later middle ages the college provided fellowships to enable scholars to study at Oxford. From its foundation the college was the responsibility of the chapter who acted as its patron and supervised it. Its warden was always a member of the chapter and almost without exception a residentiary who could be present regularly.[98] In a more general sense cathedrals had a role in training the clergy. Boys and youths entering as choristers or secondaries were educated and trained in the liturgy as they passed through the cathedral, acquiring standards they brought to their service in the Church outside the close.[99]

Cultural Achievements: Authorship, Music, Art and Architecture

For such a highly educated elite cathedral residentiaries wrote remarkably few books. Most of the little that was done was either undertaken in the course of their studies at university or compiled during their employment in royal and ecclesiastical service. Virtually none of this had any connection with their cathedrals. Few canons spent their time in residence writing books and in this they are broadly typical of the rest of the higher clergy of their age. In the early stages of their careers a number of canons wrote lectures or commentaries on law or theology as part of their study for a higher degree. Others compiled and edited formularies of documents relevant to their administrative duties in Church and state like those of William Browning and Nicholas Gosse. These were evidently considered useful and frequently passed from generation to generation of bureaucrat in the course of which they might be supplemented and expanded. It is likely that many canons would have owned or complied one. In most cases neither the commentaries nor formularies showed much originality. The academic works of the handful of outstanding scholars who spent periods in residence at cathedrals are an exception to this, though they were usually written elsewhere. Richard Fitzralph wrote several treatises, the most important being *De Pauperie Salvatoris* on the subject of Mendicant poverty, after he had left Lichfield and become

[96]   See note 62.
[97]   V. H. H. Green, *The Commonwealth of Lincoln College 1427–1977*, Oxford, 1979, 53–4.
[98]   *VCH Wiltshire*, iii, 369–85.
[99]   Orme, 'Education and Learning', 279–83.

archbishop of Armagh.[100] His contemporary, the theologian Thomas Buckingham, made a significant contribution to the study of free will in a series of commentaries and tractates while at Oxford before entering residence at Exeter.[101] The works of two fifteenth-century Salisbury canons, Richard Ullerston and Nicholas Upton will be considered in the next chapter. The books of the fifteenth century humanist scholars among the residentiaries, while reflecting their studies, were less directly related to them. Dean Fleming, a noted humanist, wrote Latin poetry. His *Lucubratiunculae Tiburtinae*,a collection in praise of Pope Sixtus IV, was written in Rome in the 1470s between his periods of residence at Lincoln.[102] Thomas Chandler, dean of Hereford, wrote four books, all in honour of his patron Bishop Bekyngton of Wells. Three have an autobiographical element; his *Libellus* compares the virtues of Bath and Wells in the light of their rivalry as the episcopal seat of the diocese. In it Chaundler praises his native city of Wells highly. His *Allocutiones* and *Collocutiones* are eulogies to William of Wykeham, the founder of Winchester and New College Oxford where both Chandler and Bekington were educated. The *Liber Apologeticus* is a mystery play chiefly notable for its illustrations. All were written before Chandler arrived at Hereford.[103] John Doget's commentary on Plato's *Phaedo* was also probably written before he took up residence at Salisbury in the 1480s. But as a resident chancellor for much of that decade his humanist learning may have been evident in the lectures he was expected to give.[104]

The historical interests of canons are reflected in the chronicle written by Adam Murimuth who spent periods in residence at Hereford and Exeter in the 1320s and early 1330s before moving to London where most of his writing was done. However, he kept a diary on which his chronicle was partly based, which he presumably kept while a residentiary and he knew of and had read the cathedral's chronicle at Exeter. The anti-papal prejudices that are a major theme of his chronicle were no doubt reinforced by his knowledge of Bishop Grandisson's difficulties with papal provisions at Exeter.[105] Most cathedrals had a chronicle or history to which canons contributed and these will be discussed in the next chapter. More remarkable than Murimuth was William Nassington, an outline of whose career suggests he was a typical canon lawyer preoccupied with diocesan

---

100 *BRUO* ii, 692–4; W. J. Courtenay, *Schools and Scholars in Fourteenth-Century England*, Princeton, New Jersey, 1987, 268.
101 *BRUO* i, 298–9, Courtenay, *Schools and Scholars*, 273–4.
102 *BRUO* ii, 699–700; Weiss, *Humanism in England*, 102.
103 M. R. James, ed., *The Chaundler Ms*, Roxburghe Club, 1916; 'Libellus et Laudibus', ed. G. Williams, *Somerset Archaeological and Natural History Society Proceedings*, xix, 99–121.
104 Cobban, *The Medieval English Universities*, 248; he was resident in 1484–5, 1487–9, the only years after 1480 for which figures survive (Salisbury D&C Communars' Accounts nos 67–76).
105 A. Gransden, *Historical Writing in England c1307 to the Early Sixteenth Century*, 1982, 29–31, 62–7; *Adae Murimuth, Continuatio Chronicarum*, ed. E.M. Thompson, Rolls Series, 1889, 1.

administration. His life was largely spent at Exeter in the service of Bishop Grandisson and where he was resident from 1333 until his death in 1359 apart from c.1344–50 when he was at York as well.[106] It was while at York that he wrote two substantial religious poems in the vernacular, the *Speculum Vitae* and *De Trinitate et Unitate*.[107] The *Speculum Vitae* was among the most popular religious poems in English and exists in forty manuscripts. It was intended to provide the laity and parish clergy with elementary religious knowledge. The poem is elaborately structured round the symbolic number seven: the seven petitions of the Lord's Prayer, the seven gifts of the Holy Spirit, the seven deadly sins and the seven beatitudes and rewards. The seven vices and virtues are discussed at some length to diagnose a penitent's sins and set out their remedies. *De Trinitate et Unitate* is a much shorter work that concentrates on the life and passion of Christ. In both Nassington drew on the pastoral problems he encountered as a diocesan administrator. The *Speculum* is part of a growing body of fourteenth-century instructional and devotional literature including Archbishop Thoresby's *Lay Folks' Catechism* and the handbooks for priests such as John de Burgo's *Pupilla Oculi*. It also forms part of a tradition of such literature produced at York under successive archbishops, notably Thoresby and Arundel. Nassington's authorship of two religious poems reminds us that not all diocesan administrators had a narrowly institutional and legal mentality as their career outlines and formularies might indicate.

Musical canons were few and far between. Responsibility for music in the cathedral lay with the precentor, but this was usually delegated to his deputy, the succentor. During the fourteenth century as more complex polyphonic music developed as part of the liturgy in honour of the Virgin Mary in the Lady Chapel, a new post of master of the choristers was created in several cathedrals.[108] The Master of the Music and of the Choristers, as he was called at Lincoln, was expected to teach singing, train the choir and compose. However, he remained a member of the minor clergy and the post was never occupied by a canon, even though it was increasingly held by graduates in the early sixteenth century. For this reason few canons at Lincoln or the other secular cathedrals were directly involved in music beyond their participation in the daily offices they attended. William Chell, who combined the posts of resident canon and succentor at Hereford from 1535, was the only exception. He is also one of the few to have

---

106 *BRUO* ii, 1339; Hughes, *Pastors and Visionaries*, 148.
107 A prose version of the *Speculum Vitae* has been published, *A Myrour to Lewde Men and Wymmen*, ed. V. Nelson, Heidelberg, 1981. *De Trinitate et Unitate* is printed in *Religious Pieces in Prose and Verse from Robert Thornton's Ms*, ed., G. G. Perry, EETS, Old Series, xxvi, 1867, 60–72. The *Speculum Vitae* is discussed in Hughes, *Pastors and Visionaries*, 148 and Pantin, *English Church*, 228–8. The context of its production is considered in Hughes, *Pastors and Visionaries*, Chapters 3 and 4 and Pantin, *English Church*, Chapters 9 and 10. Nassington's career is considered in I. J. Peterson, *William of Nassington*, New York, 1986.
108 Edwards, *Secular Cathedrals*, 163–75. The most recent discussion of cathedral music appears in Bowers, 'Music and Worship to 1640'.

studied music academically, and in 1526, soon after he graduated from Oxford, he copied a series of tracts on musical theory.[109] The other musical canons received their prebends as rewards for service, mainly to the crown. The earliest we know of, though the identification is not absolutely certain, and the most distinguished, is John Aleyn. His reputation rests on a motet of advanced style and complexity, *Sub Arturo Plebs*, which is thought to have been written in 1358 for the celebration of the battle of Poitiers by the Order of the Garter at Windsor. Aleyn was resident at Exeter at the end of his life in 1372–73.[110] Two leading fifteenth century composers were resident at St Paul's, a convenient location for combining residence with attendance in the chapel royal. Thomas Damet entered residence at Easter 1427 and remained until his death in 1436, though he was granted frequent absences. Up to 1430–31 he combined this with membership of the royal household chapel. Nine of his compositions have come down to us, all of them liturgical.[111] Nicholas Sturgeon had an almost identical career a few years later, beginning his residence at St Paul's in 1441 when he was also subdean of the chapel royal.[112] From 1442 until his death in 1454 he held the precentorship at St Paul's. Unfortunately no evidence survives to show whether he directed the music there himself or delegated it to deputies. The fact that he exchanged another benefice for the precentorship after he had entered residence suggests it was a position he wanted and that he undertook his responsibilities personally. It is tempting to think that he composed the antiphon sung on Trinity Sunday 1447 to celebrate William Booth's election as bishop of Lichfield.[113] John Pyttes (d.1467) owed his canonry at Exeter to service in Bishop Lacy's household chapel. He is unusual in that he self consciously called himself a musician on his tomb.[114] Two sixteenth-century canons were musicians, Robert Wydow at Wells and John Mason at Hereford, both of whom studied music at Oxford. Little is known about Wydow (d.1505) and none of his compositions have survived.[115] After graduating in music at Oxford in 1509 and serving as choirmaster of Magdalen College in 1509–10, John Mason became a canon of Hereford in 1525 and took up residence almost immediately. He was an active

[109] *BRUO 1500–1540* 115.
[110] *New Grove Dictionary of Music*, i, 250; B. Trowell, 'A Fourteenth-Century Motet and its Composer', *Acta Musicologica*, xxix, 1957, 65. The most recent consideration of Aleyn broadly supports Trowell's identification (R. Bowers, 'Fixed Points in the Chronology of Fouteenth-Century Polyphony', *Music and Letters*, lxx, 1990, 313–35, 320–35).
[111] *New Grove Dictionary of Music*, v, 172; Damet entered residence at Easter 1427 and is last recorded at a chapter meeting in April 1436 (GL Ms 25,513 fos 119r, 162v).
[112] *New Grove Dictionary of Music*, xviii, 309–10; Sturgeon asked to enter residence in December 1440 and was regularly present at chapter meetings until 1447 when the act book ends (GL Ms 25,513 fo. 184r passim).
[113] GL Ms 25,513 fo. 251v.
[114] N. I. Orme, 'The Early Musicians of Exeter Cathedral', *Music and Letters*, lix, 1978, 395–407, 400–1.
[115] *New Grove Dictionary of Music*, xx, 553.

composer while there; four of his works are known to have been written c.1540–47.[116] Alongside these active musicians some residentiaries had musical interests; John Orum's has already been noted.[117] Roger Keyes (d.1477) owned a book of music called *Liber Organicus*, which was probably a book of polyphony as it was placed in the Lady Chapel where there had been polyphonic music since the thirteenth century.[118] Archdeacon Smith of Lincoln showed his interest by giving pairs of organs to his prebendal church at Buckingham and the Jesus altar in his cathedral in 1528.[119]

The artistic activities of canons were almost entirely confined to patronage. Thomas Chandler is unique in that not only was he an author and scholar but he was also an artist of some considerable competence. Roger Keyes, the precentor of Exeter, has the distinction of being the only canon to merit an entry in John Harvey's *English Medieval Architects*.[120] He was appointed supervisor of the works at All Souls College Oxford in 1441, soon after construction started. His architectural reputation rests on his work at Eton College where he was master of the works from 1448 to 1450 when the chapel was built. Though it is unlikely that he designed the chapel, he was closely involved, visiting both Salisbury and Winchester cathedrals to measure their choirs and naves. He was sufficiently influential at both Eton and All Souls to determine some of the decoration. Each place contains reminders of his Devon roots and his devotion to a local Exeter saint, St Sidwell. It is while Keyes was at Eton that we get a rare glimpse of the more personal and everyday side of canons' lives. Amidst the clamour of the building site he finished a letter to the chapter at Exeter with the words 'written in haste among the stones at Eton'.[121] As patrons residentiaries could encourage artistic activity, especially church building and decoration. Other forms of artistic patronage such as book illumination are surprisingly scarce. Canons' motives as patrons were undoubtedly mixed and never explicit.[122] The principal one was religious. As educated men they would have been aware that, in the words of Robert Grosseteste, 'God is the most perfect perfection, the fullest completeness, the most beautiful form and the most splendid beauty', and that art should aspire to this level of beauty. The principal expression of this was the rebuilding of their cathedrals, which will be discussed more fully in the next chapter. There was also a didactic element to some patronage, to tell biblical stories and religious truths. A third baser motive, pride,

116 *BRUO 1500–1540* 386.
117 See chapter 7.
118 Oliver, *Lives*, 353.
119 Cole, *Lincoln Chapter Acts 1520–36*, 91–4.
120 J. H. Harvey, *English Medieval Architects*, Revised edition, Gloucester, 1984, 167–8; R. Willis and J. Clark, *The Architectural History of the University of Cambridge*, 1886, i, 396–8.
121 DRO D&C 3498 no. 24.
122 For a general discussion of this topic see T. Heslop, 'Attitudes to the Visual Arts: The Evidence from Written Sources', in J. Alexander and P. Binski, *The Age of Chivalry*, 1987, 26–32.

was identified by William Langland in *Piers Plowman*. The elaborate tomb slabs of the Lincoln residentiaries with their brass portraits, heraldic devices and rebuses were very much what Langland had in mind. He would have been equally critical of the tradition at Wells where several canons built tombs with effigies, a level of display more generally reserved for bishops in other cathedrals.[123]

As with educational patronage canons rarely initiated large scale projects because they lacked the resources, but collectively they had some impact on church building and decoration in the places they were connected with. Hugh Hopewas of Lichfield was largely responsible for embellishing his parish church at Clifton Campville, a particularly fine example of the decorated style.[124] The wealthy York residentiary William Waltham gave £40 to Beverley Minster in 1416 for the construction of the new east window in the newly fashionable perpendicular style.[125] The imposing tower of Mortonhampstead church in Devon was partly paid for by its rector Richard Penels, an Exeter residentiary, who gave 100s towards the cost in 1418.[126] A more didactic approach underlay the gift of Richard Bruton, chancellor of Wells, to the parish church of his birthplace Bruton in Somerset in 1417. As well as a set of curtains and frontal for the high altar he gave four cloth banners, two to be decorated with the miracles of Our Lady and two with the miracles of St Mary Magdalen.[127] A didactic approach also often lay behind gifts of stained glass, a relatively wide-spread form of patronage among canons, perhaps because unlike a tower or aisle it was within their means. It also offered opportunities to commemorate the donor with a figure, inscription or heraldically. Despite the massive loss of stained glass something is known of canons' contribution to its provision, particularly in their cathedrals. Dean Mamsfeld of Lincoln gave a series of twelve windows to Merton College Oxford where he was a fellow from 1288 to 1296. They are an early and important example of a standard design of the fourteenth century showing a band of figures under elaborate canopies in rich colours. Almost as remarkable is the way that Mamsfeld is depicted in each window, lest future generations should forget the donor or fail to pray for him.[128] Adam Murimuth glazed the east window in the parish church of Eaton Bishop in Herefordshire, where he also is portrayed several times. The saints Murimuth chose to depict in his window included St Michael weighing a soul, the Virgin and St John, and St Gabriel as well as the figure of Christ.[129] Thomas Overay (d.1493), a precentor of Wells, is shown kneeling in a window in the chancel of Pilton church,

---

123 Some Wells canons built tombs with effigies in the cathedral, among them Dean Godeley and William Byconnel, a practice only rarely encountered elsewhere below the episcopate.
124 Jenkins, *Lichfield Cathedral*, ii, Appendix F under Hopewas.
125 *Test Ebor* iii, 55–9.
126 *Reg. Stafford Exeter* 420–1.
127 *Somerset Medieval Wills 1383–1500*, 87–98.
128 R. Marks, *Stained Glass in England*, 16.
129 RCHM, *Herefordshire, Vol i South-West*, 1931, 60–1, plate 91.

Somerset, which was attached to the precentorship. The presence of his name on a shield in the chancel roof suggests that this was another of his benefactions.[130] Peter Carslegh's gift of a window at Winscombe church, where he was rector from 1521 to 1532, combined religious devotion, personal commemoration and artistic fashion. His window portrays three saints with his name, Peter, the Apostle, the Deacon and the Exorcist. It is decorated in the new classical style of the Renaissance with cornucopia, scrolls and putti.[131] The artistic achievements and patronage of canons contributed to the 'beauty of holiness' in their churches and cathedrals and in the celebration of the *Opus Dei* in them. In doing so it encouraged devotion and the donation earned merit for the donor with God.[132]

---

[130] *BRUO* ii, 1411.
[131] *BRUO* i, 363–4; Marks, *Stained Glass in England*, 63, 226–7.
[132] These themes are considered in R. N. Swanson, 'Liturgy as Theatre: the props', in D. Wood, *The Church and the Arts*, Oxford, 1992, 239–53.

9

A Brotherhood of Canons Serving God:
Life in the Close

Whatever their intellectual and religious interests, the immediate preoccupation of residentiaries was the running of the cathedral. This was a considerable undertaking as cathedrals were large and wealthy corporations with many estates to manage and interests to protect and pursue. On entering residence canons agreed to play an active part in the cathedral's administration. They swore an oath to 'keep chapter', that is attend chapter meetings and keep its secrets, and serve in any office to which they were elected.[1] Residentiaries were expected to take their turn in the senior offices of the chapter, the number and titles of which varied from cathedral to cathedral. They were of a broadly supervisory nature and usually included the senior financial posts. By the late fifteenth century there were five annually elected offices at Lincoln and between seven and nine at Wells.[2] This was an unusually high number but as most were supervisory, their duties were not onerous. The most important and time consuming were the financial offices, the auditors or stewards of the exchequer as they were known at Exeter. Two canons served annual terms during which they were responsible for running the chapter's estates and generally acting on its behalf. The minor clergy undertook the bulk of the day to day routine administration of the junior financial and clerical offices, some of which involved considerable responsibility. In the sixteenth century laymen, like Peter Effard, the chapter clerk at Lincoln, were increasingly employed.[3] If the Exeter canons are typical, there was always a certain reluctance to serve as steward or auditor and from time to time complaints were made about its onerous duties and the frequency with which

---

[1] For a general discussion of residentiaries' duties see Edwards, *Secular Cathedrals*, 67–70.

[2] At Lincoln two auditors of the masters of the fabric accounts, a master of the Burghersh Chantry and two keepers of the shrine of St Hugh were elected annually in the late medieval period; LAO D&C A/3/1 fos 7v, 9v, passim. At Wells two or three auditors, two keepers of the library, were elected annually and in addition two scrutators of canonical houses and two surveyors of the ornaments were sometimes chosen; *Wells HMC*, ii, 104 passim.

[3] Major, 'The Office of Chapter Clerk at Lincoln in the Middle Ages', 188.

office was held, though refusals were rare.[4] In practice at Exeter and other cathedrals with a relatively large residentiary body most canons served once or twice but those with a good business sense and proven accounting skill were repeatedly re-elected. During his fifteen years of residence at Wells between 1487 and 1502 John Vowell served as auditor seven times and as keeper of the library five times.[5] The long experience that many had in royal and ecclesiastical service was brought to the cathedral's administration. As the numbers of residentiaries declined the burdens of office fell on fewer shoulders. By the 1530s at Lincoln, where there were only five or six resident, canons had to serve in more than one office and more frequently.[6]

Cathedral statutes laid down that chapter meetings should take place weekly, though there might be short daily ones after prime. At Lichfield they were held on Fridays, at Exeter and Lincoln on Saturdays and at Salisbury whenever convenient.[7] There were also ad hoc meetings of smaller groups of canons to transact whatever business was in hand. The impression given by surviving act books is that weekly meetings were not always held, or at least their business was so routine that it did not need to be recorded, and that when there were more pressing matters meetings were called to deal with them as necessary. Even the best kept and organised act books are an incomplete record of chapter business. Meetings were normally held in the chapter house but side chapels and canons' houses were also used. Attendance at them was obligatory for residentiaries, but this was rarely observed or enforced. Canons were less regular in their attendance at chapter meetings than the daily offices. Some were legitimately absent on cathedral business but others simply did not bother, though few ignored their obligation altogether. In the 1380s and 1390s at Exeter, where there were high levels of residence, the average level of attendance was between a half and a third of the residentiaries.[8] Where there was a smaller resident body attendance was usually better, though at the extremes such as York in the late fifteenth century there might be only one.[9] Bishop Heyworth of Lichfield felt attendance at meetings was sufficiently irregular to include in his statutes of 1428 a requirement for all to be present.[10]

Much chapter business was routine, the distribution of commons, the allocation of duties in the choir for services and the correction of minor clergy for trivial misdemeanours, little of which was recorded in act books. Equally routine but of greater importance were appointments, of minor clergy, canons and dignitaries, and to benefices and chapter offices both in the cathedral and on its estates. Appointments to canonries and dignities were usually set out in full

4 Lepine, *Canons of Exeter Cathedral*, 194–5.
5 *Wells HMC*, ii, 104 passim.
6 Bowker, *Henrician Reformation*, 92.
7 Edwards, *Secular Cathedrals*, 68.
8 Lepine, *Canons of Exeter Cathedral*, 193.
9 YML H2/3 fo. 216v.
10 Kettle and Johnson, 'Lichfield Cathedral', 160.

detail. When papal provisions and competition for prebends were at their height in the fourteenth century this occupied a lot of the chapter's time as rivals tried to establish their claims and registered their provisions. Even in the fifteenth century, when papal provisions had ceased, the crown and magnates exerted pressure to secure canonries for their clients by writing to chapters, though most of these letters have been lost. The allocation of chapter farms and houses in the close received particularly detailed scrutiny as canons sought to acquire the most attractive. Questions of residence and the general management of chapter estates were also regularly and frequently discussed. The minor clergy caused trouble continuously and had to be closely supervised. Their punishments for misbehaviour in the choir, fornication, drinking and leaving the close fill many pages in surviving act books giving the impression that at times the residentiaries could barely control them. Indeed, there was a serious dispute at York, resulting in the sequestration of the vicars' property, that lasted for several months in 1411–13.[11] The disciplining of vicars was part of a wider aspect of chapter business, the maintenance of liturgical standards and the enhancement of worship. External events must have intruded into canons' discussions but have rarely left any traces. The Salisbury chapter can be seen coming to terms with the readaption of Henry VI at the end of 1470 rather cautiously as it recorded letters of patronage for cathedral offices from the restored king scarcely six months after a visit from Edward IV.[12] Earlier in Edward IV's reign, in 1463, they had discussed the rumors of treason circulating and been warned not to be caught up in them.[13] When building work was in progress this was a major preoccupation as the chapter sought to raise money.

In one random year, 1330, the Lichfield chapter settled its dispute with Sir John Swinerton, took steps to recover the 1000 marks a recently deceased canon had placed in he hands of the abbot of Tewkesbury for safekeeping, and pursued its claim against the crown for the money which it owed Bishop Langton that the bishop had given for the building of the Lady Chapel. The incomes and estates of both individual prebends and the chapter were repeatedly discussed, particularly the dependent chapels at Bakewell. Proctors to represent them at the Court of Arches and more generally in Derby, Warwickshire, and Staffordshire were appointed, rights to the wood at Arley were sold for £10 and it was agreed that the vicars' house should be rebuilt. Several minor clergy were appointed, a canon was installed and probate granted on a will. In addition the chapter recorded an account of the convocation held in 1328.[14] The scope of the interests and concerns of the Lichfield chapter was not unusual and illustrates the substantial amount of time and effort required to administer a middle ranking cathedral. The great minsters at York and Lincoln had much larger estates and interests scattered, like Lichfield's, over large dioceses. Chapter act books make

11 YML L2 (3)a fos 45r–54v.
12 Salisbury D&C Reg. Machon fos 19v, 25v–26r.
13 Salisbury D&C Reg. Newton fo. 26v.
14 Bod. Lib. Ashmole Ms 794 fos 38v–44v.

clear how time consuming the management of estates could be, especially when debts and litigation were involved as canons travelled to represent the chapter at the assizes and other courts. William Dounebrigge, an Exeter residentiary, was a skilled administrator, whose experience in royal service as an auditor of the exchequer was frequently called upon. In the late 1380s and early 1390s he represented the chapter in London on several occasions as well as travelling regularly to Cornwall.[15] Other chapters had similar figures and all retained legal advisors to protect their interests; in 1386–7 the York chapter retained two at the court of King's Bench and one at the exchequer such was scale of its business.[16] By the end of the fifteenth century it was the only chapter known to have acquired its own house in London on Fleet Street.[17] This was no doubt where its representatives stayed when parliament or convocation sat or when presenting its case in the courts. When not holding office residentiaries could expect to be asked to carry out occasional commissions. Examples are numerous; in 1496 the Wells chapter sent Thomas Gilbert to negotiate with the prior of Monacute over a disputed mill on their estate at North Cory.[18] A significant proportion of chapter business was pastoral, the exercise of spiritual jurisdiction over the parishes appropriated to the common fund which often included a number within their cities. By the end of the thirteenth century the canons of York had established their own ecclesiastical court that supervised the morals of the parishioners in its jurisdiction.[19] The fifteenth-century Lichfield canons can be seen in a similar role both in the city, where responsibility fell to the dean, and at Cannock, an appropriated church.[20] Some prebends and dignities also had pastoral responsibilities according to the nature of their endowments which conscientious residentiaries exercised.[21] A general supervision was effected through triennial visitations, though it is not clear how regularly they were carried out.

The Corporate Identity of the Chapter

[At Wells] there flourished a famous college of priests, men of honest behaviour and well learned; whereof I account it no small worship that I myself, fourteen years archdeacon of Wells, was elected one of that college.

Polydore Vergil[22]

[15] DRO D&C 3550 fos 49v, 53v, 54r, 60v, 64r, 69r.
[16] YML E1/8 (Chamberlains Accounts).
[17] YML E1/47.
[18] *Wells HMC*, ii, 144.
[19] Dobson, 'Later Middle Ages', 101–2.
[20] Kettle, 'City and Close', 160, 164–9; LJRO D30/2/1/1 fo. 88r.
[21] In 1401 the Lichfield chapter discussed the morality of those in the jurisdiction of Thomas Hanley's prebend of Gaia Major, listing those guilty of fornication and incontinence (LJRO D30/2/1/1 fos 59v–60r).
[22] Gransden, 'Wells Cathedral', 43.

From their eleventh century origins in episcopal households cathedral chapters gradually developed to become strong and largely independent corporations in the later middle ages. By the end of the twelfth century they had their own estates, administration and officials, and took collective action, and during the thirteenth century they became increasingly aware of themselves as corporate bodies.[23] But they were not yet independent corporations in a legal sense; this status evolved as the legal concepts to define it developed in the fourteenth century. Their evolution was often in reaction to external challenges, especially from their diocesan bishops. Exemption from episcopal jurisdiction for the churches appropriated to the common fund and individual prebends had been secured by the thirteenth century. The right to administer the deanery when vacant was more contentious, but at most cathedrals the chapter retained control after a struggle during the fourteenth century. Chapters were much less successful in challenging the right of bishops to visit their cathedrals, which was a major issue in the century and a half after 1250.[24] The matter was first settled in the bishop's favour at Lincoln in 1245 after a long struggle, with Exeter and St Paul's following by the end of the century without much dispute. Compromises in 1290 and 1328 gave the archbishops of York limited rights of visitation. A prolonged and bitter struggle took place at Salisbury where episcopal claims had been rebuffed in 1262 but at the end of the fourteenth century the chapter was forced to concede and visitations were regularly held in the fifteenth century. Elsewhere chapters acknowledged the rights of their bishops, in 1340 at Chichester and 1428 at Lichfield, with only Hereford remaining exempt. These disputes helped build the chapter's sense of its identity but also defined the extent of its independence. As well as conceding visitations rights chapters accepted without question the right of the bishop to appoint their members and thereby some influence from the crown and magnates who each sought to present their candidates to prebends.[25] Episcopal rights to make statutes were also widely accepted. Even so, within these limitations chapters had considerable freedom of action. Disputes with their cities also stimulated chapters' sense of identity.[26] As with bishops conflict arose from competing claims to jurisdiction, both in the close and over chapter property elsewhere in the city. Though each side guarded its privileges jealously, disputes were generally settled without rancour. At Exeter friction was caused by the mayor and corporation trying to assert their authority in the Close and by the existence of St Sidwell's fee, held by the chapter, which was outside their jurisdiction. As might be expected minor disputes arose regularly but rarely escalated into serious conflict. This happened twice, first in

---

[23] For a recent general discussion of this in the twelfth century see, E.U. Crosby, *Bishop and Chapter in Twelfth Century England*, Cambridge, 1994, 384–95.

[24] Edwards, *Secular Cathedrals*, 127–34.

[25] See Chapter 2 for further consideration of this topic.

[26] For a wider discussion on the relationship between cathedrals and their cities see Dobson, 'Cathedral Cities', and Kettle, 'Cathedral and Close'.

1283 when the precentor was murdered and the mayor and several leading citizens were implicated. The mayor was hanged for his part in the affair and the Close was enclosed soon afterwards. The second crisis was longer lasting but less bloody. Following a brawl on Ascension Day 1445 old rivalries were reawakened and the city pressed its claims to authority within the Close. Inconclusive appeals to the lord chancellor by the city dragged on until 1448 when mediation settled the issue in the cathedral's favour. Throughout the dispute the chapter defended its rights vigorously, consulting both its own records and lawyers in London.[27] On a more everyday basis much of the administration carried out by residentiaries in running the chapter reinforced their sense of corporate identity as they upheld the cathedral's rights and privileges.

The compilation of registers and cartularies from the thirteenth century was both an expression of this corporate identity and a means of developing it. By bringing together their charters and other documents chapters were more aware of their privileges and rights and better able to defend them. One of the earliest and most impressive collections is the Lincoln *Registrum Antiquissimum* which was first drawn up c.1225 and supplemented in c. 1260. At the end of the thirteenth century much of it was classified and transcribed by John Schalby, a residentiary canon and historian of the cathedral.[28] The Wells chapter began the *Liber Albus*, a register of its charters, around 1240 in response to the long running rivalry with Bath for cathedral status.[29] At Lichfield the first major compilation, the *Magnum Registrum Album* was drawn up between 1317 and 1328.[30] The keeping of chapter act books accurately recording the business done at meetings was part of this process. The earliest efforts to keep records date from the late thirteenth and early fourteenth centuries with York, Lincoln, Lichfield and Salisbury in the forefront. A miscellaneous register was kept at York from the 1290s and at Lincoln from 1305–06.[31] The first register at Salisbury followed the prompting of Bishop Martival in his statutes of 1319, though it was not regularly kept until 1331.[32] Martival had been a residentiary at Lincoln until his elevation to the episcopate in 1315 and had experienced the benefits of proper record keeping. Not all chapters developed systematic records of their business or maintained them once started. The earliest surviving at Exeter, dating from the 1380s, seems to be only a partially successful attempt and perhaps the first.[33] The physical expression of this growing self-confidence and sense of identity was the

---

27 The relationship between Exeter Cathedral and the city of Exeter is considered in M. Curtis, *Some Disputes between the city and the Cathedral Authorities of Exeter*, Manchester, 1932, and in Lepine, *Canons of Exeter Cathedral*, 321–41.

28 *Registrum Antiquissimum*, ed. Foster, i, xxv–xliv.

29 Gransden, 'Wells Cathedral', 36.

30 Savage, *Magnum Registrum Album*, xv.

31 The earliest at York, c.1290, is a miscellaneous register, YML M2/4g; the first at Lincoln dates from 1305, LAO D&C A/2/21.

32 *Hemingby's Register*, ed. Chew, 5.

33 Lepine, *Canons of Exeter Cathedral*, 191–2.

building of richly carved and decorated polygonal chapter houses that took place during the second half of the thirteenth century. The whole process can be seen clearly at Lichfield where the new chapter house was built in the 1240s. Above it was the library which contained the chapter's collection of local histories from the abbeys of Burton and Chester and the cathedral's own history, written between 1323 and 1334. While the history was being written the chapter compiled the *Magnum Registrum Album* and started its first act book.[34]

There was a strong sense of cohesion among residentiaries that contributed to a highly developed corporate identity in chapters. From their first entry into residence canons made a commitment to the cathedral and swore to fidelity and loyalty to it. They quickly became well versed in its customs and statutes, or at least what they understood them to be, and readily appealed to them at times of dispute and uncertainty. Care was taken to ensure that copies of the statutes were up dated and corrected. Familiarity with the cathedral's customs and statutes developed an awareness of its history that strengthened the sense of corporate identity. Most had a cathedral history among the chapter's charters and registers. The Wells *Historiola* was originally written in the eleventh and twelfth centuries but reworked in the early thirteenth after the episcopal see was finally settled there rather than at Glastonbury. A new version of the cathedral's foundation by the Saxon king Ine was included.[35] At Lincoln and Lichfield histories were written at the beginning of the fourteenth century. *John Schalby's Book* gives a history of Lincoln cathedral, episcopate by episcopate, from its foundation to the events of his own lifetime. Nearly twenty years in the service of Bishop Sutton (1280–99) and even longer in residence in the close (1310–33) ensured first hand knowledge and access to the cathedral's archives. Schalby's intention was to set out the position and status of the cathedral and was occasioned by a jurisdictional dispute between the canons and the dean in 1312.[36] The Lichfield chronicle was written by a vicar choral, Alan of Ashbourne, in 1323, and placed in the cathedral. At least one copy was made in the fifteenth century by Thomas Chesterfield, a residentiary who has sometimes been credited with its author-ship.[37] Versions of the York and Exeter chronicles were displayed on boards on display in the choir or nave for benefit of visitors.[38] These histories have several common elements. Most show a familiarity with the cathedral's archives and historical traditions, both written and oral, and rely heavily on the early history of Britain invented by Geoffrey of Monmouth in the twelfth century. Their subsequent chronology was usually arranged by episcopate and updated from time to time. The York tables, which were written (in Latin) between 1388 and 1397

---

34 M. W. Greenslade, *The Staffordshire Historians*, Staffs Rec Soc, Fourth Series, xi, 1982, 8.
35 Gransden, 'Wells Cathedral', 33–4.
36 See note 28.
37 See note 34.
38 Orme, *Exeter Cathedral*, 10–11; J. S. Purvis, 'The Tables of the York Vicars Choral', *YAJ*, xli, 1967, 741–8.

and intended for the instruction of the vicars choral, have a more sophisticated approach to the minster's history. They were drawn from wider sources, Bede, William of Malmsbury and a local chronicler Alfred of Beverley as well as Geoffrey of Monmouth, and contain extracts from charters and papal bulls.[39] Often contemporary with these histories were the registers of charters and other documents that chapters compiled to define and defend their rights and privileges. Soon after the Wells *Historiola* had been reworked the chapter compiled the register known as the *Liber Albus*.[40]

The liturgy reinforced this sense of history; as we have seen all but one had their own liturgical use which gave them a separate identity. Even where the Sarum use was adopted, at Chichester, St Paul's and Wells, the liturgy still gave scope to celebrate the cathedral's origins. The principal opportunity was the patronal festival which everywhere but Exeter and Wells included a canonised former bishop. Following the canonisation of the cathedral's founder, St Osmund, in 1457 liturgy and history were inextricably linked at Salisbury. Unofficial cults had the same effect. Alongside St Hugh at Lincoln there were unofficial cults at the shrines of two other bishops, Robert Grosseteste and John Dalderby, both of which flourished into the sixteenth century.[41] The lack of an episcopal patron saint did not prevent the development of a historical dimension in the liturgy as the custom at Exeter shows. The cathedral's patron St Peter was commemorated with an elaborate secular celebration on the eve of his feast for canons' servants and the choristers at which there was a bonfire and sometimes a play. Bishop Grandisson promoted three feasts with historical associations for the cathedral: the Translation of St Edward the Confessor who was closely involved in the cathedral's foundation and as the ninth lesson made clear approved the transfer of the see from Crediton to Exeter; St Boniface who was said to have been educated at the monastery in Exeter, the cathedral's forerunner; and St Sidwell, a local saint the supposed site of whose martyrdom was owned by the chapter. Patrons who were not canonised could be commemorated in obits and chantries. King Athelstan, in whose name the Exeter chapter had forged charters, was regarded as the cathedral's first founder, and had an obit celebrated on 27 October.[42] The same honour was accorded by the Wells chapter to their alleged founder King Ine.[43] The personal devotion of canons often reflected the patronal cults of their cathedals.[44] History was made vividly visible in the glazing schemes, so few of which have survived. Heraldic fragments suggest that the Exeter residentiaries deliberated in the chapter house surrounded by reminders of the

---

[39] Purvis, op. cit.
[40] Gransden, 'Wells Cathedral', 33–4, 36.
[41] Bowker, *Henrician Reformation*, 93–4.
[42] Lepine, *Canons of Exeter Cathedral*, 277–9.
[43] *Wells Communars' Accounts*, ed. Colchester, 139.
[44] For a fuller discussion of this see Chapter 7.

cathedral's founders and bishops.[45] The more complete survival of medieval glass at York demonstrates that a sense of history was an integral part of the glazing scheme. The bottom row, and the most easily visible, of the great east window contains a series of legendary and historical figures associated with the north of England and the two choir aisles tell the stories of two leading northern saints Cuthbert and William. The life of St William, a twelfth century archbishop of the Minster, would have been seen by the many pilgrims visiting his shrine.[46]

The adornment of the cathedral was another expression of corporate identity. Polydore Vergil's praise of Wells, quoted above, articulated a pride in cathedrals and the status of residentiary widely shared by canons. They were generous benefactors to their cathedrals both mobilising and contributing to rebuilding funds, though the scale of their financial contribution is difficult to quantify because most fabric accounts have been lost. Major initiatives and the bulk of the resources came from bishops, who alone had sufficient wealth for such large projects, but chapters made a significant contribution. For seventy years half the value of the prebends and dignities of the Exeter chapter was given to the fabric fund, a total of £62 9s 4d per annum, which in the later stages of rebuilding, after 1330, was the largest single source of income.[47] William Waltham and Thomas Haxey were especially generous to the fabric fund at York, giving £40 and 100 marks respectively.[48] Even when major building projects had been completed residentiaries regularly made bequests to the fabric fund for maintenance work, the standard sum being 20s–40s. The cathedral was the major focus of canons' artistic patronage. A group of thirteen canons contributed the new glass in the lady chapel at Wells; the glass is of particularly high quality and used the most recent techniques.[49] Two fifteenth-century York residentiaries, Robert Wolvenden and Thomas Parker, gave windows to the Minster. Both commemorated northern saints associated with the cathedral, Paulinus, John of Beverley and William.[50] On a more modest scale John Belvoir gave 40s towards the painting of St Hugh's shrine at Lincoln in 1391 and Thomas Morton 100s for the tabernacle on the high altar at York in 1448.[51] The most generous were placed on the cathedral's list of benefactors for whom prayers were regularly said. The Wells chapter accorded this privilege to Thomas Harrys (d.1512) soon after his death in recognition of the 200 marks he had given to the cathedral during his life.[52] The Salisbury bidding prayer lists over forty canons who had made a

[45] C. Brooks and D. Evans, The Great East Window of Exeter Cathedral, Exeter, 1988, 149–57.

[46] J. Toy, The Windows of York Minster, York, 1985, 7, 10–12, 21–4.

[47] Lepine, Canons of Exeter Cathedral, 274.

[48] Dobson, 'Residentiary Canons of York', 171.

[49] R. Marks, 'The Medieval Stained Glass of Wells Cathedral', in Colchester ed., Wells Cathedral, 139–40.

[50] J. Toy, The Windows of York Minster, York, 1985, 12.

[51] LAO D&C A/2/28 fos 41r–43r; Test. Ebor iii, 106–15.

[52] Wells HMC, ii, 232.

notable contribution, most of them fifteenth-century residentiaries.[53] This loyalty continued in death with the overwhelming majority of residentiaries asking to be buried in their cathedrals; requests for burial elsewhere were unusual. The location within the cathedral was often precisely specified, in a named chapel, in front of a favourite image or altar, or beside a patron or friend; Dean Montagu wished to be buried next to his father in the Lady Chapel at Salisbury.[54] Almost without exception extensive provisions for their souls were arranged in the cathedral to be carried out by its clergy; a solemn but grand funeral, multiple masses, an obit and perhaps a chantry.[55] Over 70 per cent of the Exeter chapter of the period 1300–1455 expressed a personal commitment to their cathedral by being buried in it, establishing an obit or chantry, making gifts or contributing to its rebuilding.[56] In doing so they acknowledged their loyalty to the foundation that gave them status, protection and livelihood.

The cohesion of residentiary chapters rested on close-knit networks of canons that grew up based on patronage and friendship often through shared diocesan administration. Though difficult to reconstruct they can sometimes be traced through association in episcopal households and service and above all in surviving wills where they can be found as executors, witnesses and beneficiaries. Jonathan Hughes' work on the clerical households in the diocese of York has demonstrated how close the ties among the minster clergy could be.[57] Similar networks can be observed at Exeter among the chapter and Bishop Stafford's circle. Four canons Richard Tyttesbury, Roger Bolter, William Fylham, and William Browning formed a close-knit group. Bolter, Fylham and Browning shared an unusual common origin in a Devon village, Ugborough, on the southern edge of Dartmoor. All four had a similar social background from the local gentry and entered the service of Bishop Stafford, though Tyttesbury was not a residentiary canon. He was the oldest of the four and the benefactor of William Browning, his clerk, to whom he bequeathed a collection of legal texts on his death in 1409. The connection between the two arose from Tyttesbury's position as rector of Ermington, where he maintained his own private chapel, which was only three miles from Ugborough, and is known to have encouraged another deserving scholar from the village. Bolter and Fylham were neighbours for most of their lives. Their association in Bishop Stafford's service continued in the cathedral close where they were both resident from the 1420s until their deaths in 1436 and 1438 respectively. Each named the other as executor and Bolter wished to be buried next to a relative of Fylham's. Their friendship survived the quarrel caused by the refusal of Bolter's nephew, John, to marry a cousin of Fylham's which resulted in John Bolter losing his place in Fylham's household. William Browning was of a younger generation and did not enter

53 Wordsworth, Ceremonies and Processions, 22–32.
54 PRO PROB 11/2A fos 48r–49v.
55 This is discussed in chapter 7.
56 Lepine, Canons of Exeter Cathedral, 281.
57 Hughes, Pastors and Visionaries, 176–97.

residence until 1435 but twenty years earlier, as a young man, had worked alongside Bolter in Bishop Stafford's service. Bolter, like Tyttesbury before him, sought to encourage able and rising young clerics and bequeathed a set of law books to Henry Webber (d.1477), a future dean and benefactor of the cathedral, who became a canon a few months before Bolter's death.[58] Further research on other chapters will doubtless reveal other clerical affinities among the residentiaries.

Relations between residentiaries were generally amicable and often close, but as in any community, there were bound to be quarrels from time to time and chapter act books record rows between canons. In 1427 the Salisbury canons had to be reminded not to use strong language to each other on pain of the loss of residence for a term; if they were violent the punishment was the loss of a year's residence.[59] These episodes were comparatively scarce and usually provoked by difficult individuals. More serious quarrels arose when a difficult individual held a dignity and the personality clash was compounded with a jurisdictional dispute. Cathedral treasurers were often at the centre of arguments over the provision of materials for the liturgy, the candles, bread and wine, which occasionally escalated. Just such a dispute clouded the last two years of Hugh Sugar's life at Wells in 1487–89.[60] Autocratic deans also provoked chapters, even a non-resident like John Prophete at York whose arrogance in the choir enraged the residentiaries who accused him of behaving more like a bishop or king than a dean.[61] The most insufferable and perhaps infamous dean was John Macworth at Lincoln, whom the distinguished historian Hamilton Thompson described as 'haughty and uncompromising'. For much of his long tenure of the office, from 1412–51, he caused dissension; the residentiaries made formal protests in 1418 and 1434 and one, Chancellor Partrich, was assaulted in 1435. Despite a temporary lull when a settlement was made by the bishop in 1438–9, the dispute was revived by Macworth in 1442 and rumbled on until his death in 1451. The episode undoubtedly damaged cathedral life while it was in progress.[62] Disagreements over canonical houses, farms and the right to present to chapter benefices occurred and are sometimes recorded in the act books. They were usually settled without rancour and orders of precedence were established to prevent future discord that were generally successful. It was more difficult to prevent divisions in the chapter during the upheaval of the Reformation. The Salisbury chapter was split between reformers and conservatives in the later 1530s.[63] At Exeter the reforming dean, Simon Heynes, antagonised the whole chapter with his

---

58 For the biographies of Bolter, Browning, Fylham and Tyttesbury see BRUO i, 215–6, 282–3, ii, 735–6, iii, 1880; for an analysis of their geographical origins see Lepine, Canons of Exeter Cathedral, 56–7; and for Bolter's household see ibid., 304.

59 Salisbury D&C Reg. Harding fo. 79r.

60 Gransden, 'Wells Cathedral', 44.

61 YML L2 (3)a fo. 122r.

62 Thomson, English Clergy, 90–8.

63 Edwards, 'Salisbury Cathedral', 185–6.

proposals which also increased his privileges.[64] Despite their differences and occasional lapses the residentiary canons managed to live a harmonious life in the close most of the time.

Capitular Life: Salisbury, 1398–1458, and Lichfield, 1481–1540

To conclude this study two complementary residentiary bodies will be examined to illustrate the range and quality of capitular life; one exceptional, Salisbury in the first half of the fifteenth century, and one typical, Lichfield in the sixty years up to 1540. The outstanding quality of the former around 1400 has long been recognised and the activities of some of its leading members have been analysed but no survey of the whole residentiary body has been undertaken.[65] The Salisbury chapter reached its late medieval zenith in the first half of the fifteenth century. The period opens with radical reform of the cathedral in the 1390s and closes with the canonisation of its founder St Osmund in 1457. The reforms began in the mid 1380s with the removal of the foreign cardinals occupying the principal dignities.[66] In 1390 Thomas Montagu became the first fourteenth-century dean to reside and together with Bishop Waltham he undertook a thorough reorganisation of cathedral life. The bishop had finally succeeded in establishing his right to carry out visitations of the chapter in 1392 and the first took place in 1394 when few defects were revealed, a tribute to Montagu's zeal. In the same spirit of reform the dean and chapter made their own additions to the statutes in 1399.[67] Regular and thorough episcopal visitations in 1404, 1418, 1440 and 1454 helped to maintain these standards.[68] The spiritual health of the chapter is reflected in the high residence levels maintained up to the 1460s. There were usually between twelve and fifteen residentiaries from the 1390s to the early 1430s. A slightly lower level of between eight and eleven resided from the late 1430s until the mid 1450s after which there was a recovery to twelve in the late 1450s.[69]

The origins and careers of the sixty canons who became residentiaries between 1398 and 1458 were distinguished and cosmopolitan. Unlike their counterparts at Exeter from 1300 to 1541 and Lichfield between 1480 and 1540 relatively few were local men from the diocese of Salisbury, approximately a third.[70] Graduates

---

64 Orme, *Exeter Cathedral*, 94–8.
65 Edwards, 'Salisbury Cathedral', 176–7; Jacob, 'Medieval Chapter of Salisbury' and 'English Conciliar Activity 1395–1418', in *Essays in the Conciliar Epoch*, 3rd edition, Manchester, 1963, 78–82.
66 Edwards, 'Salisbury Cathedral', 176.
67 Wordsworth and Macleane, *Statutes of Salisbury Cathedral*, 306–7.
68 Salisbury D&C Reg. Draper fo. 43, Reg. Pountney fos 51r–53r, Reg. Hutchins fos 3r–5r, Reg. Burgh fos 47v–52v.
69 For the residence levels see Appendix 1.
70 This figure is based on the methods used to ascertain the geographical origins of canons set out in Chapter 3.

dominated but a quarter had no university education.[71] The majority of these retired to Salisbury after a career in royal service, Peter Barton in the mid 1390s after nearly twenty years as a chancery clerk.[72] Indeed, like canons in general, most originally owed their prebends either to episcopal or royal service. Their administrative experience was similar, ranging widely among the main departments of government and diocesan offices; John Frank served as clerk of parliament from 1414 to 1423 and receiver of petitions in parliament from 1415 to 1438 which he combined with brief periods of residence at the beginning of his career.[73] Geoffrey Cruckadene acted as Bishop Hallum's official and vicar general while resident from 1409 to his death in 1420.[74] Almost all the diocesan experience of the residentiaries was gained in the province of Canterbury, the exceptions being Richard Pittes and Robert Ragenhull who had been members of Archbishop Arundel's circle at York.[75] What marks out the Salisbury chapter at this time is its connections with leading intellectual circles at court and in the Church. An important group were in the service of the outstanding patron of art and learning of the period, Humphrey, duke of Gloucester, who was a member of the cathedral fraternity.[76] Both John Fyton and Gilbert Kymer were in his service and Nicholas Upton dedicated his book, De Officio Militari, to him.[77] A notable scholar of a younger generation, Andrew Holes, regarded him as his patron.[78] Fyton was brought to Salisbury by Bishop Hallum who gathered round him some of the most active scholars of his age many of whom ended their days in the Close as residentiaries. Among these were the theologians Robert Brown, John Luke and Richard Ullerston.[79] These three were part of a larger group of seven residentiaries who attended the great church councils of the early fifteenth century. Fyton, Luke and Ullerston were at the Council of Pisa in 1409 and Brown and Fyton were at Constance with Bishop Hallum in 1415.[80] A second generation, Alexander Sparrow and John Symondsburgh, were present at Basel in 1432.[81] They brought their experience and involvement in the questions of church government and reform discussed at these councils to the Close. The chapter was not solely concerned with its own affairs but was aware of wider issues within the Church; Salisbury was the only cathedral chapter to have its own proctors at these councils.[82] Another aspect of this awareness of wider matters

---

[71] The academic qualifications of the Salisbury chapter have been compiled using the methods set out in Chapter 3.
[72] Wilkinson, Chancery under Edward III, 205.
[73] Reg. Chichele Canterbury, ii, 654.
[74] BRUO i, 524.
[75] Hughes, Pastors and Visionaries, 178–87.
[76] BRUO ii, 983–5.
[77] BRUO ii, 737–8 (Fyton), 1068–9 (Kymer), iii, 1933–4 (Upton).
[78] Ibid. ii, 949–50.
[79] Reg. Hallum Salisbury, xi–xiv.
[80] BRUO ii, 737–8 (Fyton), 1175–6 (Luke), iii 1928–9 (Ullerston), i 280–1 (Brown).
[81] BRUO iii, 1739–40 (Sparrow), 1842 (Symondsburgh).
[82] Edwards, 'Salisbury Cathedral', 177.

beyond the Close was the experience of the papal court and the new humanist learning brought to Salisbury in the 1440s by Andrew Holes.[83]

The cathedral was a centre of learning that attracted some of the most distinguished scholars of the early and mid fifteenth century. The first generation in the 1410s and 1420s included the theologians Richard Ullerston, resident from 1416 until his death in 1423, and John Luke, resident 1418–35.[84] The second generation, resident from the 1440s, were more influential and active. A remarkable group lived in the Close at this time, Nicholas Bildeston, the dean, briefly in 1438–41, and Andrew Holes, from 1446 to 1450 and 1452–3 to 1467 and perhaps his death in 1470, Gilbert Kymer from 1440 to 1462 and Nicholas Upton from 1434 to 1455.[85] The presence of these individuals made the chapter outstanding. Ullerston was the author of several theological works as well as an important reform programme for the council of Pisa. An important part of this was that the Church should be served by a resident and educated clergy.[86] Such a community existed at Salisbury and Ullerston joined them to devote the last years of his life to trying to live according to his ideal. Andrew Holes was perhaps a more distinguished scholar than Ullerston, though not an author. His residence at the papal curia from c.1432 to c.1444 put him in touch with the new humanist learning. While in Italy he acquired an extensive humanist library, one of the most important in England. Holes was highly regarded for his scholarship and austere lifestyle by at least one Italian contemporary.[87] Nicholas Upton's special interest was heraldry and knighthood about which he wrote a treatise, De Officio Militari.[88] Under the auspices of these scholars the cathedral built a new library and lecture room in 1445 in which Kymer and Upton played a leading part.[89] There was a scriptorium active in Salisbury from the late 1440s to 1460 under their patronage. Dean Kymer is known to have had two manuscripts copied for

---

83 See note 78.
84 Their residence has been calculated from their presence at chapter meetings and the surviving communars' accounts; for Ullerston Salisbury D&C Reg. Harding fo. 1 passim, Communars' Accounts nos 36–42; for Luke Reg. Harding fo. 1 passim, Communars' Accounts nos 37–45.
85 For the methods used see note 84; for Bildeston Salisbury D&C Reg Hutchins fo. 2r passim, Communars' Accounts no. 46; for Holes Reg. Hutchins fo. 47r passim, Reg. Burgh fo. 1 passim, Reg. Newton fo. 1 passim, Communars' Accounts nos 48a–60; for Kymer Reg. Hutchins fo. 2 passim, Reg. Burgh fo. 1 passim, Reg. Newton fos 1r–24v, Communars' Accounts nos 48a–57; for Upton Reg. Hutchins fo. 2 passim, Reg. Burgh fo. 1 passim, Communars' Accounts nos 46–50.
86 See Chapter 1 note no. 109.
87 M. Harvey, 'An Englishman at the Roman Curia during the Council of Basle: Andrew Holes, his Sermons of 1433, and his Books, JEH xlii, 19–38; J. W. Bennett, 'Andrew Holes: A Neglected Harbinger of the English Renaissance', Speculum xix, 1944, 314–35.
88 BRUO iii, 1933–4.
89 Salisbury D&C Reg. Hutchins fos 40r, 47v.

him at Salisbury.[90] Further encouragement to learning was given by the increase
in the number of theology lectures made in 1455.[91] The diligent preaching and
studying undertaken by Thomas Cyrcetur, another scholarly residentiary, illustrates the intellectual vigour of the chapter in this period.[92] The chapter's
commitment to study is also reflected in their supervision of De Vaux College
within the Close for which they were responsible; a visitation was carried out in
1454.[93]

A succession of conscientious resident deans lead by example, beginning with
Thomas Montagu in 1390 and continuing with John Chandler (1404–17) and
Simon Sydenham (1418–31). Though the next four deans from 1431 to 1449
were leading royal clerks all managed to spend some time at Salisbury; Thomas
Brouns was resident in 1431–2, and both Nicholas Bildeston (1435–41) and
Richard Leyot (1446–9) became resident for most cf their period in office.[94] The
tradition of longstanding resident deans was resumed in 1449 by Gilbert Kymer.[95]
In the sixty years 1398–1458 the dean was resident for a total of forty-eight years.
Under their leadership capitular life was vigorous throughout the first half of the
fifteenth century and culminated in the canonisation of the cathedral's founder
St Osmund.[96] Proposals were first put forward in 1387, but it required a sustained
commitment to bring to fruition. After the initial campaign in the late 1380s
three more were required, in 1424, 1442–4 and 1451–52 before Osmund's
canonisation was granted in 1457. At the forefront of the efforts to promote
Osmund were the leading scholars among the residentiaries, Richard Ullerston,
Nicholas Bildeston, Andrew Holes, Gilbert Kymer and Nicholas Upton. Upton
was sent to Rome as the chapter's proctor in 1452–53 after discussions with the
new bishop, Richard Beauchamp, revived the campaign. Such a lengthy campaign was expensive, costing over £700, which together with the cost of repairs
to the fabric led to an increase in the entrance fee for residentiaries. Alongside
the campaign to canonise St Osmund the chapter was engaged in other projects,
the promotion of the Sarum Use and the building of the new library. The Sarum
Use was closely, if falsely, related to St Osmund, who was widely believed to be
its author, especially by the influential Richard Ullerston. In the early fifteenth

---

[90] J. W. Bennett, 'Andrew Holes: A Neglected Harbinger of the English Renaissance',
    Speculum xix, 1944, 331.
[91] Salisbury D&C Reg. Burgh fo. 56r.
[92] For a fuller consideration of Thomas Cyrcetur see chapter 7.
[93] The educational interests and responsibilities of cathedral chapters are considered in
    Chapter 7; for the Salisbury chapter's supervision of De Vaux college see Salisbury
    D&C Reg. Burgh fos 56r–v.
[94] For Bildeston see note 85; Chandler, Salisbury D&C Reg. Draper fo. 14v passim, Reg.
    Vyring fo. 1r passim, Reg. Pountney fo. 1 passim, Communars' Accounts nos 20–35;
    Sydenham Reg. Pountney fo. 40r passim, Reg. Harding fo. 1r passim, Communars'
    Accounts nos 38–45; Brouns Reg. Harding fo. 103r–107v; Leyot, Reg. Hutchins fo.
    47r passim, Reg. Burgh fos 1r–10r.
[95] See note 85.
[96] This account is based on Edwards, 'Salisbury Cathedral', 177–8.

century it was revised and improved by Clement Maidstone (who was not a Salisbury canon) and soon afterwards adopted at Chichester and St Paul's.[97] Within the cathedral the improvement and development of the liturgy was a regular preoccupation at chapter meetings that went beyond the standard disciplining of the minor clergy. New feasts were celebrated and existing ones upgraded in importance in 1406 and 1447.[98] Individual residentiaries were also concerned to promote the liturgy; John Maidenhith (d.1407) gave the chapter £40 and William Loring (d.1416) £20 to ease the financial difficulties of the minor clergy to enable them to perform their liturgical duties.[99]

These projects bound the chapter together giving it a common sense of purpose and unity. It was strong enough to elect its own bishop in 1417, when the dean, John Chandler, a longstanding residentiary was chosen.[100] However, on his death in 1426, their election of Simon Sydenham, his successor as dean and another long standing residentiary, as bishop was overturned and the royal nominee, Robert Neville was provided by the pope, a pattern that became the norm for the rest of the century.[101] The chapter's ability to elect its own dean was preserved for a little longer. There were elections in 1382, 1404 and 1418 but thereafter external pressures lay behind the candidates chosen by the chapter.[102] The prestige of the cathedral was both reflected in and enhanced by its distinguished confraternity that included many of the greatest magnates in the kingdom from the king downwards. Henry V was admitted as Prince of Wales in 1409 with his brother Humphrey of Gloucester.[103] Queen Joan with most of the ladies of the court became members the following year, and many local knights and important clerics also joined.[104] Such influential lay and ecclesiastical support proved very useful to the chapter. In the absence of the king, the licence to elect a new bishop in 1417 was granted by John, duke of Bedford, a member of the confraternity which may account for the chapter's freedom to choose their dean.[105] Cardinal Beaufort had hardly been made a member of the confraternity before he was enlisted to help with the canonisation of St Osmund in 1421.[106] Like their colleagues at other chapters the Salisbury residentiaries were generous and loyal to their cathedral. The majority were buried in it and established obits and chantries there. As many as sixteen were sufficiently outstanding in their generosity to be regarded as benefactors and had their names added to the list of

97 Edwards, 'Salisbury Cathedral', 177–8.
98 Salisbury D&C Reg. Draper fos 32v, 33r, Reg. Hutchins fo. 54r.
99 Salisbury D&C Reg. Vyring fos 20v, 21r, Reg. Pountney fo. 9v.
100 Edwards, 'Salisbury Cathedral', 178.
101 *Salisbury Fasti*, 2.
102 Edwards, 'Salisbury Cathedral', 178.
103 Salisbury D&C Reg. Vyring fo. 17r.
104 Ibid. fo. 25r.
105 Salisbury D&C Reg. Pountney fo. 30r.
106 Salisbury D&C Reg. Harding fos 20v–21r.

benefactors in the bidding prayer, a further indication of the vigour and dyna-mism of capitular life at Salisbury during the first half of the fifteenth century.[107]

The Lichfield chapter of the late fifteenth and early sixteenth centuries cannot claim the distinction of its counterpart at Salisbury in the fifty years after 1400 but in its own way it was an active and strong religious community. The size of the residentiary body was significantly smaller; a total of twenty-three canons entered residence between 1481–1540. Between four and six were resident from the 1480s to the 1530s, rising to seven or eight at peaks in the 1480s and late 1510s, and falling to the three or four in the late 1530s. This level of residence was typical of most cathedrals, including Salisbury, during this period.[108] In contrast with the Salisbury chapter of 1398–1458, many of the Lichfield canons originated from within the diocese and were drawn from the senior gentry of Staffordshire, Derbyshire and Cheshire. The most powerful and prominent family represented in the chapter were the Dudleys; Arthur Dudley, who entered residence in 1532, was the son of Edward, lord Dudley.[109] The Staffordshire gentry families among the chapter included the Delves of Needwood and Dodyngton in Cheshire, and the Egertons of Newcastle under Lyme.[110] Members of the Derbyshire families of Fitzherbert and Beresford became canons and residentiar-ies.[111] Several of these families, including the canons, were both related to each other and associated in local government and land transactions.[112] As at Exeter throughout the later middle ages there was a strong local presence; nearly half the Lichfield residentiaries had origins in the diocese. The range of their experience was narrower than the Salisbury chapter, being confined largely to episcopal service in diocesan administration; only six had been employed by the crown and none had served in the papal curia.[113] The intellectual horizons of the Lichfield residents did not match the distinction of those at Salisbury but the chapter was concerned about books and learning. A new library was begun in 1490 and completed in 1500, continuing a tradition begun in the mid thirteenth century when the first was built.[114] Roger Walle (d.1488) was a bibliophile like Andrew Holes and he both collected and copied books ranging from the practical, Lyndwood's *Provinciale*, a canon law text, to the literary and historical,

---

107 See note 53.
108 The Lichfield residence figures are taken from Appendix 1.
109 W. N. Landor, *Staffordshire Incumbents and Parochial Records*, Staffs Rec Soc, Third Series, 1915, 140.
110 For their family backgrounds see J. C. Wedgwood, *Biographies of the Members of the Commons House 1439–1509*, 1936, 267–8 (Delves), 293–4 (Egerton); and *Inq. Post Mortem Henry VII*, ii, no. 933.
111 *BRUC* 231 (Thomas Fitzherbert); ibid. 55 (James Beresford).
112 Richard Delves and Richard Egerton were co-feoffees of Hugh Egerton before 1505 (*Inq Post Mortem Hen VII*, ii, no. 933).
113 James Denton (*BRUC* 182–3); Richard Sherbourne (*BRUO* iii, 1685); George Strangeways (*BRUO* iii, 1796); John Whelpdale (*CCR 1468–76* no. 703); Henry Williams (*BRUO 1500–1540*, 629–30); and John Yotton (*BRUC* 667).
114 Kettle and Johnson, 'Lichfield Cathedral', 166.

the *Comedies* of Terence and Thomas Elmham's *Life of Henry V*. He also owned a copy of the cathedral statutes and John Gower's *Vox Clamantis*.[115]

The cathedral was led by resident deans from Thomas Heywood in the 1480s until 1492 followed by John Yotton (1493–1512) and Ralph Collingwood (1512–21).[116] Though he was actively engaged in royal service as chancellor to Princess Mary and in Wales, James Denton (1522–33) spent several months each year at Lichfield.[117] Richard Sampson (1533–36) was an absentee dean but his successor, Henry Williams (1536–54), entered residence in September 1540.[118] All but Sampson were generous benefactors of the cathedral and their leadership and generosity was particularly important because of the financial hardships the cathedral faced in this period, it being one of the poorest of the nine. The poverty of the chapter was severe enough to restrict the number of residentiaries.[119] Decanal visitations of the cathedral in 1506, 1519, and 1522 reinforced their presence and leadership.[120] As well as the library there was some modest rebuilding, the vaulting in stone of the west end of the nave at the expense of Dean Denton.[121] Denton was also largely responsible for the liturgical adornments undertaken in the 1520s, providing new copes to replace the worn out ones still being used in 1523 and increasing the number of choristers by four.[122] During this decade the choristers finally began to live a communal life in a house built with money given by Bishop Halse (d.1490).[123] The Lichfield residentiaries were entirely typical in their desire to be buried in the cathedral, establish chantries and obits in it, and in their generosity and loyalty to it. Chief among these was Dean Heywood who was an outstanding cleric, if not a notably original one. Virtually all aspects of cathedral life were enhanced by his generosity; the Lady chapel was provided with a stone screen, the chapter house was decorated, the library begun, an organ purchased and the great 'Jesus' bell, costing £100, hung. The liturgy was developed with an obit and chantry and in 1473 an extra cursal mass and services on Fridays. The laity were encouraged by the spiritual benefits from indulgences granted to the dean in 1473 and 1482. His promotion of the cult of Jesus and St Anne in both his chantry and later a fraternity attracted pilgrims and introduced new liturgical developments to the cathedral.[124]

Relations between the cathedral and the city and diocese were particularly close at Lichfield.[125] This was partly because the city had been founded by the

---

115 *BRUO* iii, 1966.
116 Heywood, LJRO D30/2/1/2 fo. 1r passim, D30/2/1/3 fo. 1r passim; Yotton D30/2/1/3 fo. 7r passim; Collingwood D30/2/1/3 fo. 106r passim.
117 *BRUC* 182–3; LJRO D30/2/1/3 fo. 133r passim, D30/2/1/4 fo. 1r passim.
118 LJRO D30/2/1/4 fo. 124r.
119 The financial difficulties of the chapter are discussed in Chapter 5.
120 LJRO D30/2/1/3 fos 89r, 123r, 134r.
121 Kettle and Johnson, 'Lichfield Cathedral', 165–6.
122 LJRO D30/2/1/3 fos 138v–139r; Kettle and Johnson, 'Lichfield Cathedral', 164.
123 Kettle and Johnson, 'Lichfield Cathedral', 164.
124 Kettle, 'City and Close', 162–4 for a general discussion of Heywood's benefactions.
125 The rest of this paragraph is based on Kettle, 'City and Close'.

bishop and remained technically part of his manor of Longdon until the Reformation. The three chapels in the city were in the jurisdiction of the dean and chapter and the morals of the citizens were supervised by the dean in his courts. The government of the city was shared by the Guild of St Mary of which over half the residentiary body were members alongside prominent citizens, the leading gentry families of the diocese, heads of the major religious houses and other senior clerics. In 1495 three canons carried out Bishop Smith's reform of St John's Hospital, an important source of education in the city.[126] The cathedral's fraternity of St Chad had strong roots in the diocese up to the Reformation as we have seen.[127] As well as thousands of ordinary people it included members of the local nobility; in 1512 the earl and countess of Derby were admitted.[128] A new fraternity dedicated to Jesus and St Anne was established in 1487 by Dean Heywood and attracted many citizens.[129] The city was often the beneficiary of canons' charity, which seems to have been a characteristic of the Lichfield chapter unlike the Salisbury chapter of 1398–1458. Dean Heywood was outstanding among benefactors, helping to found an almshouse, repairing the three city chapels, founding a new fraternity and replenishing a decayed loan chest for the poor.[130] But Heywood was not alone; Thomas Milley refounded and re-endowed an almshouse in Lichfield for fifteen women in 1502–4 with the help of the dean and another residentiary, Thomas Reynold.[131] Two other deans helped the citizens, John Yotton left money for a preacher or an advocate for the poor in the consistory court and James Denton built a new market cross at a cost of £160 to keep the poor dry.[132] In their different ways the Salisbury and Lichfield residentiaries, especially men like Thomas Cyrcetur, Andrew Holes and Thomas Heywood, lived up to Richard Ullerston's ideal of an educated resident clergy living as a religious community; the 'brotherhood of canons serving God' that Bishop Leofric envisaged when he moved his cathedral to Exeter in the middle of the eleventh century.[133]

---

126 T. Harwood, *The History and Antiquities of the Church and City of Lichfield*, Gloucester, 1806, 403–17.
127 See chapter 1 for a fuller consideration of cathedral fraternities and the one at Lichfield.
128 LJRO D30/2/1/3 fo. 106r.
129 Kettle, 'City and Close', 163.
130 Kettle, 'City and Close', 164.
131 *VCH Staffordshire*, vol. iii, 275–8.
132 BRUC 667 (Yotton); Kettle and Johnson, 'Lichfield Cathedral', 165 (Denton).
133 F. Barlow, ed., *Leofric of Exeter*, Exeter, 1972, 9.

Appendix 1

Sources and Methods
for Measuring Residence Levels, 1300–1541

Chichester

Virtually nothing has survived to indicate residence levels here. Occasional glimpses can be found in two sources, Bishop Reade's Register and the White Act Book, the first remaining chapter act book.[1] Even the latter does not systematically record canons attendance at meetings.

Exeter

Exeter has the most complete set of materials on residence. A series of accounts enable figures to be drawn up for almost the whole period. The most important of these are the Refections Accounts, Stewards Accounts and Obit Books.[2] For a detailed discussion of them see Lepine, *Canons of Exeter Cathedral*, Chapter 4.

Hereford

Like Exeter Hereford has a rich variety of surviving medieval accounts which cover most of the period. However, they are difficult to use to draw up residence figures because of the complex system of payments residentiaries were entitled to. These came from a series of different funds each with its own set of accounts and each with a different set of qualifications for entitlement to the payments. As a consequence, the accounts often give conflicting totals of resident canons or disagree about their names and sometimes both. Caution has been used in calculating the totals used in Appendix 2 and generally the lowest figure has been included. For these reasons the Hereford figures must be regarded as provisional; further work may revise them. The principal accounts used have been: the Accounts of the Collectors of the Common Rent for the period 1302/3–1537/8, which have many gaps; the Accounts of the Reeves and Bailiffs for the period 1301–1316; the Accounts of the Receivers of Mass Pence for the period 1299/1300–1540/1; and the Accounts of the Receivers and Collectors of

---

1 *Reg. Reade Chichester*, 108; Peckham, *White Act Book*, 6 et seq.
2 DRO D&C 2777–2836 for the Stewards Accounts, D&C 3755–9 for the Refections Books, D&C 3764–72 for the Obit Books; see also the Residence Book D&C 3707 for the period 1506–41 and the Quotidian Books D&C 3761–3 for the periods 1479–83, 1486–1501 and 1523–25.

Oblations and Herriots for the period 1300/1–1345/6.[3] The accounts of the Mass Pence are probably the most reliable source though they do not list residentiaries as such (except for the period 1311/12–1361/2) but record the number of masses each canon attended per year from which their residence can be calculated on the assumption that generally most attended mass each day. Studies of other cathedrals and their residence requirements suggest that this is reasonable, though a few would have spent some time away from the city on chapter business. As canons were required to reside for thirty-six weeks a year they should have attended about 250 masses per year. This figure has been used as the broad measure of residence, though it probably slightly underestimates the total by not taking into account legitimate absences. However, for some payments canons needed only to attend matins so the Mass Pence accounts are not sufficient alone. Canons known to have attended fewer than 250 masses are recorded as being resident in these accounts; in these cases they have been counted as resident. The matter is further complicated by changes in accounting procedure (between 1372 and 1415 and between 1454/5–61/2).

Lichfield

Because of the scarcity of surviving accounts the Lichfield residence levels are entirely based on canons attendance at chapter meetings, which may cause some under-representation as residentiaries are known to have been careless in this matter. The Lichfield material indicates that most were regular in their attendance. The chapter act books are generally thorough in recording who was present at a meeting. Years where few meetings are recorded have been excluded; only those with a reasonable range across most of the year have been included. The figures have been calculated by comparing attendance at chapter meetings with the modest requirement of two month's residence; in fact most canons were present for almost the whole year. A good range of act books survive from the second half of the fourteenth century, especially from the 1370s to 1438; there is a long fifty year gap until 1481 and thereafter a more or less complete series to 1541.[4]

Lincoln

Lincoln has a long clear series of records, the Accounts of the Common Fund, which give residence levels in a straightforward manner with few major gaps over the whole period. There are some longer gaps, 1340–60, 1410–19, 1425–40 and

---

3 HCA R123a–195 Accounts of the Collectors of the Common Rent; HCA R40a–59 Accounts of the Reeves and Bailiffs; HCA R389–578 Accounts of the Receivers of Mass Pence; HCA R412–49 Accounts of the Receivers and Collectors of Oblations and Heriots. For a general discussion of the accounts and payments see Capes, *Hereford Charters*, vi–xi.

4 Bod. Lib. Ms Ashmole 794; LJRO D30/2/1/1–4.

1467–78. The fourteenth-century ones have been printed in Edwards, *Secular Cathedrals*.[5]

St Paul's

Little is known about residence levels at St Paul's. As at Chichester there are occasional isolated references which have been collected together in Brooke, 'St Paul's Cathedral'.[6] Only in the first half of the fifteenth century can any detail be added from the surviving chapter act book for the period 1411–47.[7] Unlike Lichfield for most of this period meetings and attendances are haphazardly recorded and residence figures cannot be calculated from them. Fortunately there are some scattered references which list canons present at meetings as residentiaries in the period 1411–19. From 1442 to 1447 meetings and attendance are more fully recorded from which residence figures can be produced. The names of residentiaries if not the details of their residence can be gleaned from the note of their formal entry into residence.

Salisbury

The residence levels for Salisbury are taken from two principal sources a series of accounts and the chapter act books. The Communars Accounts survive over much of the period 1300–1541 but unlike Lincoln there are considerable gaps especially in the fourteenth century where they survive only for the following years: 1343, 1347, 1350, 1361, 1369, 1370, 1371, 1377, 1380, 1381, 1385, 1391, 1394, 1398 and 1399. In the fifteenth century there are accounts for forty-one years between 1401 and 1488 after which there is a gap until 1518; seven years are covered in the period 1518–41.[8] The major problem with the communars accounts is that they are quarterly and rarely survive for more than one quarter a year. The residence requirements at Salisbury make this particularly significant; only three months a year was necessary which could be spread over the whole of it. A canon might well have been resident that year but not recorded in as many as three communars' accounts or appear earning less than the 40s commons needed to qualify for residence which he could make up in another quarter. In practice most residents were present at the cathedral for most of each of the four annual quarters but there was a minority who spent the minimum three months at Salisbury spread across the year in short periods. This accounts for some underrecording of residence. It can be partly corrected by using the chapter act books, of which fourteen have come down to us covering the period 1329–1563.[9]

5 Edwards, *Secular Cathedrals*, Appendix 1; LAO D&C Bj/2/10–16, Bj/3/1–5.
6 Brooke, 'St Paul's Cathedral', 88–90.
7 GL Ms 25,513.
8 Salisbury D&C Communars Accounts 1–89; 1–4 and 16–18 are printed in Edwards, *Secular Cathedrals*, Appendix 2.
9 Salisbury D&C Regs. Hemingby (1329–52), Corff (1348–58), Coman (1385–87), Dunham (1387–95, 1407–08), Holmes (1395–1402), Draper (1402–07), Vyring (1408–13), Pountney (1413–18), Harding (1419–35), Hutchins (1440–47), Burgh

Some, those for 1329–47 and all the surviving ones from 1402 to 1541, have been used to supplement the communars accounts employing the same method as the Lichfield act books described above.

Wells

Thanks to the efforts of the Historical Manuscripts Commission and the late L. S. Colchester much of the Wells medieval archive is in print including the main source of information on residence, the Communars' Accounts.[10] Unfortunately, these survive for relatively few widely spaced years from 1327/8–1490/1; there are only twenty-six with residence details. Attendance at some chapter meetings is known in the early 1320s and later 1380s.[11] There is very little covering the early sixteenth century beyond the records of some canons entering residence and occasional names of residentiaries.[12]

York

As with Lincoln, the York material is relatively straightforward. The residentiaries are recorded in the Chamberlains Accounts which run from 1370/1 to 1541/2.[13] There are only three serious gaps, from 1405 to 1426, 1430 to 1463 and 1492 to 1505. For the gaps some indication can be taken from the chapter act books; this has been done for 1346 and 1347, 1422, 1437, 1455, and 1498–9 using the method described above for Lichfield.[14] There is one slight complicating factor at York: its unique account system which divided the year in two from Pentecost to Martinmas and Martinmas to the following Pentecost.

(1447–57), Newton (1461–67), Machon (1468–75), Harwood's Memorials (1497–1525), and Holt and Blacker (1538–63). Hemingby's register has been printed.

10 Colchester, *Wells Communars Accounts*.

11 *Wells HMC*, i, 190, 196–8, 207–8, 295–9, 302.

12 Ibid., ii, 101 et seq.

13 YML E1/1–79.

14 YML H1/1 s. a. 1346–7, H2/1 s. a. 1422, H2/3 fos 35r–38v, 86r–89r, 216v.

Appendix 2

Residence Levels, 1300–1541

Key

The Medieval accounting period running from Michaelmas to Michaelmas has been used except where stated.

···························· Wells

- - - - - - - - - Lincoln
Figures for major residence only have been used. The Lincoln accounting period began on the feast of the Exaltation of the Holy Cross (14 September).

——————————— Exeter

–··–··–··–··–··– Lichfield
The modern calendar year beginning on 1 January has been used.

–·–·–·–·–·–· York
The York accounts divide the year into two parts Martinmas (11 November) to Pentecost (seven weeks after Easter) and Pentecost to Martinmas.

– — – — – — – Salisbury
The modern calendar year beginning on 1 January has been used.

–·–·–·–·–·– Hereford

×–×–×–×–×–×–×–× St Paul's
The modern calendar year beginning on 1 January has been used.

M Michaelmas Term
C Christmas Term
E Easter Term
J St John's Term

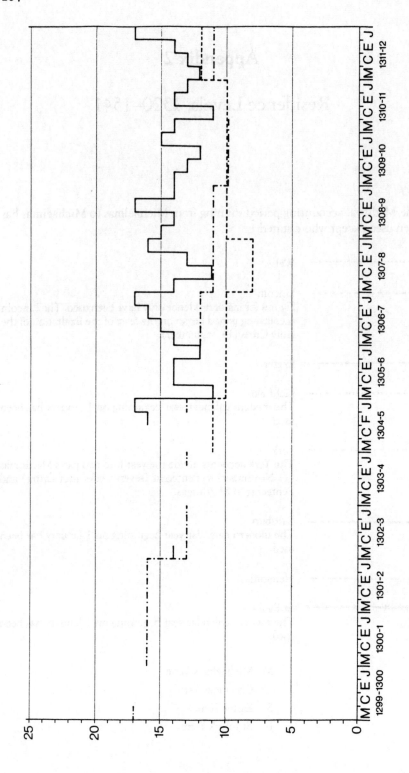

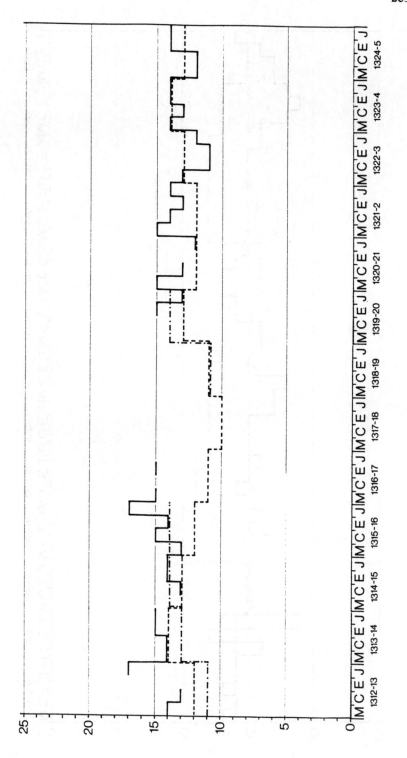

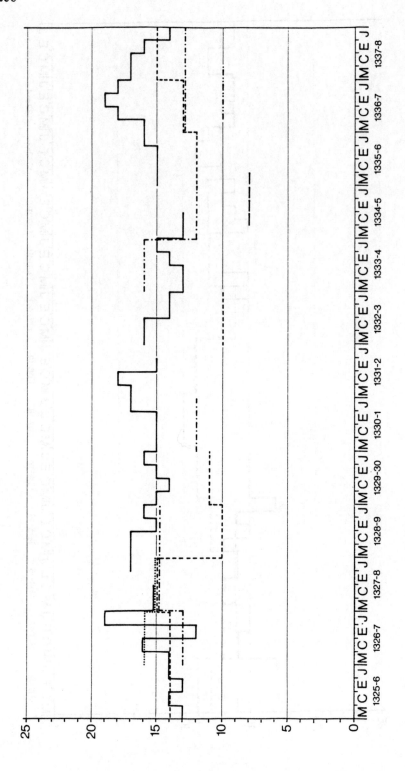

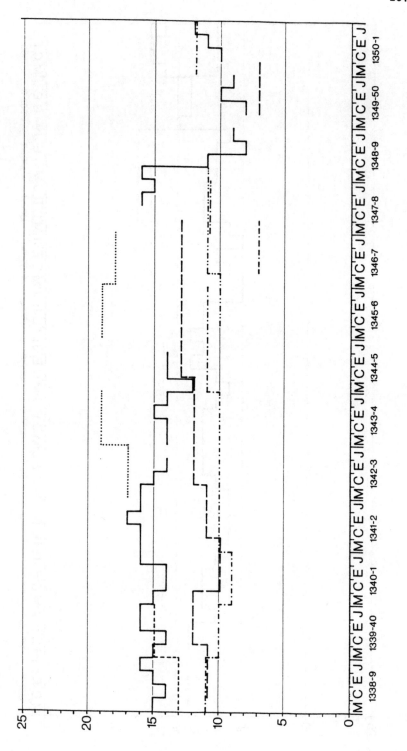

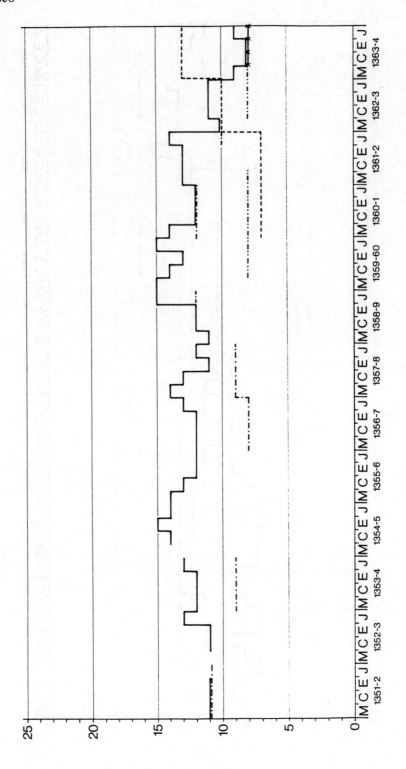

209

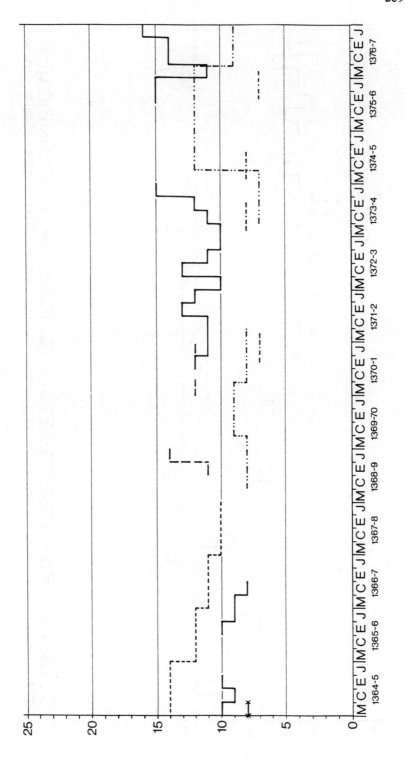

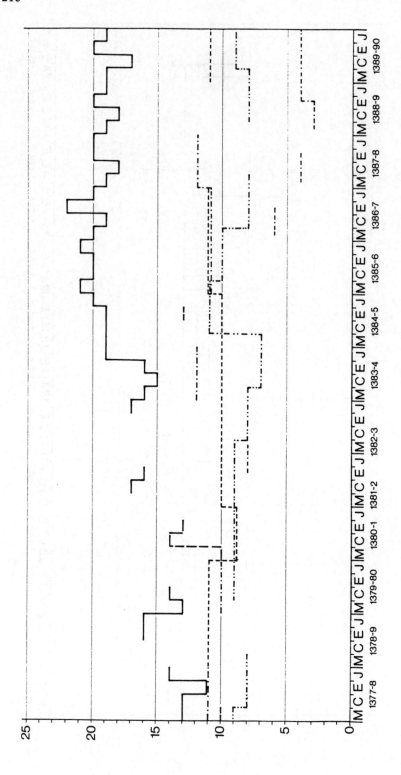

211

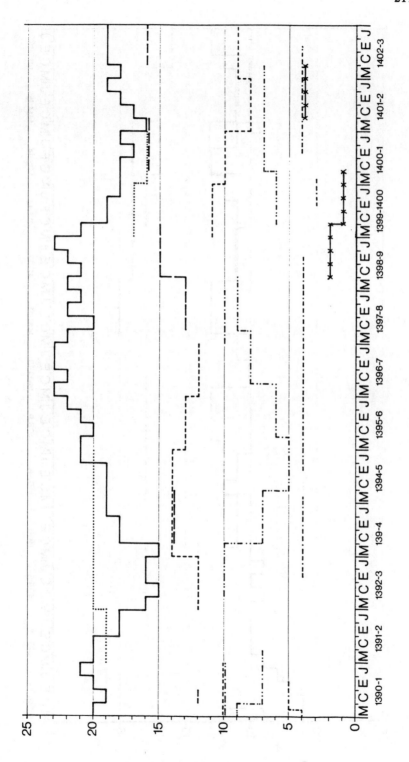

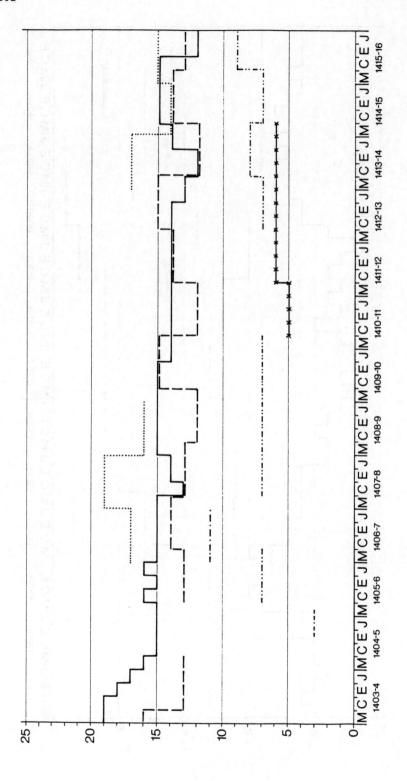

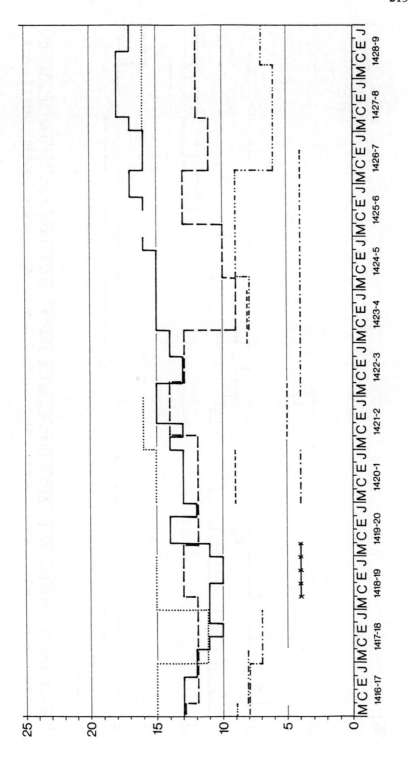

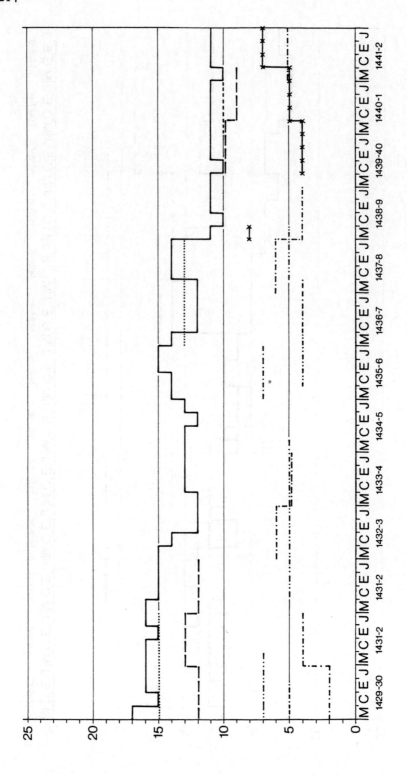

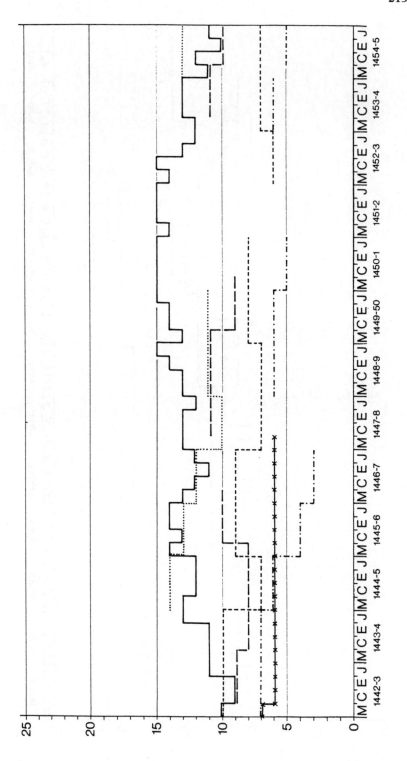

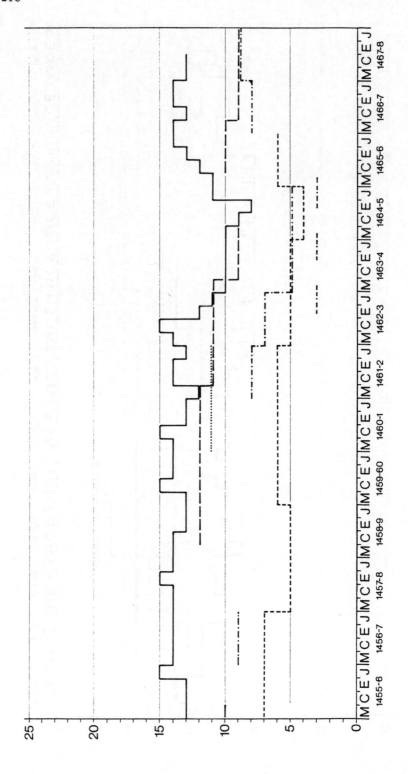

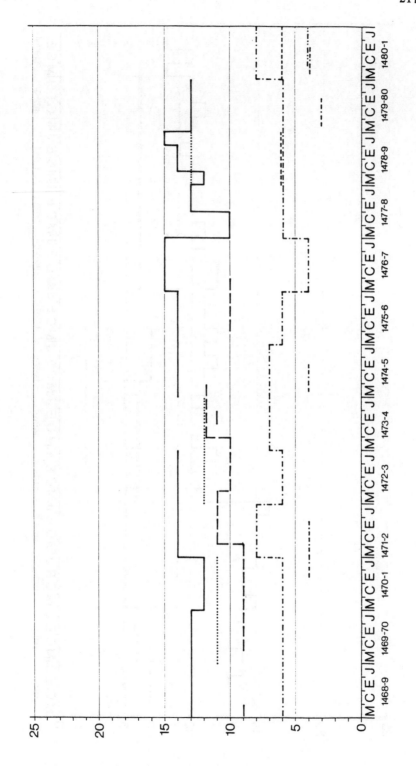

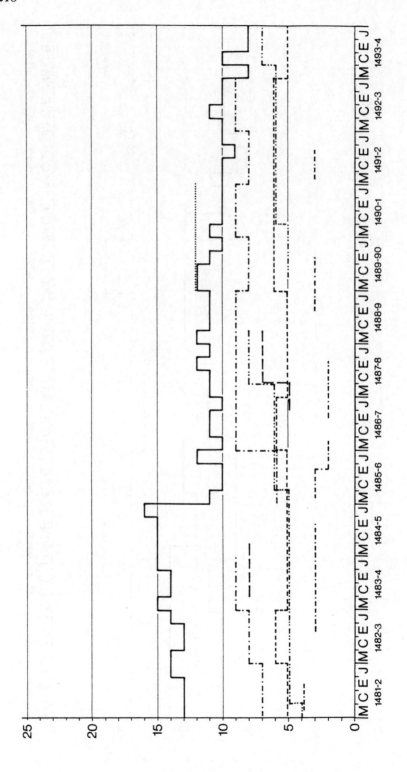

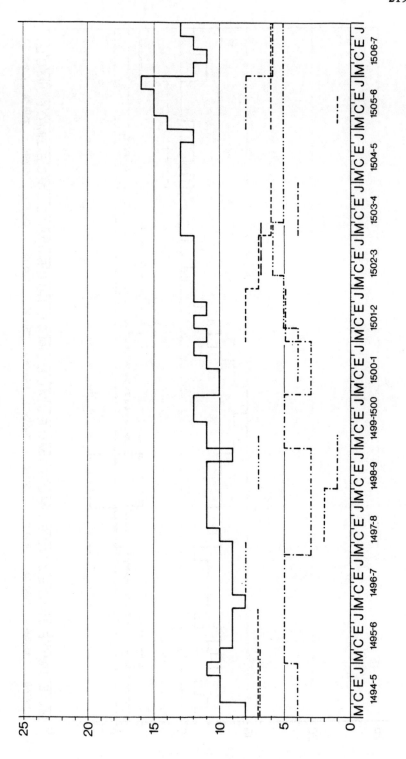

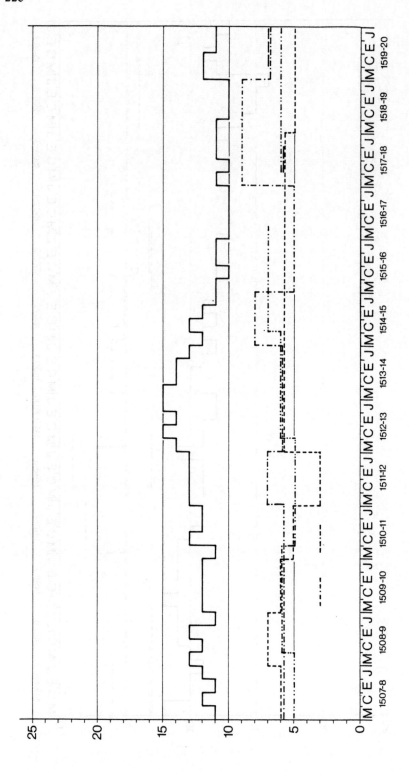

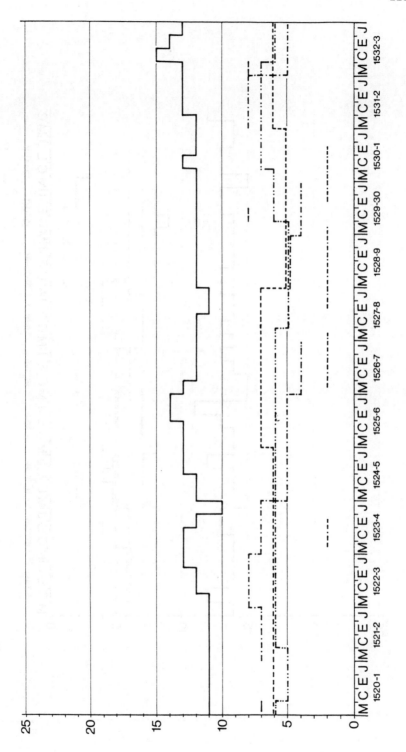

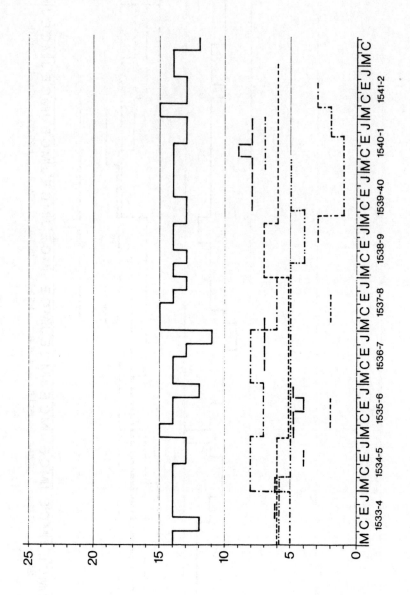

25

20

15

10

5

0

M C E J M C E J M C E J M C E J M C E J M C E J M C E J M C E J M C E J M C E J M C

1533-4 1534-5 1535-6 1536-7 1537-8 1538-9 1539-40 1540-1 1541-2

Bibliography

Manuscript Sources

Bodleian Library
  Ms Ashmole 794 (Lichfield Chapter Act Book 1321–84)
  Ms Bodley 286
  Ms Bodley 333

British Library
  Harleian Ms 220
  Harleian Ms 1027
  Harleian Ms 3300

Devon Record Office
  Chanter Ms 12 part i (Reg Neville)
  Chanter Ms 12 part ii (Reg Booth)
  Exeter Mayor's Court Rolls
    ED/M/276
  Exeter Book 51
  Exeter Cathedral Archives:
    D&C 394, 1927, 2129, 2223 (Miscellaneous Deeds)
    D&C 2777–2836 (Stewards' Accounts)
    D&C 2846 (Executors' Accounts of Dean Kilkenny)
    D&C 3498 (Miscellaneous Letters)
    D&C 3516
    D&C 3550, 3551 (Chapter Act Books)
    D&C 3625 (Cathedral Statutes)
    D&C 3764–72 (Obit Books)
    D&C 3675 (Obit Book of Vicars Choral)
    D&C 3707 (Residence Book 1506–1604)
    D&C 3761–3 (Quotidian Book 1486–1501)
    D&C 3766 (Obit Book)
    D&C 3773, 3777 (Extraordinary Accounts)
    D&C Vicars Choral 3357

Guildhall Library
  Ms 25,513 (St Paul's Chapter Act Book 1411–47)
  Ms 25,166/1–9 (Household Accounts of Dean Worsley)

Hereford Cathedral Archives
  Baylis, i (transcript of Chapter Act Book I 1512–41)
    2957, 2958
  R40a–59 (Accounts of Reeves and Bailiffs)
  R123a–195 (Accounts of the Collectors of Common Rent)
  R389–578 (Accounts of Receivers of Mass Pence)
  R412–49 (Accounts of the Receivers and Collectors of Oblations and Heriots)

Lambeth Palace Library
  Reg. Courtenay
  Reg. Arundel

Lichfield Joint Record Office
  D30/2/1/1–4 (Chapter Act Books)

Lincolnshire Archives Office
  Reg. III (Reg. Dalderby)
  Reg. IV (Reg. Burghersh)
  Reg. V (Reg. Burghersh)
  Reg. VIII (Reg. Gynwell)
  Reg. IX (Reg. Buckingham)
  Reg. XII (Reg. Buckingham)
  Reg. XXIV (Reg. Smith)
  Reg XXVII Reg. Longland)
  Lincoln Cathedral Archives:
    A/2/21–3, A/2/25–36, A/3/1–4 (Chapter Act Books)
    Bj/1/4 (Accounts of Legacies to the Fabric)
    Bj/2/10–16, Bj/3/1–5 (Accounts of the Common Fund)
    Dvi/14/1 (Accounts of the Executors of Thomas Cotte)

Public Record Office
  C1/17/322
  C47/7/6/1
  C47/52/3/124
  E179/30/12
  E179/63/12
  E179/95/100
  PROB 11/1–40
  STAC 2 28/17

Salisbury Cathedral Archives
  Registers of Chapter Acts:
    Draper 1402–7
    Vyring 1408–13
    Pountney 1413–18
    Harding 1419–35
    Hutchins 1440–7
    Burgh 1447–57
    Newton 1461–7
    Machon 1468–75
    Harwood's Memorials 1497–1525
    Holt and Blacker 1537–63
    Communars' Accounts 1–89

York: Borthwick Institute
  Reg Alexander Neville
  York Minster Library
    E1/1–79 (Chamberlains' Accounts)
    H1/1–3, H2/1–3, H3/1, L2/3a (Chapter Act Books)
    M2/4g (Miscellaneous Register)
    P1 (2) ix

Printed Sources

All books were published in London unless otherwise stated

Primary Sources

The Accounts of the Fabric of Exeter Cathedral, 1279–1353, ed. A. M. Erskine, 2 vols, DCRS, New Series, xxiv, xxvi, 1981–3.

Accounts Rendered by Papal Collectors in England, 1317–78, ed. W. E. Lunt and E. B. Graves, Memoirs of the American Philosophical Society, lxx, Philadelphia, 1968.

The Acts of the Dean and Chapter of the Cathedral Church of Chichester, 1472–1544 (the White Act Book), ed., W. D. Peckham, Sussex Record Society, lii, 1952.

Calendar of Close Rolls, 1900–55.

Calendar of Fine Rolls, 1911–49.

Calendar of Inquisitions Miscellaneous, 3 vols, 1916–37.

Calendar of Inquisitions Post Mortem, 17 vols, 1904– in progress.

Calendar of Inquisitions Post Mortem Henry VII, 3 vols, 1898–1955.

Calendar of the Manuscripts of the Dean and Chapter of Wells, ed., W. H. B. Bird and W. P. Baildon, 2 vols, HMC, 1907, 1914.

Calendar of Papal Letters, 1893–1955.

Calendar of Papal Petitions, 1896.

Calendar of Patent Rolls, 1893–1910.

Catalogue of Muniments and Manuscript Books of the Dean and Chapter of Lichfield and of the Lichfield Vicars, ed., J. C. Cox, William Salt Society, vi, part 2, 1886.

Catholic England: Faith, Religion and Observance before the Reformation, ed., R. N. Swanson, Manchester, 1993.

Ceremonies and Processions of the Cathedral Church of Salisbury, ed., C. Wordsworth, Cambridge, 1901.

The Chapter Acts of the Cathedral Church of Lincoln, 1520–47, ed., R. E. G. Cole, 2 vols, LRS, xii, xiii, 1915–17.

Charters and Records of Hereford Cathedral, ed., W. W. Capes, Hereford, 1908.

Dean Cosyn and Wells Cathedral Miscellanea, ed., A. Watkin, SRS, lvi, 1941.

Early Lincoln Wills, ed., A. Gibbons, Lincoln, 1988.

Feudal Aids, 6 vols, 1899–1920.

The Fifty Earliest English Wills in the Court of Probate 1387–1439, ed. F. J. Furnivall, EETS, lxxviii, 1882.

The Great Register of Lichfield Cathedral known as Magnum Registrum Album, ed., H. E. Savage, William Salt Society, Third Series, 1926.

Hemingby's Register, ed., H. M. Chew, Wiltshire Archaeological and Natural History Society, Records Branch, xviii, 1963.

History and Constitution of a Cathedral of the Old Foundation Illustrated from Documents in the Registry and Muniment Room of the Cathedral of Chichester, ed., C. A. Swainson, 1880.

Letters and Papers Foreign and Domestic Henry VIII, 23 vols, 1864–1932.

Lincoln Wills Registered in the in the District Probate Registry at Lincoln, ed. C. W. Foster, 2 vols, LRS, v, x, 1914, 1918.

John Lydford's Book, ed. D. M. Owen, DCRS, New Series, xx, 1974.

Monasticon Anglicanum, ed. W. Dugdale, vi part 3, 1846.

Adae Murimuth, Continuatio Chronicarum, ed. E. M. Thompson, Rolls Series, 1889.

North Country Wills, ed. J. W. Clay, 2 vols, SS, cxvi, cxxi, 1908, 1912.

Official Correspondance of Thomas Bekynton, Secretary to King Henry VI, and Bishop of Bathand Wells. Edited, from a Ms in the Archepiscopal Library at Lambeth, with an Appendix ofIllustrative Documents, ed., G. Williams, 2 vols, Rolls Series, 1872.

Ordinale Exon, ed. J. N. Dalton and G. H. Doble, 4 vols, Henry Bradshaw Society, xxxvii, xxxviii, lxiii, lxxix, 1909–40.

'The Poll Tax of A. D. 1379–80 for the hundreds of Offlow and Cuttlestone', ed., W. Boyd, *William Salt Archaeological Society*, xvii, 1896.

Registrum Antiquissimum of the Cathedral Church of Lincoln, ed., C. W. Foster and K. Major, 12 vols, LRS, xxvii, xxviii, xxix, xxxii, xxxiv, xli, xlii, xlvi, li, lxii, lxvii, lxxviii,1931–73.

The Register of Thomas de Brantyngham, Bishop of Exeter (AD 1370–94), ed. F. C. Hingeston-Randolph, 2 vols, London and Exeter, 1901–6.

Register of Nicholas Bubwith, Bishop of Bath and Wells, 1407–24, ed. T.S. Holmes, 2 vols, SRS, xxix, xxx, 1914.

Registrum Thome de Cantilupo, 1275–82, ed., R. G. Griffiths and W. W. Capes, CYS, ii,1907.

The Register of John Chandler, Dean of Salisbury, 1404–17, ed. T. C. B. Timmins, WiltshireRecord Society, xxxix, 1984.

The Register of Henry Chichele, Archbishop of Canterbury, 1413–43, ed. E. F. Jacob, 4 vols, CYS, 1943–7.

The Register of Richard Clifford, bishop of Worcester, 1401–7: a calendar, ed. W. E. L. Smith, Pontifical Institute of Medieval Studies, Subsidia Mediaevalia, vi, Toronto, 1976.

The Register of John de Grandisson, Bishop of Exeter (AD 1327–69), with some account of the episcopate of James de Berkeley (AD 1327), ed. F. C. Hingeston–Randolph, 3 vols, London and Exeter, 1894–9.

The Register of William Greenfield 1306–15, ed., W. Brown and A. H. Thompson, 5 vols, SS, cxlv, cxlix, cli–iii, 1931–40.

The Register of Robert Hallum, Bishop of Salisbury, 1407–17, ed., J. M. Horn, CYS, lxxii,1982.

The Register of Edmund Lacy, Bishop of Exeter (AD 1420–55): part I, the register of institutions together with some account of the episcopate of John Catrik (AD 1419), ed. F. C. Hingeston-Randolph, London and Exeter, 1909.

The Register of Edmund Lacy, Bishop of Exeter, 1420–55: Registrum Commune, ed. G. R. Dunstan, 5 vols, CYS lx–lxiii, lxvi, 1963–72.

The Registers of Roger Martival, bishop of Salisbury, 1315–30, ed. K. Edwards et al., 4 vols, CYS, 1959–75.

The Register of John Morton, Archbishop of Canterbury, 1486–1500, ed., C. Harper-Bill, 2 vols, CYS, lxxv, 1987, 1992, in progress.

The Episcopal Register of Robert Rede, ordinis predicatorum, Lord Bishop of Chichester, 1397–1415. Summarized and edited with explanatory and illustrative notes by Cecil Deedes, 2 vols, Sussex Record Society, viii, xi, 1908, 1910.

The Register of Bishop Repingdon, 1405–19, ed., M. Archer, LRS, lvii–lviii, lxxiv, 1963–82.

The Register of Edmund Stafford, Bishop of Exeter (AD 1395–1419): an index and abstract of its contents, ed. F. C. Hingeston-Randolph, London and Exeter, 1886.

The Register of Walter de Stapeldon, Bishop of Exeter (AD 1307–26), ed. F. C. Hingeston-Randolph, London and Exeter, 1892.

Registrum Statutorum et Consuetudinum Ecclesiae Cathedralis Sancti Pauli Londiniensis, ed., W. Sparrow Simpson, 1873.

Registrum Ricardi de Swinfield, 1283–1317, ed., W. W. Capes, CYS, vi, 1909.

Registrum Johannis Trefnant, Episcopi Herefordensis, MCCCCIV–MCCCXVI, ed., W. W. Capes, CYS, xx, 1916.

Registrum Roberti Winchelsey, Cantuariensis Archepiscopi, ed. R. Graham, 2 vols, CYS, li, lii, 1952–6.

Somerset Medieval Wills 1383–1558, ed., F. W. Weaver, 3 vols, SRS, xvi, xix, xxi, 1901–5.

Statuta et Consuetutines Ecclesiae Cathedralis Beatae Mariae Virginis Sarisberiensis, ed., C. Wordsworth and D. Macleane, 1915.

Statutes of Lincoln Cathedral, ed., H. Bradshaw and C. Wordsworth, 3 vols, Cambridge, 1892, 1897.

Taxatio Ecclesiastica Angliae et Walliae Auctoritate P. Nicholai IV c. 1291, ed. T. Astle, S. Ayscough, and J. Caley, Record Commission, 1802.

Testamenta Eboracensis, ed. J. Raine et al., 6 vols, SS, iv, xxx, xlv, liii, lxxix, cvi, 1836, 1855, 1865, 1869, 1884, 1902.

Tudor Exeter: Tax Assessments 1489–1595, ed. M. M. Rowe, DCRS xxii, 1977.

Valor Ecclesiasticus temp. Henricii VIII, auctoritate regis institutus, ed. J. Caley and J. Hunter, 6 vols, Record Commission, 1810–34.

Wells Cathedral Communars' Accounts 1327–1600, ed. L. S. Colchester, 2 vols, Wells, 1984.

Wells Cathedral Escheators' Accounts, ed., L. S. Colchester, 2 vols, Wells, 1988.

Wells Cathedral Fabric Accounts, ed., L. S. Colchester, Wells, 1983.

Wells Cathedral: Its Foundation, Constitutional History, and Statutes, ed., H. E. Reynolds, Leeds, 1881.

Secondary Sources

Archer, M., 'Philip Repingdon, Bishop of Lincoln, and his Cathedral Chapter', *University of Birmingham Historical Journal*, iv, 81–103.

Aston, T. H., 'Oxford's Medieval Alumni', *Past and Present*, lxxiv, 1977, 3–40.

Aston, T. H., Duncan, G. D., and Evans, T. A. R., 'The Medieval Alumni of the University of Cambridge', *Past and Present*, lxxxvi, 1980, 9–86.

Aylmer, G. E. and Cant, R., *A History of York Minster*, Oxford, 1977.

Ball, R. M., 'Thomas Cyrcetur, a Fifteenth-Century Theologian and Preacher', *JEH*, xxxvii, 1986, 205–39.

Bannister, A. T., *The Cathedral Church of Hereford*, 1924.

Barlow, F. *Leofric of Exeter*, Exeter, 1972.

Bailey, D. S., *The Canonical Houses of Wells*, Gloucester, 1982.

———, *Wells Manor of Canon Grange*, Gloucester, 1985.

Barr, C. B. L., 'The Minster Library', in Aylmer and Cant, *York Minster*.

Bowers, R., 'Music and Worship to 1640', in Owen, *Lincoln Minster*, 47–76.

Bowker, M., *The Secular Clergy of the Diocese of Lincoln, 1495–1520*, Cambridge, 1968.

———, *The Henrician Reformation: the Diocese of Lincoln under John Longland, 1521–47*, Cambridge, 1981.

———, 'Historical Survey 1450–1750', in Owen, *Lincoln Minster*, 164–209.

Brooke, C. N. L., 'The Earliest Times to 1485', in Matthews and Atkins, *St Paul's Cathedral*, 1–99.

Buck, M., *Politics, Finance and the Church in the Reign of Edward II: Walter Stapeldon, Treasurer of England*, Cambridge, 1983.

Catto, J. I., *A History of the University of Oxford, Vol. I: The Early Schools*, Oxford, 1984.

Catto, J. I. and Evans, R., *A History of the University of Oxford, Vol. II: The Collegiate University*, Oxford, 1992.

Cherry, B. and Pevsner, N., *Devon*, 1989.

Church, C. M., *Chapters in the Early History of the Church of Wells 1136–1333*, 1894.

Churchill, I. J., *Canterbury Administration*, 2 vols, 1933.

Cobban, A. B., *The Medieval English Universities*, Aldershot, 1988.

Colchester, L. S. ed., *Wells Cathedral A History*, Shepton Mallet, 1982.

Courtenay, W. J., *Schools and Scholars in Fourteenth Century England*, Princeton, 1987.

Crosby, E. U., *Bishop and Chapter in Twelfth Century England*, Cambridge, 1994.

Cross, C., 'From the Reformation to the Restoration', in Aylmer and Cant, *History of York Minster*, 193–232.

Curtis, M. L., *Some Disputes between the City and the Cathedral Authorities of Exeter*, Manchester, 1932.

Dictionary of National Biography, ed., L. Stephens and S. Lee, 63 vols, 1885–1900.

Dobson, R. B., 'The Later Middle Ages 1215–1500', in *A History of York Minster*, ed. G. E. Aylmer and R. Cant, Oxford, 1977, 44–109.

————, 'The Residentiary Canons of York Minster in the Fifteenth Century', *JEH*, xxx, (1979), 145–74.

————, 'Cathedral Chapters and Cathedral Cities: York, Durham and Carlisle in the Fifteenth Century', *Northern History*, xix, (1983), 15–44.

————, *The Church, Politics and Patronage in the Fifteenth Century*, Gloucester, 1984.

Dunbabin, J., 'Careers and Vocations', in Catto, *Oxford University Vol. I*.

Dunning, R. W., 'Patronage and Promotion in the Late Medieval Church', in Griffiths, *Patronage, the Crown, and the Provinces*, 167–80.

Edwards, K., 'The Houses of Salisbury Close in the Fourteenth Century', *British Archeaological Journal*, 3rd series, iv, (1939), 55–115.

————, 'Salisbury Cathedral', in *VCH Wiltshire*, iii, 156–210.

————, *The English Secular Cathedrals in the Middle Ages*, 2nd edn, Manchester, 1967.

Emden, A. B., *A Biographical Register of the University of Oxford to A. D. 1500*, 3 vols, Oxford, 1957–9.

————, *A Biographical Register of the University of Cambridge to 1500*, Cambridge, 1963.

————, *A Biographical Register of the University of Oxford, 1500–1540*, Oxford, 1974.

Fryde, E. B., et al., *Handbook of British Chronology*, 3rd edn, 1986.

Girouard, M., *Life in the English Country House*, Harmondsworth, 1978.

Given-Wilson, C., *The English Nobility in the Late Middle Ages*, 1987.

Godfrey, C. J., 'Pluralists in the Province of Canterbury in 1366', *JEH*, xi, (1960), 23–40.

Gransden, A., *Historical Writing in England c. 1307 to the Early Sixteenth Century*, 1982.

————, 'The History of Wells Cathedral c.1090 to 1547', in Colchester, *Wells Cathedral*, 24–51.

Griffiths, R. A., *Patronage, the Crown, and the Provinces in Later Medieval England*, Gloucester, 1981.

Harper-Bill, C., *Religious Belief and Ecclesiastical Careers in Late Medieval England*, 1991.

Harrison, F. Ll., *Music in Medieval Britain*, 2nd edn, 1963.

Harvey, M., *England, Rome and the Papacy, 1417–64*, Manchester, 1993.

Heath, P., *English Parish Clergy on the Eve of the Reformation*, 1969.

————, 'Urban Piety in the Later Middle Ages: the Evidence of Hull Wills', in Dobson, *The Church, Politics and Patronage*.

————, *Church and Realm, 1272–1461*, 1988.

Hughes, J., *Pastors and Visionaries*, Woodbridge, 1988.

Jacob, E. F., *Essays in the Conciliar Epoch*, 3rd edn, Manchester, 1963.

————, 'The Medieval Chapter of Salisbury Cathedral', *Wiltshire Archaeological Magazine*, li, 1947, 479–95.

Jenkins, H. T., *Lichfield Cathedral in the Fourteenth Century*, unpublished B. Litt Thesis, University of Oxford, 1956.

Jones, S., Major, K., and Varley, J., *Survey of Ancient Houses in Lincoln*, 3 vols, in progress, 1984, 1987, 1990.

Kettle, A. J., 'City and Close: Lichfield in the Century before the Reformation', in C.

M. Barron and C. Harper-Bill, *The Church and Pre–Reformation Society*, Woodbridge, 1985, 158–69.

Kettle, A. J. and D. A. Johnson, 'Lichfield Cathedral', in *Victoria County History of Staffordshire*, iii, 1970, 140–99.

Kitch, M. J., 'The Chichester Cathedral Chapter at the Time of the Reformation', *SAC*, cxvi, 1978, 277–92.

Lega-Weekes, E., *Some Studies in the Topography of the Cathedral Close, Exeter*, Exeter, 1915.

Lehmberg, S. E., *The Reformation of Cathedrals*, Princeton, 1988.

Le Neve, J., *Fasti Ecclesiae Anglicanae, 1300–1541*, ed. J. M. Horn, B. Jones, and H. P. F. King, 12 vols, 1962–7.

———, *Fasti Ecclesiae Anglicanae, 1066–1300 III Lincoln*, ed. D. Greenway, 1977.

Lepine, D. N., *The Canons of Exeter Cathedral 1300–1455*, unpublished PhD Thesis, University of Exeter, 1989.

———, 'The Origins and Careers of the Canons of Exeter Cathedral, 1300–1455', in Harper-Bill, *Religious Belief and Ecclesiastical Careers*, 87–120.

———, 'The Courtenays and Exeter Cathedral in the Later Middle Ages', TDA, cxxiv, 1992, 41–58.

McFarlane, K. B., *Wycliffe and English Non-Conformity*, Harmondsworth, 1972.

Macleod, R., 'The Topography of St Paul's Precinct, 1200–1500', *London Topographical Record*, xxvi, 1990, 1–14.

Major, K., 'The Office of Chapter Clerk', in M. V. Ruffer and A. J. Taylor, *Medieval Studies Presented to Rose Graham*, Oxford, 1950, 163–88.

Marks, R., 'The Medieval Stained Glass of Wells Cathedral', in Colchester, *Wells Cathedral*, 132–47.

———, *Stained Glass in England During the Middle Ages*, 1993.

Matthews, W. R. and Atkins, W. M., *A History of St Paul's Cathedral*, New Edition, 1964.

Mertes, K., *The English Noble Household, 1250–1600*, Oxford, 1988.

Millet, H., *Les Chanoines du Chapitre de Laon, 1272–1412*, Rome, 1982.

Milman, H. H., *Annals of St Paul's*, 1868.

Mynors, R. A. B. and Thomson, R. M., *Catalogue of the Manuscripts of Hereford Cathedral Library*, Cambridge, 1993.

Oliver, G., *Lives of the Bishops of Exeter and a History of the Cathedral*, Exeter, 1861.

Orme, N. I., *Education in the West of England, 1066–1548*, Exeter, 1976.

———, *The Minor Clergy of Exeter Cathedral*, Exeter, 1980.

———, 'The Medieval Clergy of Exeter Cathedral', TDA, cxiii, 1981, 79–102, cxv, 1983, 79–100.

———, 'Education and Learning at a Medieval English Cathedral: Exeter 1380–1548', *JEH*, xxxi, 1981.

———, *Exeter Cathedral As It Was, 1050–1550*, Exeter, 1986.

———, 'Two Saint–Bishops of Exeter', *Analecta Bollandiana*, cii, 1986, 403–18.

Owen, D. M., ed., *A History of Lincoln Minster*, Cambridge, 1994.

———, 'Historical Survey 1091–1450', in Owen, *Lincoln Minster*, 112–63.

Pantin, W. A., *The English Church in the Fourteenth Century*, Cambridge, 1955.

Pevsner, N. and Metcalf, P., *The Cathedrals of England*, 2 vols, 1985.

Portman, D., *Exeter Houses, 1400–1600*, Exeter, 1966.

RCHM, *Salisbury The Houses of the Close*, 1993.

Robinson, J. A., 'The Correspondance of Bishop Oliver King and Sir Reginald Bray', *Proceedings of the Somerset Archaeological and Natural History Society*, lx, part 2, 1914, 1–10.

Smith, D. M., *Guide to Bishops' Registers of England and Wales*, 1981.

Swanson, R. N., 'Titles to Orders in Medieval English Episcopal Registers', in *Studies in*

Medieval History Presented to R. H. C. Davies, ed. H. Mayr-Harting and R. I. Moore, 1985, 233–45.

———, *Church and Society in Late Medieval England*, Oxford, 1989.

Thompson, A. H., *The Cathedral Churches of England*, 1925.

———, *The English Clergy and Their Organisation in the Later Middle Ages*, Oxford, 1947.

Thomson, J. A. F., *The Early Tudor Church and Society, 1485–1529*, 1993.

Thomson, R. M., *Catalogue of the Manuscripts of Lincoln Cathedral Library*, Cambridge, 1989.

Victoria History of the County of Staffordshire, iii, Oxford, 1970.

Victoria History of the County of Staffordshire, xiv, Oxford, 1990.

Victoria History of the County of Sussex, ii, 1907.

Victoria History of the County of Sussex, iii, 1935.

Vivian, J. L., *Visitation of Devon*, Exeter, 1895.

Weiss, R., *Humanism in England during the Fifteenth Century*, 2nd edn, Oxford, 1957.

Wright, J. R., *The Church and the English Crown 1305–34*, Toronto, 1980.

Index of Names and Places

All the individuals listed below were canons unless otherwise identified; their dignities, if they acquired them, are indicated for ease of identification.

Index of Subjects